# Business Studies in Practice
## Second Edition

# Business Studies in Practice

## Second Edition

DAVID NEEDHAM

ROBERT DRANSFIELD

McGRAW-HILL BOOK COMPANY

**London** · New York · St Louis · San Francisco · Auckland
Bogotá · Caracas · Hamburg · Lisbon · Madrid · Mexico
Milan · Montreal · New Delhi · Panama · Paris · San Juan
São Paulo · Singapore · Sydney · Tokyo · Toronto

Published by
McGRAW-HILL Book Company Europe
Shoppenhangers Road, Maidenhead, Berkshire, SL6 2QL, England
Telephone 0628 23432
Fax 0628 770224

---

**British Library Cataloguing in Publication Data**
Needham, David
   Business Studies in Practice. – 2Rev. ed
   I. Title II. Dransfield, Robert
   658

ISBN 0–07–707292–8

**Library of Congress Cataloging-in-Publication Data**
Needham, David, 1954–
Business studies in practice / David Needham and Robert
   Dransfield. — 2nd ed.
     p.   cm.
   Includes index.
   ISBN 0–07–707292–8
   1. Business.    2. Industrial management.    I. Dransfield, Robert,
1954–   . II. Title.
HF5351.N39   1992
650—dc20                         91–47680
                                        CIP

12345CL95432

Typset by TecSet Limited
and printed and bound in Great Britain by Clays Ltd, St Ives plc

# Contents

| | | |
|---|---|---|
| | Preface | vii |
| | Acknowledgements | ix |
| 1 | Business | 1 |
| 2 | Decision making within the business | 22 |
| 3 | A business within the economy | 35 |
| 4 | Ownership and control | 49 |
| 5 | The business in its environment | 72 |
| 6 | Work and pay | 100 |
| 7 | Production | 119 |
| 8 | Marketing | 135 |
| 9 | Communication | 165 |
| 10 | Business documentation | 190 |
| 11 | Finance and financial control | 202 |
| 12 | The personnel department | 224 |
| 13 | Industrial relations in the workplace | 251 |
| 14 | Business in an international setting | 271 |
| 15 | The government and business | 291 |
| 16 | The consequences of business | 308 |
| 17 | Services to business | 331 |

# Preface

Over recent years we have seen a rapid pace of change in the business environment. Just as organizations have to respond quickly and positively to the fluctuating needs of their customers in a time of change, this book is designed to do the same. Since the first edition many of the case studies have required updating and we have responded appropriately. We have added many more and have made further attempts to integrate case analysis into the text to make the book easier to use in the classroom on a regular basis. We have also been aware of changes made by examination boards and of the development of options to support the core area of theory. In response we have incorporated information technology skills, opportunities to use a modern language in a business setting, enterprise skills and other important commercial skills.

Whenever we write a textbook we develop a number of themes which we endeavour to continue through the text. Such themes always reflect external pressures in the business environment and are, therefore, important issues for modern, responsive organizations to consider. In this book we have identified the themes of Europeanization, business ethics, the rapid growth of marketing and the increasing awareness of the consumer, concern for the environment and equal opportunities.

Finally, this book is designed to provide a sound grounding in the fundamentals of business studies, both at an initial level and also as a preparation for the approach used in our 'A' Level text. It is hoped that the material contained within will provide relevant, integrated and interesting experiences for the participants which will exemplify the true nature of the discipline.

David Needham
Robert Dransfield

# Acknowledgements

Abbey National
Alan Robinson (Huntley, Boorne & Stevens)
Banking Information Service
Barclays Bank PLC
Ben Cribb
British Nuclear Fuels PLC
British Telecommunications PLC
Darlington Borough Council
David Hayes
Derek Chapman (The Prudential)
Eva Tutchell
Export Credits Guarantee Department
Ford Motor Company
Friends of the Earth
Geoff Hale
Hanson PLC
Harrogate Advertiser
John Warner
Kim Hooper
London East Anglian Group
Margaret Walsh
Marks and Spencer PLC
Midland Examining Group
National Westminster Bank PLC
Nissan Motor Manufacturing (UK) Limited
Northern Examining Association
Northern Ireland Schools Examinations and Assessment Council
Oxford and Cambridge Schools Examination Board
Peter K Radband
Post Office Counters Ltd
*Reading Standard*
Roland Peck & Co

Scottish Whisky Association
Shell UK Ltd
Southern Examining Group
Staff and students at Darlington College of Technology
Steve Hodkinson
*The Economist*
*The Independent*
The Nestlé Company Ltd
The Women's Press
Transport and General Workers Union
Understanding Industry
Welsh Joint Education Committee

# 1

# Business

Look at the word *business*. What do you think that it means? Can you come up with a definition of the word business? One of the first steps in a Business Studies course should be to learn how to spell the word BUSINESS. Carry out a group investigation to find out how people spell business. Produce a short word processed report to show your findings. Illustrate your results by means of a chart from a graphics package.

## Starting in business

People start their own business for a variety of reasons. Some have a bright idea that they think will make them rich; others find themselves unemployed and start their own business to survive; some can only be themselves when they are their own bosses; others want to make a particular contribution to their community and can see no other way of doing it except by setting up on their own.

### Where do I get a business idea from?

Nearly everyone at some time or another thinks about setting up an enterprise of their own. You will hear people say things like: 'Someone could make a fortune out of selling such and such' or 'If I had some money, I could create a business out of making this or that'.

Where does the idea to set up an enterprise come from? Some people copy ideas that they have seen somewhere else (such as selling flowers at a busy railway station). Other people spot a gap in the market – 'Nobody round here runs a mobile disco service!' Others turn a hobby into a business—'I always enjoy making wooden toys!'

*Task*

What business ideas can you think of that could be run on a small scale in your local area?

**Figure 1.1**    Brainstorming session

Brainstorm ideas with two or three other students. Brainstorming simply means saying out loud the first ideas that come into your head and writing them down. When you have drawn up a list you can start to discuss the ideas to decide which ones are practical.

It is fairly easy to come up with ideas. It is far more difficult to come up with 'successful ideas'. A successful idea will be one that meets a real need or opportunity and where the costs of production (including your own time) will be less than the revenues. There are a lot of other factors that help to determine whether a good idea can be turned into a good business. These include making sure that the market is aware of the product, keeping regular and detailed accounts, obtaining the materials to produce the product and many other factors which will be dealt with in the chapters that follow.

## The decision making cycle

Any business decision that we make needs to be carefully followed through. If we identify a need or opportunity, we can then do something about it. For example, we may design a product on paper that meets particular requirements. We may then spend a considerable amount of time planning and making that product. We can then evaluate the finished product.

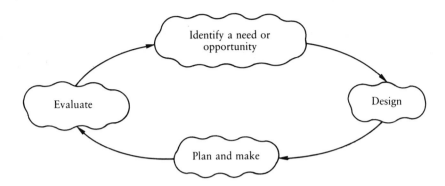

**Figure 1.2**    The decision making cycle

Of course the process we have outlined here is a simplification. Firstly, it need not take place in the order outlined. Indeed the cycle can start at any point. For example, you may be planning and making something when you suddenly identify a quite different opportunity. For example, part of the space programme involved developing heat resistant materials for space rockets. An unexpected outcome of this project was the realization that similar materials could be used to develop non-stick pans for use in the kitchen. Secondly, any of the stages in the decision cycle can interact with any other. For example, when you are designing a packet for a new cereal you will need to continually evaluate your progress.

### Case Study—ET to the rescue of women drivers

In February 1991 the RAC unveiled a new SOS device for women stranded in their cars.

The £150 gadget was christened ET because it allows drivers to 'phone home' by sending out an emergency signal for help. Research at the time showed that 55 per cent of women fear being attacked if they break down on motorways. Concern had been growing following the murder of pregnant housewife Marie Wilks as she used an emergency phone on the M50 in 1989.

The new device fits in the glove compartment. Drivers type in a personal identity number and can call help from the police, ambulance, fire brigade and breakdown service. A transmitter in the car boot flashes a message to the RAC control centre which can pinpoint a vehicle within 50 yards.

*Questions*

1. How do you think the need for the 'ET' device was identified?
2. What factors will be important in deciding whether the new product is a success or not?

3.   What modifications do you think could be made to the device?
4.   How could the product be developed for use in other areas?
5.   Can you suggest another electronic device for which you can see a need or opportunity?

## Decisions, decisions

Business activity continually involves problem solving and decision making. You will find many opportunities to try out your own problem solving and decision making skills in the activities suggested in this book. Being inventive can be very helpful. Nick Munro, a designer of kitchen equipment, came up with an idea for a highly successful egg cup one day when he was idly gazing at a bed spring. Gladys Wallace's claim to fame was that in her fifties she won a new car in a competition (in 1966!) for coming up with the now universally-known slogan 'Beanz Meanz Heinz'.

Business studies provides you with the opportunity to use in practical ways the skills and knowledge which you have learnt from other areas of study. Arithmetic can be helpful in constructing a set of accounts. Scientific knowledge is helpful in giving you a greater understanding of the properties of materials. Communication skills are essential in all areas of business activity.

### Task

Working in a small group of two or three students devise a slogan for a well known product. When you have completed the task consider how you arrived at a decision. For example, did you all share ideas? Did some people tend to dominate the discussion? Where did you get ideas from? Did you evaluate the effectiveness of different slogans? How?

### Case Study—The rise and rise of a small business

In the early 1980s, it looked as if the cinema industry was dying on its feet. Official statistics showed that fewer people were going to cinemas, many of which were closing down.

It was about this time that Robin Sanders was made redundant from his job as project organizer with an engineering company. He had been involved in research to find out the most cost-effective ways of carrying out engineering projects. By chance, he heard that the Terry Wogan Show had voted Grantham the most boring town in Britain because of its lack of leisure facilities. So Robin decided to use his experience in project-investigation (and his own newly acquired leisure!) to see if a cinema could be made into a profitable business in Grantham.

The project was to involve him in a great deal of personal financial risk. However, when he first looked at the figures for falling cinema attendances, he thought he could see something that other people had missed. Cinemas were being closed, not because films were unpopular, but because the sites the cinemas occupied in the high street could be used more profitably for supermarkets and multiple stores.

Robin felt he was on to a good thing. He worked out his costs and his likely takings as part of his business plan, but it took him a year to convince people that the plan was worth supporting. He estimated that it would cost £55,000 to build his cinema (which he decided to call the Paragon), and he was eventually given a council loan of £30,000 and a bank overdraft of £15,000.

His first few weeks in business were difficult. He had actually spent more money than he had borrowed, and so he needed profits to come in straight away in order to break even.

Fortunately, in the cinema business you take in money before you pay out most of your running costs. This helped Robin to survive. But as he now says 'The business had to work in the first few weeks or I would have gone under'.

There are other reasons for the success. Robin sited the Paragon off the high street, thus halving both the rent and the rates. He was one of the first cinema owners to computerize all his accounts and paper-work, and he was the first in this country to show different films on the same day.

The Paragon Cinema has gone from strength to strength. Profits have remained steady at around £25,000 per year and the cinema is a popular attraction. Robin says 'I will never work for anyone but myself again. The sense of achievement outweighs everything. Even if I didn't make a large profit, I would have achieved something off my own bat and proved to everyone that I can do it.'


*Questions*

1. Where did Robin's business idea come from?
2. Would you consider Robin to be a risk taker?
3. What was the biggest problem in setting up this business?
4. What sort of location was Robin looking for? Why?
5. Why is it important to choose a good location?
6. Who do you think would benefit from the setting up of the cinema?
7. Who do you think might lose out?
8. Who do you think Robin would need to consult with before setting up his business? Why?

9.  What information would Robin have needed to know about his potential customers?
10. What do you expect Robin's main costs and revenues to be?
11. Is Robin purely motivated by profit? Explain?
12. What will the success of the business depend on?
13. From studying the Paragon case study, what questions would you need to consider before setting up a business of your own?
14. When was Robin's business at its most vulnerable? Explain?
15. Why do you think that the council were prepared to support Robin?

**The story continues**

In 1987, Robin decided to find out whether there was sufficient demand in the town to justify a second screen. He had seen estimates suggesting that the population of Grantham would increase from 30 000 to 50 000 over the next ten years. He had also arrived at a point where he was having to turn customers away at one out of five shows. He consulted a local business studies teacher whose students were doing some work on market research for their business studies course, and asked for help in devising and implementing a survey.

The students first designed a pilot survey and tested it on friends and relatives. The pilot proved satisfactory, so they then carried out a full-scale survey of 115 people of different age groups, living in Grantham. The students worked in pairs, one asking the questions, the other marking off the answers on a grid. The grid was designed so that the results could be recorded and analysed easily.

A sample question and a section of the grid relating to this question is shown below.

*Question 3*

How often do you go to the cinema?
(a) More than once a week ...............................................................
(b) Once a week .............................................................................
(c) Once a fortnight ........................................................................
(d) Two or three times a year ..........................................................
(e) Never ......................................................................................

Analysis of the results indicated that age was a significant factor in determining whether people went to the cinema and what they liked to see.

Robin presented the following brief to the students. 'I would like you to carry out some research for me. The questions I would like answering are:

1. Is there a market for a second screen in Grantham?
2. What sort of people would go to the cinema?
3. How often do people go to the cinema?
4. What price are they willing to pay?
5. What sorts of films do they prefer?
6. What times do they want to go to the cinema?
7. What complaints do people have about the cinema?

I would like you to design a questionnaire, and use it to collect the information I need. You must then present a report of your findings to help me decide whether to install a second screen.'

The students spent three weeks carrying out the research and analysing the results. They then presented their findings. The key finding was that 78 per cent of those people questioned were in favour of a second screen.

On the basis of the research, Robin decided to go ahead with the new screen. This opened in late 1988, at a total cost of £65,000 for the whole extension. Robin is now considering opening up a third screen in 1992, because of the success of the other two.

*Task*

Your task is to design a research questionnaire to help find out whether there is a demand for a second, third, or even fourth screen at your local cinema. If there isn't a cinema in your area, you could do some research to see if local people would like to have one.

## Using information technology (IT)

The Paragon Cinema is an excellent example of the way in which a business can use Information Technology. Clearly, Robin uses the latest projection technology to convey sound, pictures and other images to the audience in his cinema. He also uses IT for running his day to day business. He uses the telephone to communicate with film suppliers and to let customers know what films are showing. He also uses a computer to keep his accounts, to print programmes of 'What's On' at the cinema, to keep a record of the stocks of sweets and confectionery at the cinema, to write letters and to produce leaflets.

In your business studies course you will need to use information technology in a wide range of situations. This use of IT closely reflects practice in the real world. Computers are used in small and large organizations to serve the needs of these organizations. They are used in all types of companies, in schools, hospitals, charities, local government offices and many other places of work. Computers are used to support the vital functions of business organizations.

Managers in these organizations must have control over:

- *Cash*: how much you have, how much is due to go out, and how much is due to come in.
- *Staff*: what job they are doing and how much they are paid.
- *Stock* kept up to date and valued; what is in short supply and what needs re-ordering.
- *Paperwork*: business records kept centrally; avoidance of waste and duplication.
- *Suppliers*: accounts kept up to date so that you can select which bills you pay and when.
- *Profits*: how profitable each item sold and each customer is; how profitable the business is.
- *Growth*: development of the business now and in the future.

Each of these areas needs to be managed quickly, accurately and frequently. The computer can be used to provide these three basic management needs.

Small businesses can use stand alone computers to manage these areas. A large business can link its computers together through a network. This means that personal computing is available to an employee at his or her desk which can be used for personal requirements, or it can be linked into a network which gives access to data from the company's mainframe (central) computer.

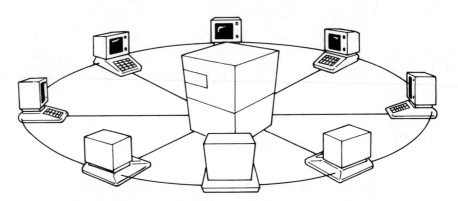

**Figure 1.3**   Computer network

### Pictures on the screen

Icons are small pictures used to represent objects and activities. They are used in several ways on Acorn computers:

- To identify (for the user) different types of file in a directory display – for example, whether it is:

  an application (an icon with no frame)
  something created within an application (an icon with a frame)
  another directory containing more files.

Icons are small pictures used to represent objects and activities. They are used in several ways on Acorn computers:
● to identify (for the user) different types of file in a directory display – for example, whether it's:

      an application

      something created within an application

      a directory containing more files.

Figure 1.4   Pictures on the screen

In recent years computers have increasingly become a tool which is easy to use by the layperson. One of the main reasons for this has been the development of Graphical User Interface (the little pictures on a computer screen). All we now need to do is point at the little picture that relates to the activity that we want to carry out. If we 'click on' to the picture we want, the computer will find the appropriate activity for us.

All we have to do to set up the computer is to push in the disc we want and then to select from a menu.

A typical business menu might read something like this:

Menu   1.  Invoicing
       2.  Stock control
       3.  Financial planning
       4.  Payroll
       5.  Production schedules
       6.  Graphics
       7.  Word processing

The first five of these are referred to in the relevant chapters of this book. The other two will now be covered in this opening chapter as you will be expected to use them regularly in the activities which you carry out.

### Word processing

There are many different types of word processing package which you will come across. Each will have its own simple manual to help you understand how to operate it. We will therefore make some general comments about word processing.

Word processors are used for producing and altering text. They show on a screen and record in memory the text that a person keys in on the keyboard.

A word processor is made up of:

1. The keyboard for typing in material and instructions.
2. A visual display unit which displays the material on a screen.
3. A disk storage unit.
4. The printer for finished text.

The basic features availabe in all word processing packages are:

• New text can be fed on to the screen. Text which is already on the screen can be moved to make space for it.
• Blocks of text can be moved from one place to another.
• Text can be spaced out to fill a whole line.
• A word or phrase can be searched for and replaced by another word or phrase, wherever it occurs.
• A header or footer can be added (a piece of text printed at the top or bottom of the page).

More expensive word processors used in business also include the following features:

• Different printing styles (such as italic).
• Text can be written in more than one column, as in newspapers.
• Graphics can be built into the text.
• A spelling checker.

*Task*

Here is an activity for which you will need to use some simple word processing skills. You will need to:

(a)  Load or call up a word processing program.
(b)  Create a text file.
(c)  Edit text using insert and delete.
(d)  Set margins.
(e)  Centre text.
(f)  Justify text.
(g)  Print text.
(h)  Save a text file.

Produce a class letter to 21 local small businesses. The letter should ask a few simple questions to find out where the business idea came from that led to the creation of the business.

For example, you might ask 'Did your business idea stem from:

1. An idea that you had seen elsewhere?
2. A hobby or personal interest?
3. A sudden brainwave?
4. Something else?'

The letters could be sent to seven retailers, seven manufacturing businesses, and seven service organizations (eg hairdressers). How will you set out the letters? Before you start to analyse the replies consider how effective the research questionnaire was. How many replies did you get? Could you have organized the research better? What did you find out about where people get their business ideas from?

## Graphics

Computer graphics packages are simple to operate once you have had the chance to practise with them. You will use them to complement the word processing activities that you do. Graphics can be used to make pictures and to show data. Activities in this book will encourage you to create pie charts, line graphs and other charts. Using a graphics package you will be able to label the axes and segments, to shade in your charts. Of course you will want to save and print this information.

Pie charts can be used to present data in a clear and often dramatic way. A circle is made up of 360 degrees. If you want to show that three-quarters of a firm's costs were labour costs and one quarter were transport costs, you would give labour a value of 270 degrees and transport 90 degrees. You must be careful to set up a pie chart accurately if it is to have real meaning. Of course a computer graphics package will do much of the work for you! But it is important that the data you feed in is accurate and relevant. Just drawing pretty pictures is a waste of valuable time.

Bar charts, which are also known as block graphs, are useful not just for showing proportions, but particularly for comparing amounts. You can easily

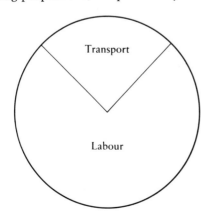

**Figure 1.5** Pie chart showing how a firm's costs are divided between labour costs and transport costs

see how one amount 'stands' in relation to another. For instance you could compare the male/female employee ratio in two firms.

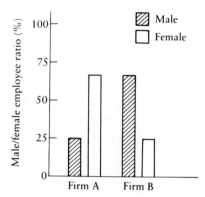

**Figure 1.6** Bar chart showing the proportions of male and female employees in two firms

Line graphs need to be drawn to scale. If you are not producing them on a computer you should use graph paper. They are particularly useful for showing how things change over time. The line graph in Fig. 1.7 shows the sales of a firm's products in the first six months of the year.

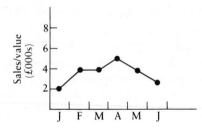

**Figure 1.7** Line graph showing the sales of a firm's products over six months

## Desk top publishing

Desk top publishing simply means producing good quality publications on your own computer. No longer do pamphlets and other short publications have to be sent out to the printers. Large, medium and even small firms can save a lot of money by developing their own in-house desk top publishing.

Desk top packages offer a range of different typefaces, the freedom to set pages out in an interesting way, the ability to place a diagram or picture on a page and many other useful features.

Desk top publishing can be used to produce newspapers, booklets, leaflets and advertisements at low cost.

*Task*

Produce a leaflet to advertise a particular brand of washing powder. In the leaflet set out graphs and charts to illustrate comparisons between your brand and other brands, e.g. of price, weight per pack, etc.

## Databases

In this book you will frequently be asked to set up a database or to use an existing database to find out information. A database is a store of facts that can be called upon to provide up-to-date information. For example, if I go into my bank and ask how much I have in my account, and whether a cheque I have written for a new computer printer has been cashed yet, this information can be called up immediately from a database. The person serving me in the bank would simply type in my account number, wait a few seconds and then read off the information from the screen.

A database will be used in all banks and building societies to store information on the state of all of the accounts. Data (information) is fed into the base (store of information) in a clear form. For instance, a company could store information about the firms it supplies credit to, e.g. it might have a record for the account of Johnson's stores. The information is stored in a number of fields—address, value of goods bought, payments and balance on the account. If Mr Johnson rings up asking for the state of his account, the firm can simply order the computer to find the balance on Johnson's account.

Under the provisions of the Data Protection Act, companies wishing to store personal information on a computer system must register with the (government appointed) Data Protection Officer. They must indicate the type of data they are storing and the use they make of it. Any individual has the right to request (on payment of a small fee) details of any information held about them by any firm and to require any mistakes to be corrected.

*Task*

Load a database package and set up a file to contain the following information. It relates to the feeding costs of animals at a zoo. The information should be entered under the following headings: animal, number, feeding cost per animal (per year) and total cost (per year).

The information should be entered as follows:

| animal | number | feeding cost per animal | total cost |
|---|---|---|---|
| elephant | 5 | £6,000 | £30,000 |
| koala | 1 | £4,000 | £4,000 |
| giraffe | 8 | £3,000 | £24,000 |
| sea lion | 4 | £2,500 | £10,000 |
| camel | 2 | £1,000 | £2,000 |
| reindeer | 6 | £1,000 | £6,000 |
| chimpanzee | 6 | £750 | £4,500 |
| ant | 200 | £15 | £3,000 |

1. Save and print the complete file in a record by record format.
2. Sort the file into alphabetical order.
3. Search the file for animals whose annual total cost of feeding is greater than £10,000.

4. In an economy drive the zoo decides to sell off the elephants and replace them with four gorillas which cost £1,000 each to feed for a year. Alter the database to show these changes.
5. Sort the file in ascending order of total annual cost to feed.
6. Why would the zoo need to periodically alter the data in this database?
7. How would the database help the managers of the zoo?

## Spreadsheets

A spreadsheet is a table of numbers which can be organized and altered on a computer. A spreadsheet is used for making forecasts and calculations – the computer does the work for you. Spreadsheets will often be used in financial forecasting. For instance, a firm will make a forecast of all the money that will come in and go out of the firm over a twelve month period.      (See Fig. 1.8.)

|  | First Quarter | Second Quarter | Third Quarter | Fourth Quarter |
|---|---|---|---|---|
| Sales Revenue | 12 000 | 20 000 | 24 000 | 36 000 |
| Costs |  |  |  |  |
| Materials | 1 000 | 1 600 | 2 000 | 6 000 |
| Labour | 3 000 | 5 000 | 6 000 | 9 000 |
| Rent | 500 | 500 | 500 | 500 |
| Energy | 100 | 160 | 200 | 300 |
| Advertising | 500 | 0 | 500 | 0 |
| Insurance | 0 | 0 | 0 | 100 |
| Other | 600 | 1 000 | 1 200 | 1 800 |
| Total Costs | 5 700 | 8 260 | 10 400 | 17 700 |
| Profit | 6 300 | 11 740 | 13 600 | 18 300 |

Total Profit: 49 940

Figure 1.8  Spreadsheet

The person using the spreadsheet can then alter the inputs, to calculate, for example, the effect of lowering the heating bill by a certain amount each month. The computer will automatically recalculate the columns to change the heating figures and the cost and profit figures for each month. It will also recalculate the total profit figure.

The beauty of the spreadsheet is the speed with which you can juggle figures around. For example, a supervisor of part-time staff at a supermarket may keep a record of who works at what time. If he or she needs an extra five staff to work on Saturday morning he or she can quickly see on a spreadsheet who is free and how much, in total, it would cost to employ them for the extra hours.

*Task*

Set out a spreadsheet to show your own income and expenditure over a four week period.

A suggested outline is:

|  | 1 | 2 | 3 | 4 |
|---|---|---|---|---|
| INCOME | | | | |
| EXPENSES | | | | |
| rent | | | | |
| fares | | | | |
| lunch | | | | |
| weekends | | | | |
| records | | | | |
| clothes | | | | |
| cinema | | | | |
| holiday | | | | |
| other | | | | |
| TOTAL | | | | |
| BALANCE | | | | |

# Presentation of your work

In business studies it is always important to present your work well. This doesn't just mean making sure that your work is tidy and attractive. It is also concerned with the content of your work. You need to be able to show that you know what you are looking at and that you are able to express your ideas clearly. An attractive folder with lots of pictures and charts will not necessarily present good business studies work. In this book we have set out a number of activities which encourage you to think and to support your arguments with clear evidence.  .

For example, if you carried out a piece of research into people's preferences for chips you may be able to present your conclusions forcefully by saying:

In a survey of 243 sixteen year olds in Skegness I found that 82 per cent preferred chips bought from the 'chippie' rather than those cooked at home. My research also indicated that 90 per cent of this sample bought fish and chips at least twice a week. Seventy per cent said that they would buy fish and chips just as often if the price rose by 50 per cent. In the light of this evidence I feel that the fish and chip shops in Skegness will continue to make profits in spite of the small increase in the price of potatoes.

Charts and diagrams can be used to support the arguments that you develop and the conclusions you reach. To conclude this chapter we will briefly discuss tables, flow charts and organizational charts.

## Tables

A table is a simple way of presenting information. Tables can be used for a variety of purposes and can present information very clearly, while being simple to set up.

An example of a table that gives a lot of information and is easy to read is a football league table including the names of teams, games played, games won, drawn and lost, the goals scored for and against and the number of points each team has (see Fig. 1.9).

| ITALY | | | | | | | |
|---|---|---|---|---|---|---|---|
| | P | W | D | L | F | A | Pts |
| Sampdoria | 31 | 19 | 9 | 3 | 50 | 20 | 47 |
| AC Milan | 31 | 17 | 9 | 5 | 39 | 17 | 43 |
| Inter Milan | 31 | 16 | 10 | 5 | 52 | 28 | 42 |
| Torino | 31 | 12 | 11 | 8 | 59 | 28 | 35 |
| Genoa | 31 | 12 | 11 | 8 | 46 | 36 | 35 |
| Parma | 31 | 12 | 11 | 8 | 33 | 30 | 35 |
| Juventus | 31 | 12 | 10 | 9 | 40 | 27 | 34 |
| Napoli | 31 | 10 | 13 | 8 | 32 | 33 | 33 |
| Roma | 31 | 10 | 12 | 9 | 41 | 36 | 32 |
| Lazio | 31 | 7 | 18 | 6 | 28 | 30 | 32 |
| Atalanta Bergamo | 31 | 10 | 11 | 10 | 37 | 37 | 31 |
| Fiorentina | 31 | 7 | 14 | 10 | 35 | 32 | 28 |
| Bari | 31 | 8 | 10 | 13 | 28 | 44 | 26 |
| Cagliari | 31 | 5 | 15 | 11 | 26 | 42 | 25 |
| Lecce | 31 | 5 | 13 | 13 | 19 | 42 | 23 |
| Pisa | 31 | 7 | 6 | 18 | 31 | 55 | 20 |
| Cesena | 31 | 5 | 9 | 17 | 28 | 51 | 19 |
| Bologna | 31 | 4 | 10 | 17 | 26 | 52 | 18 |

**Figure 1.9** A football league table – an example of a table that gives a lot of information

## Flowcharts

These show the individual stages of a process from beginning to end. The simple flow chart in Fig. 1.10 shows how a mail order catalogue works.

## Organization charts

An organization chart is used to show the relationship between members of an organization. Jim Smith has a small garage business in London. He was asked to draw an organizational chart to show how roles were set out within the organization. (See Fig. 1.11.)

Start

Customer chooses goods

↓

Agent visits customer

↓

Agent orders goods

↓

Goods delivered to agent

↓

Agent delivers to customer

↓

Payment made

Stop

**Figure 1.10**  Flowchart showing how a mail-order catalogue works

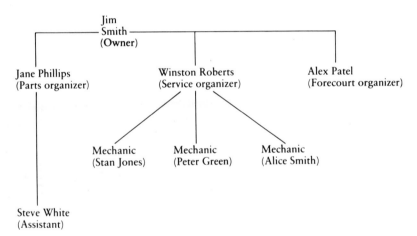

**Figure 1.11**  Organization chart of Jim Smith's garage business

## Questions

1. Complete the following sentences using the terms below:

Need or opportunity      Keyboard
Network                  Database
Evaluation               Spreadsheet
Graphical User Interface  Data Protection Act
Word processing          Flowchart

(a)  A . . . . . . can be used for storing information.
(b)  A . . . . . . . . makes it possible to link several computers.

(c)   Information can be typed into a word processor by using the . . . . . . .

(d)   . . . . . . . . . . . . . makes the computer screen easy to understand.

(e)   A business idea often stems from spotting a . . . . . . . .

(f)   . . . . . . . . . . software allows you to enter data into a cell or grid.

(g)   The . . . . . . . . requires companies wishing to store computer data to register.

(h)   Every step of the decision cycle requires some form of . . . . . . . to check on progress and to think about future developments.

(i)   . . . . . . . . a document makes it possible to alter text.

(j)   A sequence of steps can be shown on a . . . . . . .

2.   Quik Snax is a fast food chain. The following pictures give you an idea of the way in which they present their brand image. Quik Snax would like to add 'Children's Parties' to the range of products they offer. Produce an advertising leaflet to explain this service to the public. You may need to do some research first. For example, is there a fast food chain in your local town. Do they offer a similar service? What prices do they charge, etc.

**Figure 1.12**   Quick Snax burger

**Figure 1.13**  Use of logos to promote brand image

3.  A confectionery manufacturer wants a cheap, self-service mint dispenser that they can supply free to shopkeepers. The dispenser will be used to sell a new type of mint called 'Icemints'. The dispenser should fold flat when not being used, so that it does not take up too much space when being transported to shops. It should be able to hold 100 packets of mints. The illustration below shows a packet of 'Icemints'.

(a)  Sketch three possible ideas with an advertising slogan added.

(b)  Make a card model of the best idea. Use rolled up tubes of card to test your idea.

20 × 100 mm long

**Figure 1.14**  A packet for Icemints

4.  Study the data shown in the chart below. What does it show? Draw a chart or diagram to illustrate the key points that can be extracted from the data.

HOW WIMBLEDON'S WINNERS HAVE GOT RICHER

| YEAR | MEN'S WINNER | PRIZE MONEY (£) |
|---|---|---|
| 1968 | ROD LAVER | 2 000 |
| 1972 | STAN SMITH | 5 000 |
| 1974 | JIMMY CONNORS | 10 000 |
| 1979 | BJORN BORG | 20 000 |
| 1982 | JIMMY CONNORS | 41 000 |
| 1983 | JOHN McENROE | 66 000 |
| 1984 | JOHN McENROE | 100 000 |
| 1987 | PAT CASH | 155 000 |
| 1990 | STEFAN EDBERG | 230 000 |
| 1991 | MICHAEL STICH | 240 000 |

| YEAR | WOMEN'S WINNER | PRIZE MONEY (£) |
|---|---|---|
| 1968 | BILLIE JEAN KING | 750 |
| 1973 | BILLIE JEAN KING | 3 000 |
| 1975 | BILLIE JEAN KING | 7 000 |
| 1976 | CHRIS EVERT | 10 000 |
| 1979 | MARTINA NAVRATILOVA | 18 000 |
| 1982 | MARTINA NAVRATILOVA | 37 000 |
| 1984 | MARTINA NAVRATILOVA | 90 000 |
| 1987 | MARTINA NAVRATILOVA | 139 000 |
| 1990 | MARTINA NAVRATILOVA | 207 000 |
| 1991 | STEFFI GRAFF | 216 000 |

5.  Can you translate the caption of this cartoon into English? What point is
    the cartoon making about computers today?

**Figure 1.15**   French cartoon

# 2

# Decision making within the business

Every organization needs some form of structure. This will set out a chain of command and responsibility. The internal organization of a business is usually illustrated by an organogram which shows the lines of control. The organization of a business will vary greatly according to the size and type of business. A small firm will have fewer posts of responsibility and different organizations will have different officials. It would be very unlikely for a firm that concentrated on selling, for instance, to have the same group of managers as one that concentrated on production.

Because small firms employ fewer people they cannot be organized so easily into departments and management will have more general functions. In large firms there will tend to be more specialists.

## Departmental organization in large businesses

Large organizations in the UK will normally be private companies, public companies or public corporations (see Chapter 4 on ownership and control). In this chapter we will concentrate on the sort of organizational structure which we might expect in a large public company.

The company will be owned by shareholders who appoint a committee, known as a board of directors, to represent their interests. The board of directors then appoints a managing director who, like a head teacher or the principal of a college, has the job of making sure that all the various departments are running well. (See Fig. 2.1.) Every organization is different and

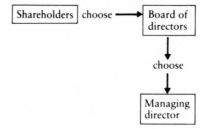

**Figure 2.1** The control structure of a large public company

any organizational structure will be aimed at meeting the particular needs of that body. The organogram in Fig. 2.2 may be found in some company structures, but you are more than likely to find something quite different.

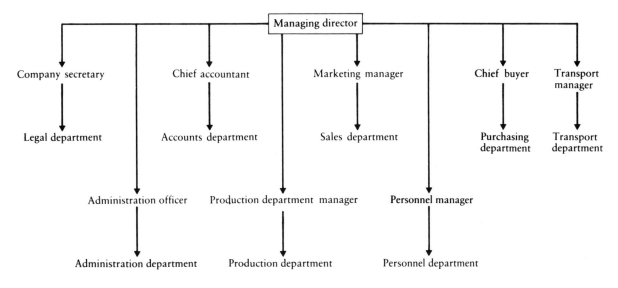

**Figure 2.2**  Organization of a possible company structure

## The company secretary and the legal department

The company secretary is responsible for all the legal matters of the company. If paperwork is not done properly, the company secretary could end up in court. For example, he or she must fill in and periodically amend all of the records and documents involved in having set up the company such as the Memorandum and Articles of Association as well as keep the share register. Other departmental managers may consult the company secretary on legal matters.

## The administration officers and the administration department

Many large firms have a central office which is responsible for controlling the general paperwork of the whole firm. This department might handle the filing of materials, the company's mail, word-processing and data-handling facilities. The modern office uses information technology to service all of the company's key areas.

### The chief accountant and the accounts office

The chief accountant is responsible for supervising the accounts department. The accounts section must keep a detailed record of all money paid in and out and present the final balance sheet at the end of the year. Modern accounts are stored on computer files and accounting procedures are greatly simplified by the use of computers.

### The production department manager and the production department

The production manager is responsible for making sure that raw materials are provided and made into finished goods effectively. He or she must make sure that work is carried out smoothly and must supervise procedures for making work more efficient and as enjoyable as possible.

### The marketing manager and the marketing/sales department

Marketing may be combined with sales or the two functions may be separate. Marketing is concerned with the finding out of what people want and then the meeting of their wants and needs for a profit (see Chapter 8). Sales is, as the name suggests, concerned with all aspects of selling to customers. In a combined sales/marketing department, the manager will be responsible for market research, promotions, advertising, distribution and the organization of product sales.

### The personnel manager and the personnel department

The personnel department is responsible for the recruitment and training of staff (see Chapter 12). It is also responsible for health and safety at work, trade union negotiation and staff welfare.

### The chief buyer and the purchasing department

The buying department of a firm is responsible for all items bought by that firm. It send for quotations from suppliers, issues orders and keeps track of the delivery of goods. It also checks that the prices, quantities and quality of goods received are as expected.

### The transport department

This department is responsible for obtaining supplies and making sure that goods are delivered in good condition, in the right place and at the right time.

### Case Study—The organization of a buying group at Marks and Spencer plc

Marks and Spencer is perhaps the world's best known high street retailer. Some of the products they sell include recipe dishes. To provide these dishes in the way that the customer requires involves getting together a team of specialists:

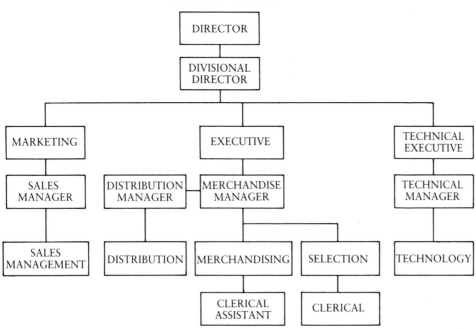

MARKS & SPENCER

THE ORGANIZATION OF A TYPICAL
BUYING GROUP

**Figure 2.3**  Personnel hierarchy in a buying group

The *selectors* must choose the recipe dishes that they want to be prepared for sale. They work with top chefs and restaurants to come up with state-of-the-art dishes. Creating a dish includes finding 'a source of excellence'. For instance, if it is an Italian dish the selectors consult with the best Italian chefs and cookery schools in search of the best ideas. When the recipe has been selected the selectors will choose a food manufacturer to make the product.

The *merchandisers* are responsible for negotiating prices, estimating the quantities of ingredients and fixing up production schedules with manufacturers.

The *technologists* work out how the dish can be made in bulk. They look at any difficulties that might arise in production. They are concerned with quality and such things as 'sell by' dates.

The *distribution manager* will be concerned with working out schedules for getting the goods to the stores.

The *marketing and sales managers* will look at how goods are selling in the shops, which lines to expand and which lines to cut.

*Questions*

1.  Explain why each of the departments described above is important to the total buying operation at Marks and Spencer.
2.  Why are food manufacturers keen to work for Marks and Spencer?
3.  How are Marks and Spencer able to maintain the quality of their supplies?
4.  Why might different specialists in the buying team need to meet regularly?
5.  Why is the role of the technologist crucial in supporting the buying group?
6.  How would you go about identifying a new recipe dish for production by Marks and Spencer?
7.  Design a recipe dish. Try it out.
8.  What problems might you have in producing this dish in bulk?
9.  How might you have to modify this dish for sale to the mass market?

## Decision making within an organization

Decisions can be made and carried out in a number of ways. In some organizations all major decisions will be taken by senior managers and passed down to junior employees. Decisions are said to pass down the line from senior management, to middle management, to the employee doing the routine work. Such an organization is said to be hierarchical. Each employee knows who their line manager is and takes commands from this official. There may be just a few layers in the hierarchy as in Fig. 2.4, or there may be many. Such organizations may be effective when work is very routine and easy to predict, but there are a number of problems with such a system.

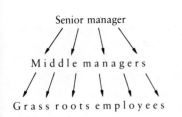

**Figure 2.4**   Organization hierarchy chart

1.  Grass roots employees may become discontented because they are not allowed to show initiative. They may grumble about the 'hierarchy' (people above them) and become uncooperative.
2.  When decisions need to be made quickly junior employees may be unwilling or unable to react. They may say things like 'I can't do anything about it. It's not my job. You'll have to wait until Mrs X. comes back'.

3.  Hierarchical organizations can become costly to run, if there are a lot of people wasting time reporting to each other.

In contrast to a hierarchical system, an organization may be based on more democratic lines. Where decisions need to be made quickly by individuals, it makes sense to give them the power and freedom to make and carry out these decisions. In such an organization individuals would be appointed to carry out tasks according to their skill and experience. They would then be expected to think and act for themselves. One way of representing such an organization would be as a circle. Each member would be an independent decision maker, although they would clearly consult with each other from time to time. An example might be a group of vets working as a partnership (see Chapter 4).

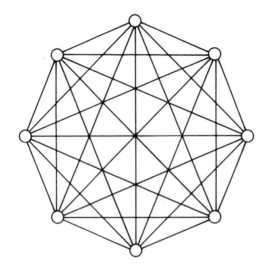

**Figure 2.5**   A circle (democratic) network

## Strategy and tactics

Every company should be clear about its strategy. This comprises the major business aims of a company. It covers the:

- What?
- How?
- When?
- Where?

For example, a supermarket chain may set out a strategy to become the market leader in out-of-town supermarket sales in the United Kingdom. To do this it might set itself the target of having a store near every major town and city in the UK by the year 2000 offering the best value for money prices to be found.

Having established its basic strategy, it will need to operate on a day-to-day level to meet these aims. In the short term it will need to alter its tactics i.e., its working practices and policies. For example, when a new rival sets out to undercut its prices, it may for a time enter into a price war in selling various key items. When rivals offer free car parking for purchases over £50, it may employ the tactic of offering free car parking for purchases over £40 and so on. The day-to-day tactics should not deflect the general strategy. From time to time the supermarket will need to re-evaluate its strategy and possibly adjust it in the light of changing circumstances.

## Management

The way in which humans use resources is not simply an instinctive reaction to a stimulus like hunger, or pain. Unlike lesser animals, humans are able to 'plan, coordinate and control'—that is, to manage resources. We are able to use our thinking skills to consider and decide how best to use resources. The management function is thus essentially that of:

- Planning
- Coordinating
- Controlling

A *skilled manager* is able to use and direct resources well. The resources may be human resources (e.g., by a personnel manager) or physical resources (e.g., by a production manager). A skilled manager will use resources wisely in order to get maximum return from a given quantity of resources. The skilled manager will handle people wisely. Some of these management skills will come naturally to managers, others will need to be learnt.

Modern organizations have grown up according to basic management principles. The managers in these organizations plan, organize and control in a way that produces consistent results, even in large and complex multinationals. In a rapidly changing world an additional quality is now required as well as management skills. We can call this additional factor *leadership*. Leadership is the ability to make things happen and to introduce *change* to organizations.

We can illustrate this need for leadership by reference to American companies. For many years companies such as Xerox (with its copier patent) and Chrysler (cars), both with a strong home market, only needed strong, efficient management to make the most of their massive market shares. Then the world changed. And kept on changing at a faster and faster rate. Management, which is all about maintaining order, proved ill-equipped to deal with change. Xerox and Chrysler reeled under the onslaught of Japanese competition. Fortunately, these companies were able to recruit leaders with a vision who were able to change the way in which the companies were run and the companies were able to fight back. Both management and leadership are therefore important in today's rapidly changing business environment.

# The de-layering of large companies

An important change is taking place in large companies in the 1990's – some layers of company organization are being stripped away. Organizational charts for a number of companies are being flattened out. Examples of companies which have implemented recent middle-management cutbacks in the UK include Boots PLC, British Petroleum, Storehouse, British Telecom, the Stock Exchange and the Trustee Savings Bank (TSB). While those organizations which are now shedding management layers are obviously trying to cut costs, most also argue that they need to improve communications, reduce red tape and increase their responsiveness to customer demands.

We can, for example, apply this argument to BP. For any company, but particularly one with a wide geographical spread and wide range of product types, decentralization of one kind or another is essential. Most decisions, especially tactical decisions, cannot be taken effectively at head office which may be miles or continents away. They have to be taken immediately, on the spot, by people who know all the circumstances. There is often no time to ring back to head office, even if head office had any understanding of that particular problem.

## Case Study—Who to employ

Fashion Design is a company that produces clothes for fashion designers. An independent designer comes up with an idea for a new garment, displays it at fashion shows and takes orders. If the orders are substantial then they ask Fashion Design to produce the garments in bulk. Fashion Design is made up of a managing director, a sales department with a manager and three sales representatives, an accountant, a personnel manager, a distribution manager and three van drivers, an office manager and three clerical staff, and a production manager in charge of two chargehands and 120 machinists.

The business has done well over the years but is now going through a period of rapid change. There is fierce competition both within the domestic trade and also with foreign competitors. The nature of production is changing. Before, it was possible to set up a regular production pattern and systems to ensure that work ran smoothly. Today, designers are demanding far more flexibility in garment manufacture. One day the production line needs to be set up in a particular pattern, the next the system needs to be quite different. It is necesssary for the production manager to organize new systems and to quickly persuade the machinists that the new way needs to be put into effect.

The existing production manager has been struggling with the changes and has asked for early retirement. It is necessary to find a replacement immediately. The job has been widely advertised and three applicants for the post are to be interviewed next week. The three candidates for the job are described below.

*Jessie Hanson has been working in the trade for twenty years. She has been working for a similar company for a smaller salary. She has built up a good working relationship with the machinists at her current place of work. The company she works for uses a more traditional method of production where they rarely reorganize the production line. They are able to do this because they are a smaller firm employing fewer workers and turning out fewer garments.*

*David Lucas has just graduated from college where he has studied Production Management and Fashion. At college he did a six months' work experience placement with the leading fashion clothes manufacturer in France. He is familiar with all the latest techniques but has had no position of responsibility.*

*Sally Davies is a production manager in a factory producing fashion shoes. It is a product requiring a great deal of flexibility. No sooner has she got a product up and running than she has to switch to the next latest fashion. In the early days she made a few mistakes in trying to get her machinists to adapt too quickly. However, she learnt from her mistakes and now has a good reputation in her own business for getting things done and being able to compete with the toughest competition.*

*Questions*

1. Draw an organogram to illustrate the organizational structure at Fashion Design.
2. What evidence is given in the article to suggest that Fashion Design will benefit from a new production manager?
3. What problems might be caused by appointing a new production manager?
4. Do you think that Fashion Design would be better suited to a hierarchical or a democratic form of organization? Explain your answer.
5. What qualities would you look for in the new production manager?
6. What questions would you ask at the interview to try and find out which of the candidates is most suitable?
7. Which of the three applicants do you think would be most suitable for the production manager's job, given the evidence available? Why?

# Making decisions

Is it better for just one person to make a decision or a larger group? It depends on the situation. The more people there are inolved in the decision-making process, the more points of view to be heard, the easier it is to thrash problems around. However, the more people there are involved, the greater the chance of disagreement and time wasting. It has been suggested that the best group size is five people because:

- the odd number means that there will always be a majority view (e.g., 3 against 2, or 4 against 1).
- the group is big enough to avoid mistakes resulting from lack of information.
- the group is small enough to involve everyone.

## Meetings

Meetings are an important place for making decisions. The organization of meetings is dealt with in greater depth in Chapter 9. Henry Mintzberg, in his book *The Nature of Managerial Work*, found that in large organizations managers spent 22 per cent of their time at their desk, 6 per cent on the telephone, 3 per cent on other activities (including time spent in the toilet), but a whopping 69 per cent in meetings. That means that most managers spend more of their waking hours from Monday to Friday in meetings at work (on average 35 hours per week) than with their families at home (on average about 25 hours).

Meetings need to include representatives of those involved with a particular decision. When people feel cut off from the decision-making process they may become alienated from an organization. Meetings can provide attenders with a feeling that they are important. Mark McCormack, of International Management Group, got so fed up with staff wanting to be included in meetings that he set up a company-wide meeting. Its purpose was not to discuss company business, but simply to make everyone feel good because they were all invited.

# Questions

1. Complete the following sentences using the words below:

   | | |
   |---|---|
   | Organogram | Tactics |
   | De-layering | Strategy |
   | Board of directors | Democratic |
   | Shareholders | Management |
   | Hierarchical | Marketing |

   (a) In the 1990s several large public corporations have been . . . . . . . . their organizations by stripping off excess middle managers.

(b)  An . . . . . . . . is a chart illustrating 'who does what' in a company.

(c)  . . . . . . . are the day-to-day decisions made by a company, made in the light of changing circumstances.

(d)  . . . . . . . . is concerned with planning, coordinating and controlling an organization.

(e)  A . . . . . . . . organization makes it possible for each member of the company to have a say in decision making.

(f)  The major decisions that a company makes will be thought through in its . . . . . . . . This will include the *what*, *when* and the *how*.

(g)  . . . . . . . . is concerned with anticipating and meeting customers' needs and wants.

(h)  The real owners of a public limited company are its . . . . . . . .

(i)  A . . . . . . . . organization is made up of a number of carefully structured positions of responsibility.

(j)  The shareholders of a company will be represented by its . . . . . . . .

2.  Who would you expect the following employees to report to in a large public company?

(a)  a salesperson
(b)  a machine minder
(c)  the production manager
(d)  a director
(e)  a buyer
(f)  the managing director
(g)  a word-processor operator
(h)  a trainee accountant
(i)  a lorry driver

3.  What would you consider to be the five main departments of the following?

(a)  an insurance company
(b)  a leisure centre
(c)  a chocolate manufacturer
(d)  a supermarket

4.  You are the managing director of a company that produces tin boxes for packing biscuits and other products. Up to now you have just had one factory in the West Midlands. However, you have recently taken over another firm with two factories in South Wales. You have decided to reorganize the management structure of the company to cut down on the number of managerial posts. Look at the organograms in Figs. 2.6–2.8 and decide how to reorganize the company. Draw a new organogram to illustrate your new organization. Why have you made the changes?

(a)  Which of the three factories do you think that it would be easiest to streamline?

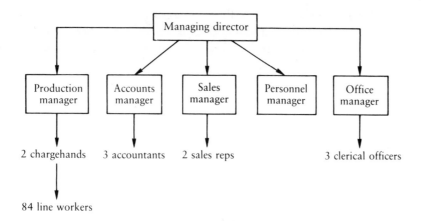

**Figure 2.6**  Organization of West Midlands factory

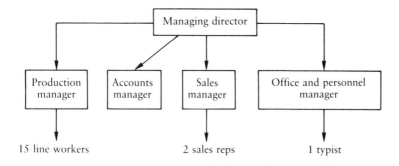

**Figure 2.7**  Organization of Cardiff factory

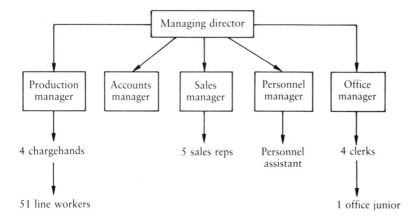

**Figure 2.8**  Organization of Neath factory

(b)  How do you think the nature of the three factories might be different?

(c)  How would you go about making changes? Why might this not be easy?

(d)  Look at someone else's plans for restructuring. How do they differ from your own? Discuss them. Is it possible in the light of this fresh insight to modify your previous plans.

5.  In 1980, Vickers and Rolls-Royce merged (joined together) to form one company. The most important task for the managing director was to make the company competitive in international markets. A strategy was set in place to meet this target.

    It was decided to have large chunks of the business represented at board level by 'barons' i.e., the managers of the various divisions (operating parts) of the company.

    However, this soon led to problems. Each of the 'barons' was concerned with fighting for the interests of their own division. Their first concern was to protect and/or expand their own empire. They found it difficult to think corporately (i.e., to think in terms of the whole company).

    However, at board level it is necessary to take care of the whole business in the interests of the shareholders.

    In 1985, the company reorganized its board structure. The new board consisted of the managing director, chairman, finance director and the commercial director. From that time if a 'baron' wanted to carry out a major change they would have to approach the board who could come up with a quick decision.

    (a)  Who does the managing director of a company represent?
    (b)  Who do department heads within an organization represent?
    (c)  Why might it be a problem to have department heads on the board of a company?
    (d)  Highlight what you consider to be the major benefits of the changes that are mentioned in the article.

# 3

# A business within the economy

A business operates within the wider economy. Each and every day a business owner makes many decisions. These decisions are influenced by what is going on in the wider economy. For example, if prices are rising then the individual business owner may be forced to push his or her prices up in order to cover rising costs. If, on the other hand, increased competition from other businesses is pushing prices down then the business owner may need to respond likewise.

The economy is a system which decides how scarce resources will be used.

## Resources

In any society resources will be scarce relative to the need for them. A resource is a means of support. It is any feature of our environment that helps to support our well being.

There are two main types of resource:

1.  Physical or natural resources—such as soil, climate, water, minerals, forests and fisheries.
2.  Human resources—people and their various skills.

## Opportunity cost

Businesses use up resources which are scarce. If society had all the land, labour, raw materials and other resources that it needed to make all the goods that people could possibly want, then we could produce goods without making sacrifices. However, resources are scarce and therefore when we produce an item we are taking away resources from something else. This is a major problem for all societies. The real cost of using resources for one purpose is the next best use to which they could be put. The opportunity cost of any activity is the next best alternative given up.

## Case Study—Houses versus a shopping precinct

This case study represents a typical business problem from society's viewpoint.

You live in an area in which there are 1300 homeless families. There are 12 500 people on the council house waiting list. Within this area there is a 17 acre site which is the last large piece of land available for council development. This land has been derelict for ten years.

A property development company has asked to buy this land for £20 million to build a shopping precinct, a car park and 150 houses for sale.

Housing groups are angry about this scheme. They put forward the following arguments:

1. It would fail to provide cheap housing at a time of real need.
2. There is no proof of the need for a shopping precinct.
3. The property development scheme will not make full use of the land.
4. There is an alternative housing plan that would involve building 410 houses, two-thirds of which would be for rent. A council spokesperson has said that public opinion over the two plans is 'neck and neck', but a spokesperson for a homeless families campaign says the local public are firmly in favour of the 410 houses plan.

### Questions

1. What alternative uses of the land are mentioned in the case study?
2. What would be the real cost if the land was used as a shopping precinct and private housing estate? (Who is the cost to? Are there different costs to different groups and individuals?)
3. How would you go about deciding which scheme was best?
4. Is it possible to provide a scheme that is best for everyone? Or will there always be gainers and losers?
5. What is the best use of the land for the people in the area?
6. What would be the best use of the land for the wider economy?
7. What sort of information is needed to make an effective planning decision? How could this information be collected?

# Economic systems

The problem of scarcity exists in all societies. For example, a piece of plastic can be used to make many end products. However, at any one time there is not enough plastic to meet all the uses to which it could be put. As a result of scarcity is is necessary for a society to decide how scarce resources will be used. Important questions to consider are:

1. What will be produced?
2. How will it be produced?
3. For whom will it be produced?

## Questions

Look at the following newspaper headlines and split them up according to whether they raise a 'what', a 'how' or a 'for whom' issue:

1. 'Pensioners to get higher benefits'
2. 'Textiles in decline while leisure centres boom'
3. 'Bring back craft skills'
4. 'New technology boosts output'
5. 'Teachers to lose out in new pay deal'
6. 'UK to produce more machine tools'
7. 'Wages increase for key workers'

## Systems for making economic decisions

A system is needed to sort out these three types of problems.

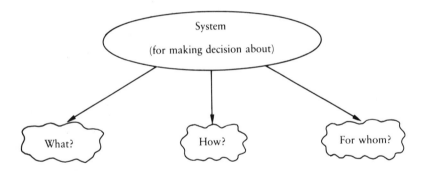

**Figure 3.1** System diagram

In the distant past these decisions were made by custom and tradition. For example, the way that crops were grown and shared out was decided by folk tradition. In most parts of the world traditional economies have given way to three major systems.

1. The centrally planned system.
2. The free-market system.
3. The mixed system.

### Central planning

In a centrally planned system many of the decisions are made by a central planning organization. Smaller groups such as factories and other business units submit their plans to a local committee. The local plans are then fed back for approval at the centre. The central organization might then decide what resources will be made available to each local area and in turn allocates resources to each factory, farm or other productive unit. (See Fig. 3.2—factories, farms, cinemas and shops are just some examples of units that might use up resources.)

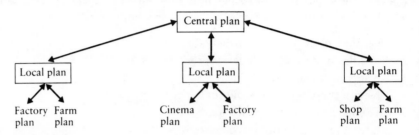

**Figure 3.2** How a centrally planned system works

Up until the end of the 1980's most of the Eastern European countries had centrally planned systems. Today, however, many of them have shifted in the direction of the free market. Examples of countries that still operate a planned system include China and Cuba.

### The free market

In a free market the decisions about what, how and for whom are made by consumer and producers; the government does not intervene.

Consumers decide what they want to do with their money. They use money to vote for the products that they want to buy. If everybody wants to buy a copy of *Business Studies in Practice* then the McGraw-Hill Book Company will print more copies and may be able to put the price up. If a product sells well firms will be inclined to produce it. But if no one wants the product firms will stop making it, since under the market system firms will seek to make profits from the goods they sell.

Producers are forced to pay attention to the wishes of consumers in order to survive. Of course producers can, and often do, try to manipulate consumers into buying their goods. Advertising can be very persuasive. For example, in late 1991 Maureen Lipman returned to our screens to inform us of the new BT share issue.

### Questions

1. In recent years the demand for videos and take-away meals has increased. How have producers responded?
2. In 1990 the price of borrowing money increased. How do you think this affected the housing market?

3. In recent years the demand for black and white television sets and push along lawnmowers has fallen. How have producers responded?
4. Every year the fashion industry spends a lot of money on advertising clothes. How do consumers react?
5. What factors decide whether consumers have more power to keep prices low or producers have the power to push prices up?
6. List five advantages that you think that (a) the free market has over central planning and (b) central planning has over the free market.

## The mixed economy

The mixed economy combines elements of both the free-market and the central planning systems. Some decisions are made solely through the private sector, while other decisions are made by the government. The UK is an example of a mixed economy: some parts of industry are owned and run by the government but large chunks of the business world remain in private hands.

## Questions

Which of the following products are produced/handled mainly by government-owned businesses and which by privately-owned businesses?

1. Coal
2. Bread
3. Electricity
4. Cinema entertainment
5. Bank notes
6. Fish
7. Insurance
8. Vehicle licences
9. Railway journeys
10. Banking services
11. Sewage disposal
12. School meals
13. School textbooks
14. Airline flights
15. Bus journeys
16. Teaching services
17. The police service
18. Telecommunications
19. Computers
20. Glass

# Production

Production is adding value to something. The farmer grows potatoes and takes them out of the ground. The transport company takes these potatoes to the store, where they are then sold to the retailer. The retailer sells them to the fish and chip shop. We buy them as chips. Each stage involved in bringing them to us meant the adding of value to the potato. Just imagine if we had to grow them, harvest them, scrub them, slice them and fry them every time.

Production includes a wide range of occupations including acting, playing professional football, selling ice-cream, running a flower shop, working as a buyer in a department store, acting as a paid childminder and thousands more.

Each of these occupations is concerned with adding a bit more value to something to turn it into a product that is finally purchased by a consumer who derives satisfaction from it. When we go to Wembley to watch David Platt play for England we also rely on the ticket seller, the car park attendant, and the police officer patrolling the crowd. Each of these adds a significant amount of value to our enjoyment of the game.

In the last quarter of the twentieth century we have seen a steep decline in the numbers of people employed in manufacturing in the UK. For example, in 1979 there were 6.9 million employees in manufacturing—by the end of 1990 there were only 5.1 million. Manufacturing has been replaced by service industries as the main source of employment. Today you will find that most people are employed in a service occupation such as hairdressing, office work and leisure industries. Carry out a survey among members of your class. What sorts of jobs do members of your families do? What percentage are involved in manufacturing? Show your results in a word-processed document with suitable graphics.

Much of the growth in employment has been centred around various 'growth poles'. For example, towns such as Harrogate in North Yorkshire and Peterborough and Grantham in the East Midlands have boomed. Parts of the South-East of England and East Anglia have been growth poles. In Scotland many jobs in the computer industry have been created around Stirling in an area now known as 'Silicon Glen'. In Wales many firms have set up along the 'M4 Corridor'.

Production is normally classified under three headings: primary, secondary and tertiary. Primary industry is concerned with taking out 'the gifts of nature', i.e. extracting natural resources. The secondary sector is concerned with constructing and making things. The tertiary sector is made up of services. There are two parts to this sector:

1.   Commercial services which make trading (buying and selling) possible.
2.   Direct services to people (e.g., your hairdresser gives you a personal service).

Table 3.1 shows occupations in the different sectors—you should add to these lists. (Where would you put farming, manicure, retailing, clothes making, oil drilling, publishing, car assembly, painting and decorating, computer programming, typing, giving golf lessons?)

**Table 3.1** Examples of occupations in the different sectors of industry—add to these lists yourself

| Primary | Secondary | Tertiary | |
| --- | --- | --- | --- |
| | | Commercial services | Direct services |
| Mining | Building | Insurance | Police |
| Fishing | Chemicals | Banking | Hairdressing |
| Forestry | Food processing | Advertising | Photography |

## Case Study—The end of the line for the Trabant

In 1990 the new Germany was created. What had previously been East Germany had been a centrally planned economy. West Germany had been a mixed economy in which prices had been free from government interference.

Before the joining together of the two parts of Germany, a car known as the Trabant had been virtually the only type of car available in East Germany. More than three million Trabants had been sold since production began in the late 1950s. The same model of car was sold from 1964 to 1991. There was no other car available and because people could only buy the one model there was no competition. The planners saw no need to change the design because they could sell every car that they produced. The car was functional (i.e., it served the purpose of getting a driver from place A to place B), it was cheap to run and it was more or less repairable with a hammer, a ball of string and chewing gum. However, it was an environmental disaster. It was made largely from a cheap fibre-glass material called Duroplast, which is everlasting. The car was noisy, gave off a lot of fumes, and the only way to destroy the cars was to burn them which gave off poisonous fumes.

Before the joining together of the two Germanies there was a long waiting list for the Trabant (some people waited for twenty years). After re-unification nobody wanted to buy a Trabant. The customers deserted to buy Western cars. The Trabant was obsolete in a modern market. It was no longer possible to continue producing an obsolete car at a cost of 11,000 Deutschmarks (£3,700) and to sell it for 9,000 Deutchsmarks. In May 1991, the company was forced to close down and lay off 9000 employees.

*Questions*

1. Why do you think that so little change was made to the Trabant over the years?
2. What would be the benefits to (a) producers and (b) consumers of sticking to the standard model?
3. Why would a free market force change?
4. How could the Trabant survive in a free market?
5. What problems do you think would have been caused by the disappearance of the Trabant?
6. Explain in detail why you think that the disappearance of the Trabant has been a good or a bad thing for (a) people living in what was East Germany and (b) the world economy.

## The firm as a system within the economy

Any business organization will turn inputs into outputs by using a number of processes.

**Figure 3.3**

For example, in baking bread:
The inputs will include—flour, yeast, water, electricity/gas, human skill, an oven, baking trays and so on.
The processes will include—measuring, sifting, mixing, kneading, heating and cooling.
The output will be the finished bread. However, in addition we should also consider as outputs the wages of the employees, the satisfaction of consumers, taxes paid to the government and so on.

The firm itself can be seen as part of a larger productive system. The national economy produces outputs using the inputs of individual organizations.

## Interdependence

If we look at the working of any business we will notice interdependence both within the firm and between the firm and its wider environment (see Fig. 3.4). Huntley, Boorne and Stevens makes a wide range of tin boxes of many different shapes and sizes. These boxes are used for packaging biscuits, sweets, tea and many other products.

### An example of interdependence—inputs, processes and outputs at Huntley, Boorne and Stevens

If we look at the working of any business we will notice interdependence both within the firm and between the firm and its wider environment (see Fig. 3.4). Huntley, Boorne and Stevens makes a wide range of tin boxes of many different shapes and sizes. These boxes are used for packaging biscuits, sweets, tea and many other products.

Huntley, Boorne and Stevens also have an aerosol line which is highly automated. As well as specialist management staff there is a wide range of other specialist jobs resulting from extensive division of labour. Specialist staff include:

1.  Sales people
2.  Design artists
3.  Engineering designers
4.  Printers
5.  Factory-floor workers
6.  Engineers

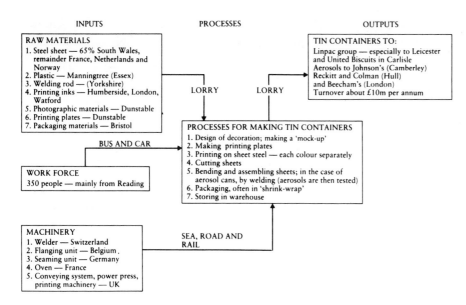

**Figure 3.4** Inputs, processes and outputs at Huntley, Boorne and Stevens Ltd

| | |
|---|---|
| 7. Buyers | 10. Lorry drivers |
| 8. Office workers | 11. Canteen workers |
| 9. Cleaners | 12. Secretarial staff |

If we go on to study the inputs of the business we can see that inputs come from various parts of the UK and the world. If we look at the processes involved in production we can see a wide range of specialist, yet interdependent, tasks. If we look at the outputs of the firm, we notice that many outlets are supplied and eventually products will be distributed all over the world.

We can see that the process of manufacture and distribution is held together by a transport network. In addition, the firm will have to use a wide range of specialist business services including banks, insurance services, import/export agencies, translation services and postal and telecommunications facilities. Business takes place in a wide environment. Changes in Bristol and Belgium can be as important to your organization as changes in your own neighbourhood.

## The aims of a business

What are the main aims of business? Although making a profit can be very important there are other considerations.

People as a rule will only tie up their money in a business if they are satisfied with the return they get from it. Making a profit is important. However, you will find many people who are prepared to take a cut in their earnings to set up in business. Why? They will often say that personal freedom is very important—the freedom to make your own decisions.

A business organization can be made up of many people, each with their own ambitions and aims. Motivations in the running of a business might include:

- *Maximization of sales*. In some large companies the salaries earned by managers may depend on the size of the business. They have an interest therefore in seeing the business expand. High sales also mean that competitors may make fewer sales.
- *Prestige*. For some people the image and name of their company can be very important. The company may spend a lot of money on public relations so that it is well thought of.
- *Survival*. In some businesses the aims of the firm may just be about surviving. An old-established company may, for instance, have the objective of keeping the business in the family or keeping on its employees.
- *As a hobby or interest*. Some people can afford to run a small business at a loss. There is enjoyment in running the thing for its own sake.

### Case Study—Joseph Robinson's grocery store

When Joseph Robinson retired from the Civil Service he hoped to buy a small book shop in Harrogate where he lived. However, he found that there was already too much competition in this field and in any case rents in the town centre were too high. Instead, he bought a small corner shop with living quarters at the back for £42,000. It cost him £1,000 to stock his shop and a further £800 for fixtures. He sold his existing house for £50,000 and had additional savings of £22,000, which were invested in the building society at a rate of interest of 10 per cent.

Joseph has made some calculations based on his monthly business:

| | |
|---|---|
| Cost of new stock each month | £800 |
| Value of sales each month | £1,300 |
| Expenses per month | £400 |

He opens the shop, which sells general groceries, at about 9 a.m. on most days. He closes for an hour at midday and then works to any time between 6 p.m. and 8 p.m. He has made many friends and plans to run the shop for at least five years.

*Questions*

1. Is Mr Robinson's business venture financially sound?
2. Can you foresee any potential pitfalls?
3. What do you think is Mr Robinson's main business aim?
4. How could you judge whether Mr Robinson is being successful?

5. Do you think that Mr Robinson is using his capital in the best possible way?
6. How will other people benefit from Mr Robinson's activities?

## The government and business

In a mixed economy the government plays an important role in steering that economy.

The public sector is that part of the economy which is government-owned. The private sector is that part of the economy which is owned by private citizens.

Some of the ways in which the government plays an important part in business life include:

1. Setting out rules and laws for some of the things that can and can not be done.
2. Encouraging some activities through subsidy and discouraging other activities by taxes or fines.
3. Running some business activities through its own business organizations.

## en France
## ☐ EMPLOI
### Moins d'ouvriers, plus de cadres

D'apres une enquête de l'Insee portant sur la période mars 1984–mars 1987, le nombre d'ouvriers a diminué de 2,8% alors que les effectifs de l'encadrement augmentaient de 2,3%.

La diminution des emplois ouvriers touche plus particulièrement les ouvriers non qualifiés, leurs effectifs régressant d'environ 4% par an pour l'ensemble des activités. Cette baisse atteint même 6% dans les secteurs de l'industrie et du BTP. La chute reste en revanche moins importante pour ce qui est des ouvriers qualifiés (−2%, toutes activités confondues).

Chez les cadres, l'enquête, qui recouvre les établissements de plus de dix salariés, constate un accroissement du nombre des ingénieurs et cadres techniques (+2,3%) ainsi que des personnels administratifs et commerciaux (+1,7%).

Cette étude indique par ailleurs que les employés sont en baisse (−0,4%) au contraire des profondeurs intermédiaires qui progressent de 1%. Dans cette dernière branche, les professions de santé, du travail social et du clergé accusent la hausse la plus importante avec +3,5%.

Les tâches les moins qualifiées régressent également dans les emplois administratifs pendant que les professions liées à l'informatique enregistrent les plus fortes hausses.

Figure 3.5  Working in France

Read the article above and then complete the table overleaf, indicating by a tick whether there has been an increase or decrease in the number of jobs in each sector or category. The first one has been done for you.

| Sector/category of job | Increased | Decreased |
|---|---|---|
| Manual workers | | ✓ |
| Salaried staff | | |
| Unskilled workers | | |
| Semi-skilled | | |
| Engineers | | |
| Administrators | | |
| Caring professions | | |
| Unskilled jobs | | |
| Jobs in IT | | |

## Questions

1.   Complete the following sentences using the words below:

Mixed economy                    Interdependence
Centrally planned economy        Division of labour
Free-market economy              Resource
Opportunity cost                 Public sector
Specialization                   Private sector

(a)  A . . . . . . . . is a 'means of support'.
(b)  The . . . . . . . involves each member of the workforce concentrating on a specialized task.
(c)  By . . . . . . . . we mean the next best alternative that is sacrificed.
(d)  In a . . . . . . . . major decisions are fed through a planning agency.
(e)  A . . . . . . . . combines elements of central planning and the free market.
(f)  In a . . . . . . . decisions are made by producers.
(g)  The . . . . . . . . is the government-owned sector of the economy.
(h)  The . . . . . . . . is made up of privately-owned businesses.
(i)  The . . . . . . . . of economic units is one of the basic facts of business life.
(j)  . . . . . . . . involves individual workers concentrating on given skills.

2.   In the late twentieth century, production in the United Kingdom depends heavily on the service industry. In 1990, the percentage of employees in each major industrial sector was:

Primary        4%
Secondary      32%
Service        64%

(a) Give one example of a job in:
   (i) the primary sector
   (ii) the secondary sector
   (iii) The services sector
(b) Using examples show how commercial services are essential to the smooth running of the economy.
(c) 'Manufacturing is still important to the United Kingdom economy.' Explain why you agree or disagree with this statement.
3. The table below shows the employment by sector in a town in Northern Ireland.

| Sector | 1970 | % employed 1980 | 1990 |
|---|---|---|---|
| Primary | 8 | 6 | 4 |
| Secondary | 45 | 41 | 37 |
| Tertiary | 47 | 53 | 59 |

Table 3.2  Employment by sector in a Northern Ireland town 1970–1990 (the table does not include the unemployed)

(a) Give examples of occupations that would be included in the primary, secondary and tertiary sectors.
(b) Draw a bar graph to show the distribution of employment between sectors in 1990.
(c) Draw a line graph to show the change in employment in the three sectors over time.
(d) Analyse the information to explain the way in which the employment pattern has changed over time.
(e) What further information would you require to make a more detailed analysis?
(f) What use could be made of statistics dividing the workforce into employment by sector?
4. Which of the following are centrally planned economies?
(a) Tanzania (b) China (c) Kenya (d) The UK (e) South Africa (f) India (g) Hungary (h) The Soviet Union (i) Hong Kong (j) Italy (k) North Korea (l) South Korea (m) Germany (n) Jordan (o) Mexico (p) Albania (q) Cuba.
5. Sarah Jones has left her highly paid job working for a merchant bank to set up her own enterprise producing toys for disabled children. Why might Sarah have made this decision? Apart from the profit motive what other aims may business organizations have?

## Coursework

1. What are the principal factors that encourage people to set up a small business? Carry out a piece of research in your local area which will

provide you with evidence to answer this question in respect to ten small businesses.

2.  The illustration below shows a derelict piece of land in an inner city area. It is an area where there are a number of groups who feel that they do not have enough facilities. These include:

    ● teenagers
    ● the unemployed
    ● pensioners

    How would you go about deciding which of these groups to develop the land for. Design and plan a new development for this area. What facilities will you include? What considerations do you need to bear in mind (e.g., safety). Draw out your plans in detail before presenting your ideas to the class.

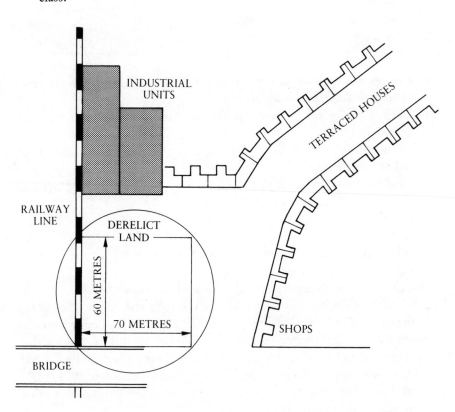

**Figure 3.6**   Diagram of derelict piece of land in an inner city area

# 4

# Ownership and control

**Case Study—The story of Marks and Spencer plc**

Michael Marks arrived in the north of England in 1881 from Russia as a Jewish immigrant. He started off as a hawker (a person who sells from door to door), going around the mining villages selling buttons, needles, ribbons and other small items. He adopted a slogan which he tied on his tray: it said, 'Don't ask the price, it's a penny'. He had this slogan to avoid complications as he could not speak much English.

After he had become quite successful he hired a stall at Leeds market and, as this brought in profits, he started to hire stalls at different markets. He decided that to become more successful he would have to find a partner. In 1894, he became partners with Tom Spencer. Spencer put in £300 to become a partner.

Soon they had 24 stalls at markets and 12 shops. They each began to specialize in specific jobs. Spencer would mainly work at the warehouse and organize administration, whereas Marks specialized in buying goods and looking for new places from which to sell. Their shops were all 'penny bazaars'.

Unfortunately, Spencer became an alcoholic and as a result less reliable. They decided to open up the company into a private company with Marks and Spencer being the major shareholders. Michael Marks remained with the business whereas Spencer retired and left to run a chicken farm. Marks was therefore an executive director (i.e., someone who made decisions and saw that they were carried out), while Spencer was willing to sit back and be a non-executive director.

Michael Marks and Tom Spencer died and Simon Marks (Michael's son) began to develop an important role in running the company. His boyhood friend Israel Sieff also began to play a large part. Simon married Israel's sister and Israel married Simon's sister.

In the early 1920s, Simon Marks went to America to learn about retailing. When he returned he decided that he wanted to change the image of Marks and Spencer giving it a more up-market image. He decided to expand into a whole chain of stores, and to start buying from manufacturers in bulk, so getting a discount, as opposed to buying from wholesalers.

To get the capital for doing this, the company decided to become a public company and sell shares on the Stock Exchange. From here, Marks and Spencer grew to the size it is today and developed the image and quality it still maintains. There are now a large number of shareholders and it is controlled by a board of directors.

The four stages in the growth of Marks and Spencer are summarized in Table 4.1.

**Table 4.1** The development of Marks and Spencer

| Type of business | Ownership | Control |
| --- | --- | --- |
| One-person business | Michael Marks | Michael Marks |
| Partnership | Michael Marks and Tom Spencer | Michael Marks and Tom Spencer |
| Private company | Marks and Spencer and other shareholders | Michael Marks and other executive directors |
| Public company | Shareholders | Directors, including Sieff family |

*Questions*

1. List the four stages in the growth of Marks and Spencer.
2. Explain why Marks and Spencer went through these four stages of growth. (Why did Michael Marks need to take on a partner? Why did the business need to become a private company and later a public company?)
3. What are (a) the advantages and (b) the disadvantages of bringing more people into a company?
4. What do the following terms that were used in the passage mean?
   (a) slogan                 (f) executive director
   (b) hire                   (g) non-executive director
   (c) specialize             (h) discount
   (d) administration         (i) manufacturers/wholesalers
   (e) shareholder            (j) Stock Exchange
5. Explain why ownership and control are not always in the same hands in a public company.

The Marks and Spencer story is one of the best known examples of the growth of a one-person business to a huge multi-national concern.

There are many types of business organization and each of these types has its own distinct features.

The UK has a mixed economy and this means that, as well as many businesses being privately owned, there are others which are run by the state (see Fig. 4.1).

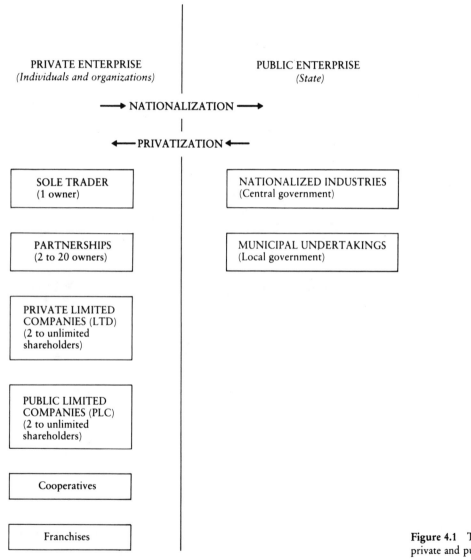

**Figure 4.1** The different types of private and public enterprise

## Private enterprise

### The sole trader

This is the most common form of business ownership and the easiest to set up. A sole trader is a business owned by one person though, of course, this business might employ a large number of people. Many new sole trader businesses are currently being set up by young people. Popular lines of business are ones involving art, design and technology—such as fashion design, mobile hairdressing and graphic design. Young people today are starting up as sole traders in many other areas too—for instance, in electronics and computing, in engineering of all kinds, in services such as plumbing, tiling, roofing, plastering, joinery, electrical contracting and landscape gardening.

Table 4.2 outlines some of the advantages and disadvantages of this form of business ownership.

**Table 4.2** Advantages and disadvantages of being in business as a sole trader

| Advantages | Disadvantages |
|---|---|
| Easy to set up as no special paperwork is required | Having unlimited liability endangers personal possessions |
| Generally these are small businesses, so less capital required | Finance can be difficult to raise |
| Speedy decisions can be made as few people are involved | Small scale limits discounts and other benefits of large-scale production |
| Personal attention is given to company affairs | Prices are often higher than those of larger organizations |
| Special services can be offered to customers | Ill-health/holidays etc may affect the running of the business |
| Cater for the needs of local people | |
| Profits do not have to be shared | |
| Business affairs can be kept private | |

The pressures of competing with larger units cause many sole traders to go out of business. In order to overcome the risks of being small, an owner may look to expand his or her organization by taking in partners.

### Partnership

Partnerships generally have to have between 2 and 20 members, though there are some exceptions. It is advisable to draw up a Deed of Partnership with a solicitor which lays down how profits and losses are to be shared and specifies the duties of each partner, e.g. how much capital each partner should contribute, the duties of partners, how profits will be drawn, procedures for introducing new partners and for settling disputes, etc. The Partnership Act of 1890 established rules which partners could refer to as a last resort, in cases where the Partnership Deed does not cover all problems and difficulties (and when no deed has been drawn up).

Limited, or sleeping partners, may be introduced to a partnership and have limited liability as long as they take no active part in the running of the business. However, there must always be at least one partner with unlimited liability.

Partnerships are common in a wide range of business areas. In addition to those listed under sole traders, they are also widely found in shop ownership and in professional practices e.g., vets, doctors, solicitors, dentists, etc.

Table 4.3 outlines some of the advantages and disadvantages of this form of business.

| Advantages | Disadvantages |
|---|---|
| Capital from partners | Unlimited liability (except for sleeping partners) |
| Larger-scale opportunities than for the sole trader | |
| Spreads responsibilities and decisions | Disagreements between partners |
| | Limitation on number of partners |
| Members of family can be introduced to business | Partnerships have to be re-formed if partner dies |
| Affairs can still be kept private | |
| Reduces the responsibility of a one-person business | |

**Table 4.3**  Advantages and disadvantages of a business partnership

## Private limited company ('Ltd')

The owners of limited companies are called shareholders because they each own a share in the business. Private companies must have at least two shareholders, but there is no upper limit to the number of shareholders and companies can expand by selling more shares. However, the shares of private companies are not quoted on the Stock Exchange and they are not allowed to advertise the sale of shares publicly. There is also a danger of issuing too many shares and thus having to divide the profits between large numbers of shareholders. The liability of shareholders is limited to the value of their shareholding and, to warn creditors about the dangers of dealing with these companies, 'Limited' (or 'Ltd') appears after their name.

All limited companies must comply with the Companies Acts of 1948 and 1980 and register with the Registrar of Companies. In order to register a prospective company, two documents have to be completed. These are the Memorandum of Association and the Articles of Association.

The Memorandum of Association outlines the relationships of a company with the outside world. For example, it would state the name of the company, the purpose of the company and what the company actually does.

The Articles of Association state the internal rules determining the company's organization, including rules regarding meetings and the voting rights of shareholders. They also include the list of directors and other internal matters. Shareholders can vote to change the articles.

Once the articles and memorandum have been received by the Registrar of Companies, together with some other paperwork, the Registrar will provide a Certificate of Incorporation and the private limited company will start trading. (See Fig. 4.2)

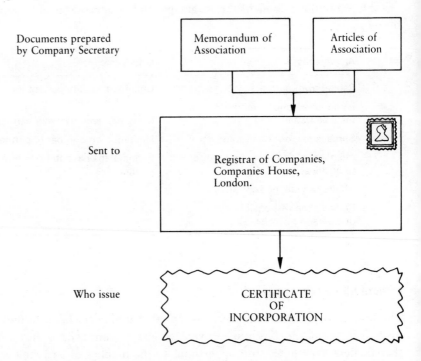

**Figure 4.2** The process of becoming a company

Table 4.4 outlines some of the advantages and disadvantages of being a private limited company.

If a company needs to get more capital in order to expand, it may consider 'going public' and having its shares quoted on the stock market. This became easier to do in 1980, when the Stock Exchange created the Unlisted Securities Market (USM) to enable smaller businesses to sell shares to the public.

**Public limited company ('plc')**

These have the opportunity to become larger than the other forms of private business organization. They are allowed to raise capital through the Stock Exchange, which quotes their share price.

| Advantages | Disadvantages |
|---|---|
| Money from shares | Cannot sell shares on the stock market |
| Firm grows bigger | Accounts not private |
| Limited liability | Limitations on capital |
| Specialist managers can be employed | A lot of administrative work is required |

**Table 4.4** Advantages and disadvantages of the private limited company

**Figure 4.3** The Stock Exchange

Only two persons are needed to form a public limited company and there is no stated maximum number of shareholders.

The process of becoming a public company is in many ways similar to that for becoming a private company. A memorandum of association and articles of association, as well as a variety of other legal documents, have to be approved by the Registrar of Companies who will then issue a Certificate of Incorporation as evidence that the company is registered.

The public company will then have to issue a prospectus, which is an advertisement or invitation to the public to buy shares in the company. The issuing of shares then takes place and the Registrar of Companies issues a Trading Certificate. Business can then start and share prices will be quoted on the stock market.

Table 4.5 outlines some of the advantages and disadvantages of this form of business ownership.

Shares may be issued:

- when a new company is formed;
- when a nationalized organization is privatized;
- when a public limited company wishes to raise additional capital;
- when a private limited company wishes to become a public limited company.

**Table 4.5** Advantages and disadvantages of the public limited company

| Advantages | Disadvantages |
|---|---|
| Limited liability for shareholders | Formation can be expensive |
| Easy to raise capital | Decisions can be slow and 'red tape' can be a problem |
| Operates on a large scale | |
| Easy to raise finance from banks | Problems of being too large |
| Employs specialists | Employees and shareholders distanced from one another |
| | Affairs are public |

Without the stock market, public companies could not operate on the scale that they do and the selling of a variety of securities helps both industry and the government. Figure 4.4 shows types of shares and securities sold on the stock market. Risk capital is money that is invested in a company in return for a share of the profits made (if any). The element of risk is that the return on the investment depends on the fortunes of the company concerned. Loan capital is money that is lent to a business for a period of time. Interest needs to be paid to reward lenders.

Shareholders who risk capital receive dividends as a return on their shareholding. These are provided at a set percentage of the original sale price of the share. If a share was sold for £1 (par value) and the dividend is 10 per cent, the shareholder will receive 10p for each share he or she holds.

However, if the market value of that share rises to £2 and the dividend is 10 per cent, the shareholder will receive 10p per share which is only a 5 per cent return on his or her capital. This would be a low yield and shareholders would have to consider alternatives unless they expected the market price of the share to rise and/or expected a higher dividend in future years.

The benefits to the shareholder of holding shares are:

1. possible increases in the share price (a form of capital gain).
2. dividends received.

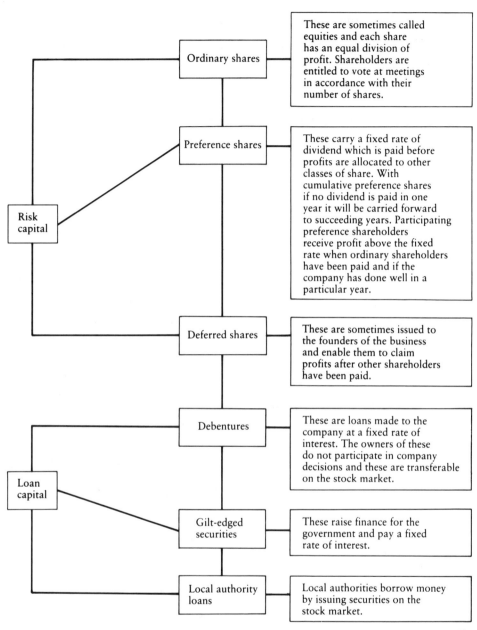

**Figure 4.4** Types of shares and securities sold on the stock market

3. being a part owner of a business concern.
4. the right to vote at shareholders' meetings.
5. the pleasure of speculation.
6. perks associated with some shares, e.g. discounts on goods.

### Case Study—The power of the shareholder

It is often said that shareholders have little power in companies today and that power rests with the Board of Directors. However, sometimes shareholders do get angry about the way in which the business is being run. In 1991, the Midland Bank was one of the four main high street banks. In the late 1980s, Midland had lurched from one problem to another. They had bought some American banks which had lost money because of poor harvests in agricultural areas, they had made losses on debts to developing countries and an attempt to merge with the Hong Kong and Shanghai Bank had failed.

A typical newspaper report of the annual shareholders meeting in May 1991 stated that: 'Angry shareholders at Midland Bank's annual meeting fiercely criticized Sir Kit McMahon, the departing chairman and the rest of the board of directors for the dismal performance of the bank. The most enthusiastic clapping followed a call for the director in charge of UK banking to resign.'

The outbursts were a reaction to Midland's surprise announcements of falling profits and a halving of dividends.

One shareholder said to the meeting: 'It's not fair to say the Midland has had a bad year. It has had six bad years. The only hope for this bank is a takeover. Once, when I was a boy, Midland was the leading bank. The bank has been brought low and who has brought it low if not the directors?'

Another shareholder said: 'You directors pay yourselves fancy salaries for leading this bank from one disaster to another. The director of UK banking's contract should be terminated here and now without compensation'.

In 1990, the chairman's salary was £295,703 and the director of UK banking earned £429,216.

*Questions*

1. Why is it important to have annual shareholders' meetings?
2. Who should have the main say about the way in which the company is run. Explain your answer using examples.
3. Is it fair to blame the directors for the performance of a company?
4. How can the directors be made accountable for the decisions that they make?
5. What is meant by the terms:
   (a) reduced profits
   (b) halving of dividends
   (c) shareholder
   (d) director
   (e) chairman
   (f) termination of contract?

## Big Bang

On 27 October 1986, changes which became known as the Big Bang took place, bringing fundamental changes to the way in which the Stock Exchange was run. One of the main reasons for the changes was to increase competition between dealers in shares. The separation of 'brokers' and 'jobbers' was abolished (a jobber was a wholesaler in shares who did not meet the public). Also, the idea of a minimum commission was stopped, so that dealers in shares could make deals which gave themselves as little profit as they liked (a dealer wanting to do a lot of business could now compete for business by only making a little profit on each deal). A broker is a person who buys or sells something for someone else. A stockbroker buys or sells shares for a member of the public.

## Multinationals

A multinational company is one that operates in a number of countries. Most multinationals are public companies but there are also a few large private companies, such as Mars. Some giant public companies such as Shell, Tate and Lyle and Marks and Spencer, have manufacturing and sales outlets in many countries. These business units are sometimes called *multinationals* and have greater powers to control and change prices because of their size and because they can switch their operations between countries. Because they employ so many people they can sometimes influence national policy decisions.

If we look at the top ten European industrial companies, according to the value of sales made, we can see that they are very large in terms of value of sales (turnover), numbers employed and the value of the things that they own (total assets). See Table 4.6.

| Company | Country | Turnover (£m) | Assets (£m) | Employees |
|---|---|---|---|---|
| Shell | UK/Holland | 64 779 | 56 371 | 134 000 |
| BP | UK | 29 641 | 31 615 | 119 850 |
| Daimler-Benz | Germany | 28 075 | 20 363 | 339 875 |
| Fiat | Italy | 24 682 | 26 129 | 286 294 |
| VW | Germany | 24 018 | 18 459 | 257 561 |
| Siemens | Germany | 22 465 | 20 901 | 361 800 |
| BAT | UK | 21 636 | 11 555 | 311 917 |
| Unilever | UK/Holland | 21 566 | 11 420 | 300 000 |
| Nestlé | Switzerland | 19 354 | 13 220 | 196 940 |
| Philips | Holland | 19 000 | 15 819 | 305 000 |

**Table 4.6** Top ten industrial companies by turnover

*Task*

Enter the data above into a database. You should also include the following information: Shell and BP are oil companies; Daimler-Benz, Fiat and VW are all in the motor vehicle industry; Nestlé and Unilever are in food retailing; Philips and Siemens are in the technology and telecommunications sector and BAT is in a variety of sectors. The operating profits of the ten companies in 1990 (£m) were: Shell—6931, BP—2524, Daimler-Benz—1343, Fiat—2288, VW—812, Siemens—372, BAT—2197, Unilever—1982, Nestlé—2054 and Philips—746.

1. Save and print the complete file in a record-by-record format.
2. Organize the file into order of profitability.
3. Search the file for companies that employ more than 300 000 employees.
4. Organize the file in ascending order of capital employed.
5. Which company makes the greatest amount of profit per employee?
6. Which company makes greatest profit for each pound's worth of capital assets employed
7. Which company makes greatest profit as a percentage of turnover?
8. Which of the figures you have looked at gives the best indication of how efficient a company is? Why?

## Co-operatives

The co-operative movement began with the Rochdale Pioneers in 1844. These were a group of workers who clubbed together to buy things to sell in their own shop. The idea behind a co-operative is that the profits from the business should be shared among the people that have bought from the shops. The more you buy the bigger share of the profits that you get. Customers own the business and receive dividends in relation to how much they spend. This type of co-operative is known as a retail co-operative.

In recent years, the term 'workers co-operative' has become widely known. This term has been used to describe factories where the workers have tried to run the business by taking on the responsibility of organizing, owning and managing it. Producers' co-operatives have become quite popular as a way of organizing small businesses in the 1990s. Small new co-operatives are organized by groups of people who want to share the responsibility of running a business. They work in co-operation, although some people will need to take the important management decisions after discussing ideas with fellow co-operators. Co-operatives can be found in all types of business, including bicycle repair, specialist shoe manufacture, clothing, food processing, agriculture, and road haulage.

Producers' co-operatives are run in the interests of the employees rather than for shareholders. Employees run the co-operative and make the decisions.

They are thus working for themselves. A problem for such an organization may be that of raising capital. Banks will lend to such an organization provided that the business plan is sound. Co-operatives will often be set up in industries where only a little capital is required.

Some modern co-operatives are made up of groups with considerable managerial expertise. Members of the co-operative must decide on the hours to be worked, the products to be produced, methods of production and marketing, as well as the distribution of profits.

## Franchising

An important development in the UK during the last fifteen years has been the development of franchising, particularly in retailing but also in manufacturing and other sectors. A franchising company, such as Thornton's confectionery company, sells the franchise, i.e. the sole right of selling its products, to private individuals. The person taking out the franchise puts up the capital but is usually supplied with equipment, training, merchandise and a well known name to trade under.

## Building societies

The organization of building societies is somewhat different from that of other businesses. Traditionally they did not set out to make a profit and are supervised by the Registrar of Friendly Societies rather than the Registrar of Companies.

In the 1990s there are fewer and fewer building societies, as the smaller ones are swallowed up by merger with larger societies. Today the banks and building societies are competing vigorously to take over business from each other. In the past building societies tended to act as a middle body taking money from savers and re-lending it to individuals and firms that wanted to buy property. The building society would lend by means of a mortgage, which is a long-term loan often repayable over a period of 20 or 25 years usually to purchase a house. The building society would then hold the deeds of the property until such time as the mortgage had been repaid. If the borrower ran into financial problems the building society could then resell the house. The building societies charge interest to borrowers of money and pay out interest to people who save money in the building society.

Nowadays all the main banks also offer mortages and so there is some healthy competition in this field. In their turn, the major building societies are offering many traditional bank services such as cheques, cash-dispensing machines and standing order services. Building societies and bank accounts are becoming increasingly similar. Indeed, one of the major building societies, the Abbey National, went public offering its shares on the Stock Exchange in 1989.

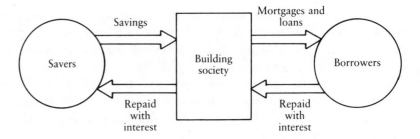

**Figure 4.5**   Savers and borrowers

## Public enterprise

### Public corporations

In the UK the government still owns a number of industries and businesses on behalf of the people. Most of these are in the form of 'public corporations'.

A public corporation is set up by an Act of Parliament. Examples of public corporations include the Bank of England and British Coal. Once a public corporation has been set up, the government appoints a chairperson to be responsible for the day-to-day running of the industry.

There are a number of reasons why public corporations have been set up:

1.   To avoid wasteful duplication (i.e., the same thing being done twice). In the nineteenth century, for example, there were three railway lines between Leeds and Harrogate. This may be seen as a waste. Imagine the problems caused by having three water companies operating in your street.
2.   To set up and run services which might not be profitable. Would a private company supply post, electricity, gas and water to a small remote village?
3.   To gain the benefits of large-scale production. It may be better to have one big firm producing lots of output than to have several smaller firms. When there is only one firm the government as owner might be less likely to charge high prices than a private firm.
4.   To protect jobs. The government might see itself as having a responsibility to protect jobs even though this might mean lower profits.
5.   To control industries which are important to the country such as coal, steel and the railways.

## Privatization

Since 1979 a number of public corporations have been privatized. This means that they have been sold to shareholders. There are a number of reasons for this, including the following:

1.   Some people argue that state-run firms are not efficient because they do not have any real competition and do not have the threat of going bankrupt because the government will always pay off their debts.

2.  It is argued that in a modern society as many people as possible should have shares in businesses. The idea is that everyone—not just the very rich—should become shareholders and therefore people have been encouraged to buy just a few hundred pounds' worth of shares in enterprises like British Telecom and British Gas. In 1979 when Margaret Thatcher became Prime Minister there were three million shareholders in the UK, when she left office in 1990 there were eleven million.

When a public corporation is set up, an independent body is also formed to protect consumers' interests. Consumers can take their complaints to this body; for example, the Post Office Users' Council will take up complaints made by users of the Post Office, such as those about the late delivery of letters.

The government has the power to make major decisions about how public corporations should run—for example, when a decision is made to close down large sections of the railway network or to close down coalfields. The chairperson and managers will decide on day-to-day matters such as wages and prices, timetables and the purchase of machinery.

Whereas a limited company has to make an annual report to its shareholders, a public corporation must present its annual report to the appropriate government minister, who then makes a verbal report to Parliament. At this time Members of Parliament can make criticisms or voice support for the way the corporation is running. A committee of MPs has the job of studying the running of each public corporation and of reporting on its operation.

## Municipal undertakings/local government

In the UK certain services in local areas are supervised by locally elected councils. These councils may run some forms of business organizations such as bus services and public toilets. Local councils receive money from two main sources: a grant given to them by central government, and a local tax (Council Tax). Local councils often subsidize loss-making activities such as local parks which provide a real benefit to the community. Many local services have recently been privatized. Refuse collection, leisure centres and the local bus service is increasingly likely to be in the hands of a private firm that has contracted to do the business for the council. Of course, the private contractor's contract will be reviewed and will only be renewed if the work is good and the price is not too high.

### Case Study—Franchising

Mary Watson had worked for a local builder as a contract plumber for several years. She worked long hours and the work was irregular. In September 1990 she saw an advertisement in a national newspaper:

**Figure 4.6** Franchise advertisement

Using her savings and a loan from the bank Mary was able to buy a franchise. SuperRod provided her with a three week training course and equipment (an electric plumbing device that quickly unblocks drains and pipes and a van). She was given the monopoly of selling her services within a 10 mile radius and the right to trade and advertise a 24 hour service. In return Mary had to hand over 12 per cent of her profits to SuperRod.

*Questions*

1. Make a list of what you consider to be six advantages and six disadvantages to Mary of taking on the franchise.
2. Make a list of what you consider to be the main advantages and disadvantages for the company granting the franchise.
3. What lines of business is franchising most suitable for, why?
4. Are there any lines of business that franchising would be inappropriate for, why?
5. If you needed a plumber in a hurry how would you go about getting one? Would a franchise plumber be at an advantage in getting your custom?
6. Identify an area of retailing which would be suitable for franchising. How would you go about organizing such an operation?

**Case Study—How share buying works**

A member of the public can buy or sell shares by asking his or her bank manager to approach a broker/dealer on his or her behalf, or by going direct to a broker/dealer in person. The broker/dealer will be a member of a firm that operates at the Stock Exchange. Nowadays much of the work involving share dealing is carried out through computer terminals. If Jane Smith asks her broker/dealer to buy shares in Shell, then the broker/dealer will consults a visual display unit showing the prices at which other broker/dealers will be prepared to sell shares. Firms that are prepared to deal in stocks and shares are known as market-makers. As Jane Smith wants to buy Shell shares her broker/dealer will look for the name at the top of the display screen showing firms offering Shell shares. The name at the top of the screen will be the market-maker selling Shell shares for the lowest price. The price of the shares will be shown in pence. There will always be at least two market-makers for a share, but there may be as many as twenty.

If Adrian Manley wishes to sell ICI shares then he will ask his broker/dealer to sell them for him. The broker/dealer in this case would consult another visual display unit. The market-maker offering the highest price for ICI shares would now appear at the top of this screen. Broker/dealers earn a commission for dealing in shares. The system whereby market-makers make deals by computer link-up is known as the Stock Exchange Automated Quotation System (SEAQ system) and the visual display units are known as SEAQ screens.

On the day the deal is done a contract note will be sent to the investor.

*Questions*

1. What is an investor?
2. What does a broker/dealer do?
3. What does a market-maker do?
4. How do market-makers compete?
5. Why is competition on the Stock Exchange important?
6. How do SEAQ screens aid trading?
7. Why might a Stock Exchange dealer charge a low commission?
8. Why does a contract note need to be sent out on the day a deal is struck?
9. Why might someone want to buy shares: (a) when the price is falling and (b) when the price is rising?
10. How does the existence of a Stock Exchange support the operation of public companies?

**Case Study—The privatization of the electricity industry**

The operations of the electricity industry consist of four main functions:

- *Generation*: The production of electricity at power stations.
- *Transmission*: The bulk transfer of electricity at high voltages through a central transmission system known as the national grid.
- *Distribution*: The transfer of electricity from the national grid and its delivery, over local distribution systems, to consumers.
- *Supply*: The wholesale purchase of electricity from generating companies and its sale to the customer, using the transmission and distribution systems to deliver the power.

Before 31 March 1990, the responsibility for carrying out these functions in England and Wales was in the hands of public corporations. Of these the Central Electricity Generating Board produced most of the electricity generated. It also owned and operated the transmission system known as the national grid. Twelve area electricity boards distributed the electricity and sold it to customers within their own areas.

*The new structure*

In 1990 the electricity industry was privatized. A number of public limited companies have been set up with shares traded on the Stock Exchange. Under the new structure, the Central Electricity Generating Board's businesses have been transferred to four companies. Three of these—National Power plc, PowerGen plc and Nuclear Electric plc, are involved mainly in power generation. These companies will now compete with each other and other generators. However, nuclear stations have been kept in the public sector under Nuclear Electric.

The national grid is now owned and run by the National Grid Company plc, which is itself owned by the 12 regional electricity companies. Distribution of electricity in a local area is now in the hands of the 12 electricity companies. The 12 companies will take supplies from the national grid and then feed these supplies to their customers through their own distribution systems. The 12 companies will have to make their systems available to private suppliers who want to supply electricity in their areas. Each of the regional electricity companies and any other supplier is now able to compete to supply customers, although the market will not be wide open until 31 March 1998. At present competition has only been introduced into the supply business for large customers.

In time all consumers will, in principle, be able to obtain electricity from whichever source they choose.

Each of the electricity companies is required by law to supply premises within its area with electricity on request. Charges that they make are currently subject to government price control.

The 12 companies are also involved in other business activities such as selling cookers, central heating systems, and other electrical app-liances from showrooms. They also offer an advisory service on how to conserve energy. In addition they are beginning to become involved in electricity generation.

*Questions*

1. Who are the main groups of consumers of electricity?
2. How are they likely to be affected by the privatization process?
3. In what parts of the electricity industry do you expect competition to become fiercest? Why?
4. Do you think that competition is a good thing in this industry? Make a list of the advantages and disadvantages.
5. Who owns the electricity companies?
6. What do you think will be the owners' main aims for these companies?
7. How do you think these aims will differ from those of the previous owners?
8. Draw a diagram to show the organization of the electricity industry today.
9. What safeguards does the government need to impose on the electricity companies to protect the public?

**Case Study—The cycle shop co-operative**

Joanna, Max and Sammy first met at the local Job Club. They had recently become unemployed but each had some savings in the bank. One afternoon they sat down together and discussed the skills that each had and tried to identify a need or opportunity in the local area that would enable them to use these skills. Joanna said that she had recently been asked to repair and respray bikes for friends. Max said that he felt that because a lot of people cycled in the town there would be a steady demand for cycle repairs. Sammy said that with their savings they could also buy a few bikes which they could hire out. It seemed like a good idea.

They enquired about premises and found a very small shop not far from the centre of town. They bought ten bicycles for hire and advertised their repair and respray service in the local paper. They were surprised how popular the business was. In the summer months there was a strong demand for the hire service and they quickly expanded to 15 bicycles. There was also a regular demand for cycle repairs and they had to move to larger premises to store all of their stock and work in progress. Up to this time the three owners had been happy to pool their resources and share the takings at the end of each week. However, as the business expanded they felt that they should have a clearer organizational structure.

They decided that every Friday afternoon they should have a regular meeting to discuss business affairs. Each member of the organization was to be called a 'co-operator'. Each co-operator should work for the same number of hours and take an equal share of the profits. Each co-operator should have an equal vote at the weekly meeting. Joanna was to be in charge of the repair and respray service, Max was to be in charge of the hire service. Sammy was to be in charge of the accounts, advertising and promotion and would also help the others out when needed. Any new member of the organization would have equal rights as a co-operator.

*Questions*

1. List four advantages and four disadvantages of co-operation.
2. Is co-operation a suitable form of organization for all businesses?
3. Was co-operation a suitable form of organization for Joanna, Max and Sammy?
4. What other forms of business organization could they have used?

# Questions

1. Complete the following sentences using the words or terms below:

| | |
|---|---|
| Producers' co-operative | Public corporations |
| Sole trader | Privatization |
| Partnership | Franchising |
| Private company | Multinational company |
| Public companies | Limited liability |
| Nationalization | |

   (a) The process through which the government takes control over industries from the private sector is known as . . . . . . . .
   (b) When workers set up a business organization which they run themselves they are said to have formed a . . . . . . . .
   (c) A . . . . . . . normally has to have between 2 and 20 owners.
   (d) A . . . . . . . produces and distributes goods in many countries.
   (e) The process whereby the state sells off state industries to shareholders is known as . . . . . . . .
   (f) Shareholders in companies can only lose the value of their shareholding. They are said to have . . . . . . . .

(g)   A typical form of business ownership for an ice cream seller or a window cleaner would be as a . . . . . . . .

(h)   In the UK most nationalized industries take the form of . . . . . . .

(i)   . . . . . . . is a system whereby you can buy the local monopoly to sell a product or service which is nationally advertised.

(j)   In a . . . . . . . shareholders can only sell shares with the permission of the board of directors.

(k)   Secondhand shares in . . . . . . . can be traded on the Stock Exchange.

2.   Which of the following are in the private sector and which in the public sector?

| | | |
|---|---|---|
| (a)   British Coal | (g)   British Telecom |
| (b)   Private companies | (h)   The Bank of England |
| (c)   Partnerships | (i)   Virgin plc |
| (d)   Municipal enterprises | (j)   Public companies |
| (e)   Public corporations | (k)   British Airways |
| (f)   British Rail | (l)   A producers' co-operative |

3.   Which of the following would be reasons for privatization and which arguments for nationalization?

(a)   to reduce government control over the economy.

(b)   to give consumers greater choice.

(c)   to control industries of strategic importance.

(d)   to create wider share ownership.

(e)   to provide a social service.

(f)   to control dangerous competition.

4.   Figure 4.7 on page 70 shows 14 town centre business premises. Which ones are partnerships, public limited companies, private companies, sole traders, public corporations and privatized organizations (that are now public limited companies)?

5.   British Gas is an industry which benefits from large scale production. Local bus services can be run on quite a small scale. Does this make the case for privatization stronger in the latter example?

6.   Anna Neidzwiedzka wants to start up a small business producing T-shirts. She is not sure whether she has sufficient capital to start up on her own. Advise her on the advantages and pitfalls of taking on a partner.

7.   Why do you think that large cutbacks are made in public corporations in the run-up to privatization?

# Coursework

This section on business units provides many opportunities for coursework. Overleaf is a suggestion for a groupwork assignment and several other suggestions for individual work.

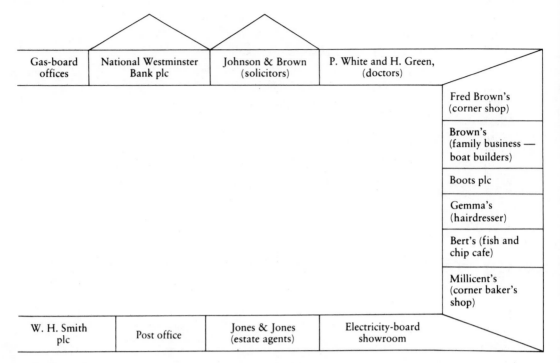

**Figure 4.7**  Fourteen businesses in a town centre

### Groupwork—Study of a local firm

The focus for the work should be an investigation of the firm. Working in a group try to brainstorm suitable questions to ask, e.g.:

- What does the firm produce?
- Who owns the firm?
- What factors of production are used?
- How much do factors cost?
- How is production organized?
- Who owns the company?
- Who makes the decisions?
- What competition does the firm have?
- What else would you ask and why?

Having brainstormed as many questions as possible, you can then split up into groups and choose a set of questions which fit together to research a particular theme.

**Individual work**

1. Interview a typical sole trader, e.g. a window cleaner, corner shop owner, decorator or hot dog seller. Pose your assignment as a question, e.g. 'What are the advantages of being a sole trader?' or 'What type of market is served by the sole trader?'
2. Similar exercises can be done with local partnerships, co-operatives and private companies. A suitable research question might be, 'How is a partnership set up?' or 'How does a partnership operate?'
3. An interesting piece of coursework might be to study how a company goes public. This can be done through the newspapers and by writing to the company for a prospectus. The privatization of a public corporation could be handled in a similar way.

# 5

# The business in its environment

We live in a world which shapes our responses to almost everything we encounter. Such influences upon our pattern of behaviour include factors such as the family, the community we live in, our ethnic background, local opportunities, the law and many others. Whenever we make a decision to do something these influences will affect us.

In the same way business activity also takes place against a background of competing influences and throughout the world people from various cultures and backgrounds involved in creating goods and services are affected by a vast array of influences in their environment. Looking at business life can therefore only be seen against a wide background of *interdependence* and *interrelationships* which affect the decisions which businesses make.

Just as your environment is subject to a process of change, the business environment is also constantly changing. Some changes may be very minor and not radically affect a business's performance; other factors may have a dramatic impact upon the operation of the organization, such as the Single Market. If businesses are to be successful they cannot ignore the changes taking place all around them. In order to meet their objectives they have to adapt and take account of competing influences such as:

1. Consumers
2. Suppliers
3. Other producers/market influences
4. Central government
5. Local government
6. Trade unions
7. Local residents
8. Technology
9. Others

Though each of these influences is examined in further detail in other chapters, it is worth introducing them at this stage and examining them as part of an integrated case.

### Case Study—Francesco's hair salon

Francesco owns his own hairdressing business, employing three full-time members of staff. He runs his own town centre hairdressing salon (see Fig. 5.1) and over the years has built up a steady group of customers. However, he is aware that unless he charges competitive prices and offers a good friendly service, customers will go elsewhere. His suppliers provide him with materials and equipment. If they raise their prices he will have to pass on the increases to his own customers. He usually buys his equipment on credit and so depends on the goodwill of his suppliers.

In the town centre there are three other salons offering similar facilities to Francesco's. It is important to keep an eye on their methods and any improvements they make.

The way that Francesco runs his business is controlled by certain Acts of Parliament. He can only work six days a week and he must look closely at health and safety at work. He pays value added tax (VAT) on the value added by his business, as well as tax on his earnings which is calculated from the books which he keeps and annually presents to the Department of Inland Revenue.

The local council also exercises control over his activities—he had to apply for planning permission to extend his business, he must be careful how he disposes of waste and he also pays a business rate to the council.

Francesco's employees do not belong to a trade union but he is aware that if he does not offer acceptable conditions, he will find it hard to recruit the right sort of labour.

**Figure 5.1** Francesco and his hair salon

The business is located in a largely non-residential part of town. Francesco did, however, have a complaint from a neighbouring shop because some of his customers were parking their cars across the shop's loading bay.

*Questions*

1. List the influences mentioned in the case study which affect the way Francesco runs his business.
2. Briefly describe what might happen if Francesco ignored some of these influences.

## Factors/bodies which influence business activity

### Demand from consumers

The consumer is the final user of the product, whether it be a good or service. If a business wishes to be successful it must respond to the wishes of its consumers by engaging in marketing activities. (See Chapter 8). Doing so will help it to identify the demand for its products. The demand for a product means the actual amount that will be bought at a given price. Common sense tells us that more of a product will be bought at a cheaper price than at a higher price. For example, market research on the number of people who would use a new swimming pool produce the following results:

| Price for adults | Demand for use the facility per week |
|---|---|
| £4 | 100 |
| £3 | 150 |
| £2 | 250 |
| £1 | 800 |
| 75p | 1200 |
| 50p | 1400 |
| 40p | 1500 |
| 30p | 1600 |

Apart from price, other main influences on demand include the following:

*Tastes*

As time moves on, new products become more fashionable and popular, while others go into decline.

### Case Study—Changes in tastes

Just a few years ago compact discs were unheard of in the UK. Today their sales exceed over £400 million per annum.

Low-alcohol lager is set to become one of the successes of the 1990s. Sales have grown five-fold since the mid-1980s

Telecommuting is a concept of the 1990s. More people today prefer to live in villages and work from home and over two million people do at least part of their work from home with a telephone link. Telecommuting alleviates some of the problems of working mothers, helps to free streets of traffic, saves the employer space and allows people to improve the quality of their lives.

Figure 5.2   BT logo

Over recent years there has been a steady increase in demand for mineral water. A number of reasons have been put forward for its popularity such as the fashion for foodstuffs with no additives, the distaste for tap water, which for the Londoner has on average already passed through eight other Londoners beforehand, increased foreign travel which has introduced more people to mineral water, etc.

Though many toys have basically remained the same for many years, they are constantly being rebranded to reflect changing trends from the media. Ghostbusters was closely followed by the Teenage Mutant Hero Turtles.

Work in a small group to consider the answers to the following questions and then report your answers back to the rest of the class.

*Questions*

1.  Make a list of products which you regularly use which were probably not available for your parents when they were your age.
2.  Consider what products are going to be subject to an increase in demand over the next few years. Make a list of these products and, for each one, briefly state why you think they are likely to become fashionable.

*Income*

The more money people have, the easier it is for them to buy products. The amount of income people have to spend on goods is known as their disposable income and is their pay minus taxes and other deductions.

*Advertising*

Advertising campaigns influence customers' preferences and affect their demand for particular commodities.

*Price changes in other goods and services*

A change in the price of one commodity may have implications for substitute goods. If the price of butter doubled, demand would increase for margarine.

*Price of complementary goods*

Some products are used together so that the demand for one is linked to the price of another. For example, if the price of bricks goes up this might affect the demand for materials used to make mortar.

## Suppliers

Most organizations are part of a complex chain of production and are therefore influenced by what goes on at the previous stage. For example, a change in the price of raw materials from suppliers might lead to price changes for thousands of producers. Rising fuel costs during the early stages of the Gulf conflict led to price rises for many products. Price rises for products leads to wage increases of workers seeking to maintain living standards. Improved technology may also affect supplies and enable organizations to supply materials at a lower cost. Relying upon one supplier may become a problem. It is not unheard of for a large manufacturer to have its production affected because of a shortage of vital parts from a relatively small supplier which has run into financial difficulty or has industrial relations problems.

## Other producers/market influences

A *market* is a situation in which buyers and sellers come into contact. Whereas some markets are dominated by just a few organizations or even just one, others are characterized by a large number of small producers. This is a major influence on business behaviour. A firm's prices, profits and policies will be affected by the nature and *level of competition* it faces. There are various degrees and types of competition from those industries in which firms are very competitive, to producers who might be in a position to control a market for their own benefit.

A business that does not face direct competition is said to have a monopoly. A monopoly does not have outside pressures on it to compete and will be able to determine its own prices. We must not, however, assume that all monopolies are inefficient. Monopolies will often put a lot of money into research and development to maintain their market dominance.

A market in which there are a large number of small producers, each of whom sells a similar commodity, and which is easy for organizations to enter would be highly competitive. In this type of competition producers have little control over their price and need to charge similar prices to those of their competitors if they are to survive.

There are many stages between a highly competitive market and a monopoly. (See Fig. 5.3.) There may be just a few firms dominating a market or hundreds. Many businesses will seek to capture larger market shares by trying to make their products different to those of their rivals.

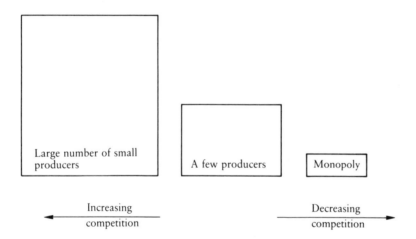

**Figure 5.3** The stages between a highly competitive market and a monopoly

## Question

The railways are an industry characterized by a lack of competition; banking is an industry dominated by just a few organizations; road haulage is an industry in which there are many producers. Make a list of organizations and indicate which of these three categories you feel they fall into and briefly state why.

## Central government

The central authorities set up a legal framework within which businesses operate. As we shall see later, there are a wide range of laws which constrain the activities of businesses. The theory is that though businesses should be encouraged to produce goods and services, they should not exploit consumers. The government therefore establishes the rules of the game. For example, the Monopolies and Mergers Commission investigates monopolies and proposed mergers which it is felt would operate against the public interest.

## Local government

A small local business or a plant of a larger business must take in to account local by-laws and rules. The local authorities are responsible for looking after the interests of local residents. Business activity is thus constrained by a wide range of local influences, including the protection of the local environment and planning permission specifications. An example of this might be when a redevelopment project can only take place if it fits in with the style of the existing architecture.

## Trade unions

These can be looked on as both an internal and external influence on the business. The local branch of a trade union can be seen as part of a larger national movement. Bargaining may take place between a group of employers and trade union representatives. Trade unions are dealt with in more detail in Chapter 13.

## Local residents

Local people may interact with a firm in a number of ways:

1.   As consumers
2.   As workers
3.   As shareholders
4.   As neighbours.

In each of these situations the firm will have to take account of their interests.

## Technology

Technology today plays a fundamental role in all of our lives, whether it is used at home, at work or for leisure purposes. In the business world the use of computers, microelectronics and telecommunications has completely transformed the ways in which organizations operate. Modern technologies have improved the ability of managers to manage and have made businesses more efficient and cost-effective. Organizations today which do not respond to new technologies either do so in order to emphasize the nature of the manufacture of their product, e.g. Morgan Motor Company or jeopardize their future.

*Question*

Explain how you think the following might use modern technology:

(a)   travel agent              (d)   small shop
(b)   medical profession        (e)   author
(c)   schools                   (f)   insurance company

## Others

The world in which businesses operate is rarely static. Events constantly influence the ways in which businesses compete and the successes they achieve. Whether it is the law, the economy, pressure groups, environment organizations or international influences, businesses must be aware of how their actions affect other organizations and equally of how the actions of others affect them. In addition to this, businesses today have to accept basic obligations to contribute to a more healthy community by taking into consideration the effects of their actions upon others, particularly in areas such as labour relations, consumerism and environmentalism.

# Developing the business

In order to manufacture a product or provide a service in response to the many changing environmental influences, a business will have to make two major decisions.

1.   Where should the business be located?
2.   How large should the business be?

## The location of the business

One of the earliest decisions any entrepreneur has to make is where to locate his or her business. Some businesses locate themselves where they happen to be or at the site which appears to be the best at the time. For example, William Morris started manufacturing cars in Oxford because that was where his cycle business was located. Many businesses, however, choose the wrong spot and this can lead to a host of problems later.

   Though costs play an important role in location, and a good location might be the one where costs are minimized, this is not always the case. For example, a large multiple store will probably want branches in city centres where property costs are at their highest. We must, therefore, say that the best site for locating a business will be the one where the business gains the *maximum advantages* from its location.

*Question*

You wish to open a video shop in your neighbourhood. Working in groups, think of a good place to locate this business and list the factors which have influenced your choice. Report your findings back to the class.

*Factors affecting location*

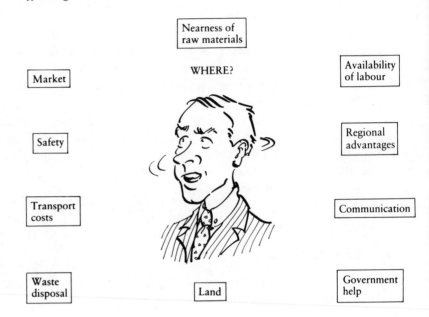

**Figure 5.4** Factors affecting the location of a business

*Market*

Service industries such as entertainment, banks and accountants have to locate near to their markets to be available for their customers. Many manufacturing industries locate close to their markets, particularly if they produce bulky or fragile items which are expensive to transport. Centres of population therefore tend to attract *bulk-increasing* consumer goods industries. These are industries where the output is more expensive to transport than the raw materials; so, in order to minimize transport costs, the businesses are located near to the market. (See Fig. 5.5.) For example, London is ringed by consumer goods industries.

**Figure 5.5** Bulk increasing industries are better placed near their market

*Raw materials*

Some businesses use a lot of heavy and bulky raw materials in the construction of a product which is a lot smaller and lighter than the ingredients which have gone into it. For example, finished steel is a lot lighter than the ore, limestone and other materials which have gone into its manufacture. If the raw materials are bulky and expensive to transport it will therefore be in the entrepreneur's interest to locate near to them. These industries are known as *bulk-decreasing* industries, as their output is substantially cheaper to transport than their input. (See Fig. 5.6.)

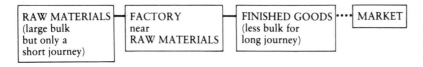

Figure 5.6  Bulk decreasing industries are better placed near their source of raw materials

*Transport costs*

Different industries will have different transport requirements. Two major influences will be the pull of the market and the pull of the raw materials. These will be largely determined by whether the industry is bulk-increasing or bulk-decreasing, though for many industries, in practice, markets will be spread out and raw materials will come from several suppliers.

*Land*

Land costs vary considerably from area to area and some firms will need a larger square footage than others, wholesalers for example. Sometimes the geology or climate of land needs to be looked at to see if land can support heavy weights or has the right climate to produce certain goods. Jersey has an ideal climate for producing tomatoes early in the season. Manufacturing chocolate in a hot country can be problematic. Mars confectionery company occasionally have to shut down their 'Mars Bar' line in very hot weather. Milford Haven has an ideal deep water anchorage for an oil terminal.

*Labour*

Labour and skills are more readily available in some areas than in others. Though the availability of labour is not always considered to be an important locational influence, if a firm moves to an area with a limited labour supply it could be saddled with relocation expenses and expensive training costs. 'Footloose' industries are organizations not specifically dependent on other locational factors, which are attracted to areas of cheap labour. They often move to suburbs to utilize cheap female labour rather than move to areas of heavy unemployment.

**Figure 5.7** Would you live here?

### Safety

Some industries have to locate their premises well away from high-density population levels and their choice of location is limited. These would include nuclear power stations, munitions factories and some chemical plants.

### Amenities

There are five standard amenities to be considered: gas, electricity, water, disposal of waste and drainage. Aluminium smelting uses vast quantities of cheap power and takes place where there is cheap hydro-electric power. Industries such as food preparation and paper production use considerable reserves of water. Certain industries produce considerable waste and the costs associated with the disposal of this might affect their location. Underestimating the cost of amenities can be very costly in the long run.

### Communications

The accessibility of motorways, ports and airports has become an increasingly important locational factor over recent years. A good infrastructure can often encourage a business to move to a region. Many towns have expanded and boomed partly as a result of good communications. The M4 corridor between London and South Wales has been hugely successful. A lot of companies, particularly if they have extensive overseas operations, locate their head offices in the South East because of its infrastructure and yet have their manufacturing units elsewhere.

### Regional advantages

Locating in an area which contains similar businesses, suppliers and markets may be a considerable advantage. Local research facilities, technical college expertise and commercial skills may be of use. Living surroundings may also be important. The quality of schools, local housing, leisure and recreational facilities help to maintain the quality of staff and keep them happy and motivated.

### Government

One of the aims of any government is to achieve balanced economic growth. However, unemployment rates vary considerably between regions. Governments attempt to reduce this disparity in unemployment rates by providing locational inducements to influence the location of industry. Over the years, areas have been designated with a certain status according to their needs, for example, Special Development Areas and Enterprise Zones. A wide range of support has been extensively provided in these areas. A criticism of such areas has been that they make the problems worse in neighbouring areas and that the new industries created have not been very labour intensive. In the 1980s many local councils also tried to boost industry within their boundaries. They often did this by advertising in national newspapers and magazines. Some researched the facilities that new businesses were looking for and then built factory units to suit their needs.

- **Enterprise zones**. Decaying inner-city areas have many problems, including high unemployment. When the old industries went into decline in these areas new industries were not quick to move in. Enterprise zones such as Clydebank, London (Isle of Dogs) and Liverpool (Speke) provided a major encouragement for firms to move into these areas.

### Case Study—Locating in Darlington

#### Questions

1. Look at Darlington's location on a map. Using both the text overleaf and the map, explain why Darlington would be a good place to locate a business.
2. Describe how the locational advantages outlined in the case study differ from the advantages which businesses have if they locate in the area in which you live.

**Figure 5.8**   Locating in Darlington

3.  Using another language produce a promotional leaflet highlighting the locational attractions of the area in which you live.
4.  Explain why local authorities produce promotional literature and describe how this might benefit their area.

## The size of the business

Every entrepreneur must aim for the scale of production which suits the business best. This level of production is achieved when unit costs are lowest for the output produced. Many businesses thrive as they become larger and the advantages they gain are known as *economies of scale*.

Most advantages of being large are *internal economies*, enjoyed by the firm as it grows, benefits from becoming larger and making the most of its situation. However, *external economies* outside the direct control of the firm also take place as the firm benefits from the overall growth of the industry and its effect upon the locality. (See Fig. 5.9.)

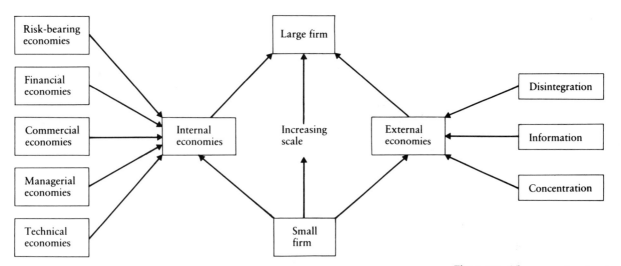

**Figure 5.9** The economies of scale that come into play as a small firm becomes a large one

## Internal economies of scale

Through being large a business can gain many financial benefits. The most obvious is that they can produce goods more cheaply per unit. There are a number of internal economies.

### *Technical economies*

Techniques and equipment can often be employed in large-scale production which cannot be adopted by small-scale producers. For example, a firm might have two machines which produce 1000 units per week; as the firm gets larger these machines might be able to be replaced by one machine which is technologically more advanced and produces 2500 units per week, at lower unit costs. (See Fig. 5.10.)

**Figure 5.10** Mass-production techniques allow low-cost production (Source: Ford Picture Library)

*Labour and managerial economies*

In large organizations highly-skilled workers can be employed in jobs which fully utilize their specialist skills, whereas in a smaller business they might have to be a 'Jack of all trades'. Large organizations can employ specialist staff such as accountants and marketeers. Such expertise will increase efficiency and their cost will be spread over a larger output.

*Commercial economies*

As production is on a large scale, raw materials may be purchased in bulk and bulk discounts from suppliers will reduce their unit cost. The cost of transport per unit will be much lower with larger loads. Larger firms may be able to organize their retail outlets or have a financial stake in their suppliers and thus collect profit at other stages.

*Financial economies*

Large firms tend to be a more secure investment than smaller firms and they find it easier to borrow money. Their reputation and reliability can often gain them loans at preferential rates of interest.

*Risk-bearing economies*

Large firms have the option of carrying out a range of activities, rather than putting all of their eggs in one basket. They might product diversify and produce a range of products so that if some do badly others might still sell well. Alternatively, they might market diversify and sell goods in different markets such as overseas markets. They might also benefit from spreading their risks in the supply of raw materials and use several suppliers rather than just one.

## External economies of scale

There are a number of reasons why the environment in which a business is operating may improve.

*Concentration*

As firms within an industry grow larger in a locality, a concentration of special services develops. These might include local college courses, a skilled work force and a reputation.

*Information*

Larger industries can set up special information services to benefit producers, e.g. the Building Trade Journal, the Motor Research Association.

*Disintegration*

Firms producing components might be attracted to areas of specialized industries, as well as firms able to help with maintenance and processes, e.g. software houses for the large computer companies in the Thames Valley.

### Case Study—Clockwork Trains Ltd

Clockwork Trains Ltd have responded to the general growth in interest in modelling among young people, as well as the market response to branded toys with a massive expansion programme. The figures overleaf in Table 5.1 have been drawn from the business:

*Questions*

1. Examine the figures carefully. Briefly explain what economies of scale have taken place and then describe how they might help both Clockwork Trains Ltd, as well as their consumers.

Table 5.1

|  | Yearly Output | Number of Machines | Number of Employees | Number of Products | Cost of Manufacture per unit £ |
|---|---|---|---|---|---|
| 1988 | 11240 | 52 | 21 | 3 | .63 |
| 1989 | 17842 | 61 | 26 | 7 | .59 |
| 1990 | 26427 | 64 | 31 | 12 | .53 |
| 1991 | 41322 | 70 | 39 | 18 | .45 |
| 1992 | 50000 | 74 | 42 | 20 | .40 (forecast) |

2.  What other figures could you extract from the table, e.g. output per machine, labour productivity, etc? Explain what these figures tell you about the larger company.
3.  Describe the benefits of working for a large organization and compare them to the benefits of working for a small manufacturer.

## Integration

Organizations can obtain the benefits of economies of scale through a gradual build-up of their business. *Organic growth* of this kind is, however, often a slow process. A quicker and more dynamic form of growth is through mergers or take-overs which involve the *integration* of a number of business units under a single umbrella organization. Amalgamation increases size and enables companies to benefit from economies of large-scale production. A decision to merge might be aimed towards increasing the benefits of specialization or towards diversifying in order to minimize risks.

### Horizontal integration

This type of merger is where one company takes over another which produces goods of a similar type and which is involved at the same level of production. Companies will benefit from increasing economies such as having only one head office and this will also reduce competition. (See Fig. 5.11.)

**Figure 5.11** Example of horizontal integration

### Vertical integration

Products are made in stages and often stages are carried out by separate firms. This type of merger is where a firm either takes over a supplier or an outlet for its products, which is involved at a different level of production. A *backward vertical integration* would be the take-over of a supplier and a *forward vertical integration* would be the take-over of an outlet. (See Fig. 5.12.)

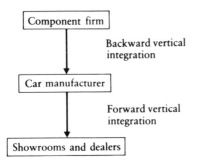

**Figure 5.12** Example of vertical integration

*Lateral integration*

This is where two businesses merge which produce similar products that are not perfect substitutes. These types of mergers are directed towards maximizing risk-bearing economies. (See Fig. 5.13.)

**Figure 5.13** Example of lateral integration

*Conglomerate integration*

Another way of maximizing risk-bearing economies is for a firm to acquire businesses which are not connected in any way with its present activities. A conglomerate integration provides a perfect form of diversification. (See Fig. 5.14.)

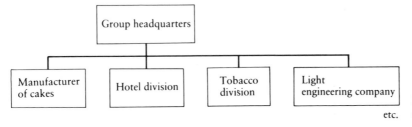

**Figure 5.14** Example of conglomerate integration

*Multinationals*

Large companies will seek to expand their markets overseas and this often leads to opportunities to manufacture or assemble goods abroad. In many cases they will develop by taking over companies in other countries. It is estimated that exports from the United States are only equivalent to about a quarter to a sixth of the goods produced by factories located overseas by their multinationals.

### Case Study—Hanson PLC

Hanson PLC is a massive British/American industrial management conglomerate employing 80 000 people worldwide. Its subsidiary and associated companies enjoy leading market positions and well-established brand names.

**Figure 5.15**   Hanson PLC logo

Hanson PLC attributes its success to its philosophy of channelling capital investment to where it will be most profitable. While doing this it maintains a decentralized management structure which provides those in charge of the business with real responsibility.

In the UK their activities include Imperial Tobacco which boasts such brands as Embassy, John Player Special, Superkings, Lambert and Butler, St Bruno, Castella, Panama and Henri Wintermans. They also include Ever Ready batteries which have a volume of sales which exceeds that of their three nearest competitors combined, as well as Seven Seas which is the world's largest supplier of vitamin and mineral supplements in capsule form. Other activities include ARC, Greenways, Butterley Brick and Crabtree Electrical in the building products industry and their other industrial products include Switchmaster, Berry Magicoal and SLD Pumps.

In the US and overseas some of Hanson PLC's most prominent companies include SCM Chemicals, Peabody Coal, Kaiser Cement, Grove cranes, Ames Tools, Faberware cookware and Jacuzzi whirlpool baths and spas.

The feeling at Hanson PLC is that the diverse mix of profitable businesses provides a solid foundation from which they can exploit the opportunities which lie ahead.

*Questions*

1. The case illustrates many of the activities of Hanson PLC. Working in groups, produce a statement commenting upon:
   (a)  the scale of its activities

    (b)  the conglomerate nature of the organization
    (c)  its overseas operations.
2.  Comment upon the philosophy of Hanson PLC and explain why such diverse activities help it to maximize risk-bearing economies of scale.
3.  Explain the benefits which Hanson PLC receives from both its conglomerate organization and its overseas operations.

## Diseconomies of scale

Despite the enormous advantages associated with large-scale production, the majority of business units in the UK tend to be small. Small companies often supply large companies with components and have the ability to provide specialist goods with low overheads. Small firms are important in areas such as haulage, agriculture, retailing, building and professional services. In these areas it is possible to start with a relatively small amount of capital, make rapid decisions, compete with firms of similar size and provide for the personal reqirements of customers. Large organizations are more difficult to manage and these inefficiencies are known as diseconomies of scale. These disadvantages of large-scale production are a predominant factor in many businesses wishing to remain relatively small.

### Human relations

Large numbers of workers are always likely to be difficult to organize. Personal contact between senior staff and shopfloor workers will be reduced and this can often lead to problems of industrial relations. Large firms tend to be involved in more industrial disputes than smaller firms.

### Decisions and coordination

The sheer scale of production may limit the management's ability to respond to change and exploit the market. The improvement of products may involve considerable delays and cost while a production line is being fitted. Decisions need to be discussed extensively throughout a firm and this might involve considerable paperwork, large numbers of meetings and wasted time. It is also difficult for large organizations to provide a personal interest in satisfying customer demands.

### External diseconomies

Public displeasure with a particular industry can turn into action which can affect output. For example, boycotts of goods from other countries such as

South Africa, only stocking items which will be approved of by the public such as 'dolphin-friendly' tuna fish, or real ale in response to the Campaign for Real Ale.

### Case Study—A business in its environment

Deborah Gomez (see Fig. 5.16) is the owner of the Waverley Gap Service Station which is located on a stretch of motorway on which there are no exits for 27 miles, giving her considerable *monopoly powers*. She is able to charge prices which are 15 per cent higher than the national average for petrol sales. However, weighed against this, she has to pay higher than average wages to attract staff. She is able to operate the firm on a 24-hour-a-day basis, but must keep a daily check on sales figures because the *turnover* is so high.

She buys in her supplies of fuel from a well-known *multinational* oil company. Because her demand for petrol and accessories is so high, she is able to negotiate a sizeable *trade discount*. However, she finds that prices tend to fluctuate because of frequent price wars between the giant companies.

Because of the importance of the product, Deborah is not affected by regulations restricting Sunday trading. However, her pumps are regularly checked by the local *trading standards department* and her cashiers are only allowed to work the regulation number of hours in the day. She is also bound by local by-laws to keep her premises tidy and safe.

**Figure 5.16** Deborah Gomez and her service station (Source: Kim Hooper, Reading)

*Questions*

1. (a) Explain the following terms from the case study:
      (i)   Monopoly powers
      (ii)  Turnover
      (iii) Multinational
      (iv)  Trade discount
      (v)   Trading standards department
   (b) Explain one advantage and one disadvantage of the location.
2. Explain four different groups which might have an external influence on the activities of the garage.
3. (a) What do you learn from this case study about the following:
      (i)  the demand for petrol?
      (ii) the supply of petrol?
   (b) Explain at least four ways in which Deborah could increase the sale of her petrol.
   (c) Why is she able to gain a trade discount?
4. (a) Why might the multinational consider buying up the Waverley Service Station?
   (b) What advantage does the Waverley have as a result of being owned by a sole trader?
5. Explain how you think Deborah's activities are influenced by having to take account of external influences?

## Case Study—Locating a tin box factory

Firms belonging to a particular industry need to take many factors into consideration when deciding upon the location of plant or factory. Important factors to consider are:

1. The cost of transporting the finished product to the market.
2. The cost of transporting raw materials to the plant or factory.
3. The cost of labour travelling to work.

The firm will locate its plant where these costs, taken together, are minimized. We assume that production costs within the factory are constant wherever the factory is located. In the following simulation, a tin box manufacturer is comparing the advantage of locating nearer to its labour supply, to its markets and to the source of its raw materials. The purpose of the exercise is that you should compare the transport costs involved and then provide a recommendation. This is done by calculating the transport costs in producing tin boxes at each of the four possible places, A, B, C and D (see Fig. 5.17) and choosing the two with the lowest cost.

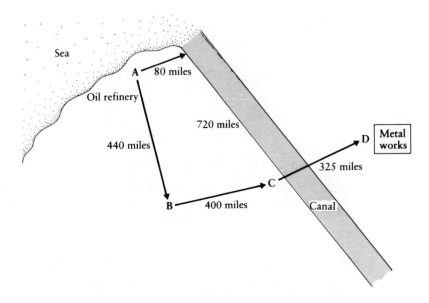

**Figure 5.17**  A, B, C and D are
the four possible locations for the
tin-box factory

To simplify the task, it has been assumed that a market exists for the
tin boxes only at B, C and D, but workers would have to commute
from B if the factory was to be located at A. A labour force is therefore
only available at B, C and D.

For each thousand tin boxes produced:

1.  It costs 10p per mile to transport the required labour from B to A.
2.  Transporting oil from the refinery at A costs £12 per mile by road
    and 20p per mile by canal.
3.  The cost of transporting tin boxes is £6 per mile by road and 20p
    per mile by canal.
4.  Tranporting metal from the metal works at D costs £9 per mile by
    road and 30p by canal.

Work out the transportation costs of locating the factory at either A,
B, C or D by filling in Table 5.2. Some parts of the table will be blank.
For example, there will be no costs for transporting metal to D.

**Table 5.2**  Table for working out
the costs in different locations.

|  | A | B | C | D |
|---|---|---|---|---|
| Labour transport costs |  |  |  |  |
| Oil transport costs |  |  |  |  |
| Metal transport costs |  |  |  |  |
| Market costs |  |  |  |  |
| TOTAL |  |  |  |  |

*Questions*

1. Which is the location with lowest cost?
2. Which is the location with the next lowest cost? Would the business necessarily locate at the site with the lowest cost?

**Case Study—Falling demand**

Firms operate against a background of what is happening to other firms and to the economy in general. In business studies we talk about a multiplier effect of upturns and downturns in business activity. In the United Kingdom in the late 1980s and early 1990s there was a downward multiplier effect.

The *multiplier effect* occurs when an original change in demand goes on to create further changes in demand in a given area. If the government spends £50 million in the North East and workers who receive this income re-spend some of it in the North East, this will help to create further income and jobs in the area. If, in the end, total spending in the area rose by £100 million, the multiplier would be two. The opposite occurs with a downward multiplier effect.

The recession led to a downturn in demand across a range of manufacturing and service industries. Unemployment rose and house prices fell.

*Questions*

1. What sort of factors would cause an upward multiplier?
2. What sort of factors would cause a downward multiplier?
3. Make a list of industries you would expect to have suffered from the recession in the 1990s.
4. If you were the manager of a retailing firm in a recession, how would you react to this change?
5. Is it possible for anyone to benefit from a recession?

# Questions

1. Complete the following sentences using the terms below.

| | |
|---|---|
| Bulk-increasing industry | Take-over |
| Bulk-decreasing industry | Demand |
| Technical economy | Supply |
| Financial economy | Industrial inertia |
| Risk-spreading economy | External economy |
| Merger | Monopoly |

   (a)  A . . . . . . . . occurs when one firm buys at least 51 per cent of the shares of another.

(b)    Furniture manufacture is an example of a . . . . . . . .

(c)    . . . . . . . . is the quantity of a product that consumers are prepared to buy at a given price.

(d)    A . . . . . . . . exists when one firm controls the production or sale of a good.

(e)    An example of a . . . . . . . . of scale would include the division of labour.

(f)    An example of a . . . . . . . . of scale would be diversification of output.

(g)    An example of a . . . . . . . . of scale would be the ability of a large firm to borrow money at a lower interest rate.

(h)    The . . . . . . . . of a good is the quantity that producers are prepared to sell at given prices.

(i)    . . . . . . . . occurs if firms do not change location after their original locating factors have disappeared.

(j)    An example of an . . . . . . . . of scale is the development of a technical college in a city.

(k)    The manufacture of beer is an example of a . . . . . . . .

(l)    A . . . . . . . . occurs when two firms voluntarily join together.

2.  In the late 1980s the Welsh Development Agency ran an advertisement on television to the tune of 'Cwm Rhondda':

'Dunlop. G Plan. Revlon. Berlei . . . British Airways. Hotpoint. Kraft. Kelloggs. Esso. Hoover. Sony . . . Metal Box. Ferranti. Ford.

Made in Wales. Made in Wales. And there's room for many more (many more). And there's room for many more.'

(a)    Put the firms from the jingle into a table using the headings shown below. (The details for Sony have been filled in to start you off.)

**Table 5.3**

| Name of company | Products made | Country of company's head office |
| --- | --- | --- |
| Sony | Tape recorders, televisions, electrical equipment | Japan |

(b)    What questions would a firm producing motor cars want answering before it decided whether or not to set up in Wales?

3.  Which of these are examples of (i) horizontal integration, (ii) vertical integration, (iii) lateral integration and (iv) conglomerate integration?

(a)    Coca Cola buys up a firm that produces equipment which takes the salt out of sea-water.

(b)    Two cat-food manufacturers combine.

(c)    A holding company buys up several unrelated businesses.

(d)    An oil company buys a chain of petrol stations.

(e)    An examination board buys up a paper manufacturer.

(f)    A bank buys up a factoring company.

(g)   Two cigarette giants combine.
(h)   A Japanese car manufacturer buys up a British car manufacturer.
(i)   A brewery takes over a distillery.
(j)   An exporting agency buys a small shipping company.
(k)   An insurance firm buys up several estate agents.
(l)   Two banks combine.
(m)  A biscuit firm buys up a tin-box manufacturer.
4.  The local council has given a property-development company permission
    to develop a new shopping facility which will be the largest in Western
    Europe. Choose a location on the map in Fig. 5.18. Explain why you have
    chosen this location.

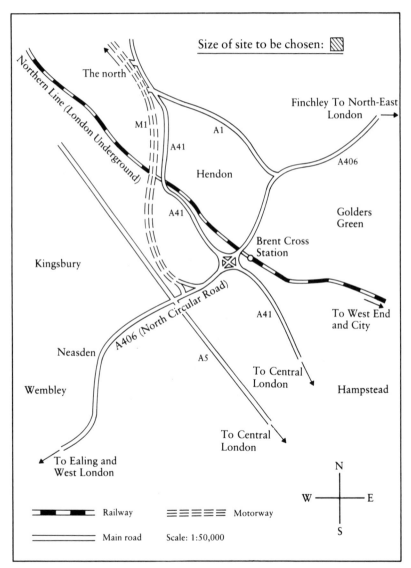

**Figure 5.18**  Where should the
shopping centre be built?

5. Nissan decided to locate in Europe in 1981 and the choice of Sunderland was announced in 1984. Working in groups make a list of factors which might have influenced Nissan's choice of location. Report your findings back to the class.

6. Scunthorpe FC and Hull Kingston Rovers are two of many clubs which have either moved from their traditional sites over recent years or are considering doing so. Outline the benefits clubs might obtain by moving to new sites and describe where these sites ought to be located.

7. Small firms continue to exist despite pressures from larger units. In what fields do small firms predominate and why are they so successful in these areas?

8. Using recent examples where possible, outline the various types of integration and merger.

9. Planco Ltd would like to expand its operations and is investigating the possible routes of expansion shown in Fig. 5.19. Choose one route suggested in the diagram. Explain why this might be an appropriate way for Planco Ltd to expand.

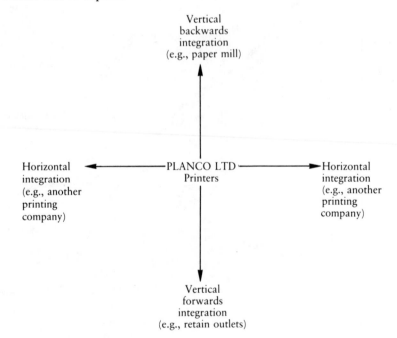

**Figure 5.19**   Planco Ltd (Source: Midland Examining Group)

## Coursework

1. How do local businesses compete?

    A group of students set out to study how firms in different lines of business compete with each other. Some of them looked at how souvenir shops in Windsor competed with each other, others looked at the competition between taxi firms, and a third group studied jewellery shops. They then pooled their results to look at the nature of competition. The group looking at souvenir shops found that location was the most important factor in giving a business a competitive edge. A souvenir shop needed to be on the main tourist route close to Windsor Castle. Other important elements of the competition mix were window display, cleanliness of the shop, variety of items sold, opening hours and service. The students were able to glean their information by preparing a questionnaire and interviewing shop-owners and customers. The group was surprised to find that price was only a minor factor in competition because tourists were not really aware of price differences for items such as postcards.

The group looking at taxi firms found that price was more important, particularly for regular users of taxis. Reliability and location were also important because taxi firms needed to be close to their calls. Other important factors included the telephone number (5555, for example, is easy to remember), the presentation of the cab, and the politeness of the driver.

The group studying jewellery stores found price to be particularly important in terms of value for money; window display, opening hours and the timing of sales were also important.

From doing this particular piece of coursework students discovered a lot about the nature of competition. In order to answer their main question, 'How do firms compete?' the students had to think out carefully the questions they were to ask in order to collect a lot of good information.

Do your own piece of coursework looking at price and non-price competition between a set of businesses in your area, e.g. hotels, coach companies, video shops, etc. To do this exercise well you must carefully construct the subset of questions that enable you to answer the title question.

2.   Are big schools efficient?

Interview your head-teacher, economics teacher, other teachers, parents and pupils to answer the above question.

You should first review your notes on economies and diseconomies of scale. See how the various economies of scale relate to the topic.

What is the optimum size of a school? What is the optimum size of class for different subjects?

What inefficiencies—technical, managerial, financial, risk-spreading, etc.—begin to set in as the size of the school increases? Highlight inefficiencies in school organization.

# 6

# Work and pay

Look at the picture below. What type of work are the people in the picture doing? Make a list of ten factors which may affect the level of wages earned by the people in the picture.

**Figure 6.1** At work

Now make a list of five groups of employees that you would expect to get higher wages than those in the picture and five groups that would get lower wages. Set out a list of factors which would explain why some people earn higher wages and a list of factors which would explain lower wages. Do you think that these differences can be justified?

There are many reasons why people receive different wages. These reasons include differences in levels of education, training and skill. Fig. 6.2 shows part of an advertisement for a highly paid job requiring a high level of skills and experience.

**CHIEF ACCOUNTANT**
**THE NETHERLANDS**
C.£30–35,000 (equivalent) + car + benefits

**Figure 6.2** The Chief Accountant of a company is paid more than those in jobs for which fewer skills are required

## Calculating pay

The amount paid for a normal working week is referred to as a 'basic' wage or salary. Many workers receive extra benefits on top of their basic wage, either in money or some other benefit. Look through job advertisements in a national newspaper. Make a list of the non-money benefits of different jobs. Do some types of jobs offer more benefits than others. Can you explain why?

Not all workers receive a wage or salary. For example, salespeople may be paid on a commission basis. They are paid according to their success in selling.

The main ways of calculating pay are shown below. Sometimes elements of these methods are combined.

### Flat rate

This is a set rate of pay, based on a set number of hours, for example, £100 for a 20 hour week. Pay is easy to calculate and administer, but it does not provide an incentive to work harder.

### Time rate

Under this scheme, the worker receives a set rate per hour. Any hours worked above a set number are paid at an 'overtime' rate.

### Piece rate

This system is sometimes used in the textile and electronics industries, among others. Payment is made for each item produced which meets a given quality standard. The advantage of such a scheme is that it encourages effort. However, it is not suitable for jobs which require time and care. Also, the output of many jobs such as service occupations is impossible to measure—for example, how could you measure the output of a teacher, a bus driver or a doctor.

### Bonus

A bonus is paid as as an additional encouragement to employees. It can be paid out of additional profits earned by the company as a result of the employee's effort and hard work. Bonuses may also be used as an incentive to workers at times when they might be inclined to slacken effort, e.g. at Christmas and summer holiday times.

### Commission

This is a payment made as a percentage of the sales a salesperson has made.

### Attendance records

In order to make up pay packets, it is necessary to keep a fair record of how much work is being done. Today, most wages for large employers are paid by bank multiple giro. Large firms can now make out giro payments through computer discs.

- **Multiple giro**. The wages department of a firm has a record of the bank and bank account numbers of each of its employees. A wages clerk then simply fills in a multiple giro form authorizing the firm's bank to make payments to its employees' bank accounts.

There are several ways in which a record can be kept of attendance at work.

#### Clock-cards

Large firms will often have a clocking system so that the employee 'clocks on' and 'clocks off'. Each employee picks up his or her card on arriving at work and punches it into the clocking device. Employees may have to clock off and on again when they take a lunch-break and then off again when they finish work.

At the end of the week the wages department will have a clear picture of how much to pay individual workers.

#### Time books

Smaller firms may keep a time book. Employees simply sign in and out of the book.

#### Time-sheets

This method is often used when workers do not always work at the same place each day, e.g. contract workers, such as painters and decorators, film crews, road builders, etc. The sheet is filled in each day and is signed by the supervisor to prove accuracy.

## Flexitime

Flexible working time (FWT) is increasingly used in modern work. At 'peak' times all members of staff will be at work. Outside these 'core' hours, there is more flexibility and staff have a certain amount of choice about when they work, provided they work a minimum number of hours.

The firm's working day is divided into three sections:

1. *Band time*. This is the total period for which the business is open, e.g. 8 a.m. to 8 p.m.
2. *Core time*. This is the period in which all the members of the firm are expected to be working, e.g. 10 a.m. to 12.30 p.m.
3. *Flexible time*. This is the period of time in which workers can select the hours they work, e.g. 8 a.m. to 10 a.m. and 2 p.m. to 8 p.m.

If, for example, employees are expected to work 36 hours in a five-day working week and they work 20 hours of core time, then they choose the other 16 hours in which they work. Some workers may prefer to work more in the morning, others in the afternoons. Other workers may vary their hours.

The advantages of flexitime are as follows:

1. It gives employees more control of when they work. Employees may enjoy this type of freedom. Flexibility also enables them to fit in private

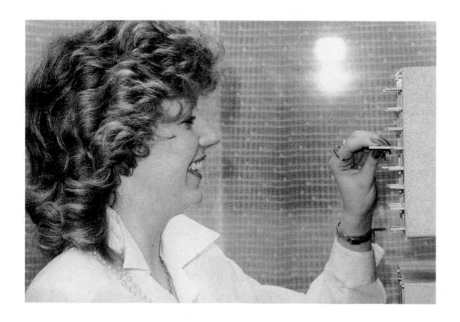

**Figure 6.3** Clocking in on a flexi-meter (Source: Kim Hooper, Reading)

engagements such as hair and dental appointments and taking the children to and from school.

2.  At least for the basic core time, all the workforce is operating together.

Staff may be responsible for keeping their own record of the hours they have worked, or they may 'clock in' and 'clock out'. (See Fig. 6.3.)

*Shift work*

In many industries it is important to have machinery working continuously in order to use it most profitably. This is true of industries such as textiles, chemicals, steel, coal-mining, food processing and many others. There are a number of ways of doing this. In some textile businesses, for example, there are distinct day and night shifts. In the North Sea oil industry, production workers may work on a rig for two weeks and then take a two-week break. In the chemical industry, workers sometimes work the day shift for one week, followed by a week on the night shift.

Employees will be paid higher rewards to work unsocial hours.

## Gross and net pay

Gross pay is the total amount earned by an employee *before* any deductions have been taken off. It includes the basic pay, plus any additional payments such as bonuses and overtime.

Net pay is the total amount received by an employee *after* any deductions have been taken off. This figure shows take-home pay.

Net pay = gross pay − deductions

A typical pay slip illustrates the difference well. Fig. 6.4 shows one belonging to Milorad Rajic who works in the accounts department of Tasty Sweets plc. We can look at it one column at a time.

### Column 1

1.  The name of the company.
2.  The employee's basic month's pay.
3.  Milorad has worked some overtime.
4.  If we add (2) and (3) we get Milorad's gross pay.

### Column 2

5.  The employee's name.
6.  Milorad is a married man with a mortgage. He will be entitled to some tax free pay as an allowance each month. He will have to pay income tax on any earnings above this allowance each month.

| Column 1 | Column 2 | Column 3 | Column 4 |
|---|---|---|---|
| Pay advice | NAME | Ref. No (Quote on any query) | 27 NOV 92 |
| (1) TASTY SWEET PLC | (5) M RAJIC | 27 2687 2017 | |
| BASIC PAY/ADDITIONS | DEDUCTIONS | PAY CUMULATIVES | |
| (2) BASIC PAY  1052.25 <br> (3) OVERTIME  40.50 | (6) TAX CODE 0450H 209.96 <br> (7) NAT.INS  78.41 <br> (8) SUPERANUATION 63.13 <br> (9) UNION  4.00 | THIS YEAR | YOUR NET PAT HAS BEEN CREDITED TO YOUR ACCOUNT AS STATED BELOW: <br> (17) BANK  NAT.WESTMINSTER <br>  SORTING CODE  06 17 25 <br>  ACCOUNT NUMBER  76256905 |
| | (10) NAT.INSURANCE NO. <br>  YT82034B <br> (11) DATE OF PAYMENT <br>  28 NOV 92 <br> (12) INCOME TAX YEAR <br>  92/93 <br> (13) PAY PERIOD  08 <br> (14) ENTER 'X' IF FINAL <br>  PAY PERIOD IN TAX <br>  YEAR  ☐ | | MR M RAJIC |
| TOTAL PAY <br> (4)  £1092.75 <br>  ADDITIONS | (15) TOTAL DEDUCTIONS <br>  £355.50 | (16) NET PAY  £737.25 | |

**Figure 6.4** Typical payslip (The numbers in brackets refer to the explanatory notes)

7. As well as income tax, employees have to pay a compulsory National Insurance contribution to the government. This money goes towards providing benefits like pensions and unemployment benefit.
8. Milorad also contributed £63.13 towards his company's pension scheme.
9. Milorad is also a member of a trade union to which he pays a monthly subscription.
10. Milorad's National Insurance number.
11. The date on which money will be transferred to Milorad's bank account by giro payment.
12. The tax year runs from 1 April 1992 to 31 March 1993.
13. The pay period is for the eighth month, i.e. November.
14. An 'X' would appear in this box in March.
15. The total amount of deductions.

## Column 3

16. Net pay, i.e. gross pay minus deductions.

**Column 4**

17.  A statement of the fact that the money is being paid by multiple giro into Milorad's bank account.

In addition to the above details, the pay slip would typically show the overall amount of gross pay, tax, superannuation and National Insurance paid in the financial year up to that date.

### Case Study—Celia Lim's budget

Celia Lim works as an insurance broker. She has drawn up a budget of her likely income and spending for 1991 which is shown below.

Budget of Celia Lim for 1991

| Income | | | Spending | £15,000 |
|---|---|---|---|---|
| Basic pay | £12,000 | | Saving | £? |
| Commission | £9,000 | | | |
| | | £21,000 | | |
| less | | | | |
| Deductions of 20% | | | | |
| of income | £? | | | |
| | ? | | | ? |

*Questions*

1.  Suggest two possible deductions from Celia's income.
2.  Calculate, showing working, the amount that Celia expects to save.
3.  Why do you think Celia might find it difficult to budget?
4.  What would happen to Celia's net pay if her gross pay rose by 25 per cent?
5.  How does Celia benefit from deductions from her pay?

## Statutory deductions from pay

These are some compulsory deductions from pay.

## Income tax

This is paid through the pay-as-you-earn system (PAYE). People of working age are sent a tax form to fill in. They have to state the name of their employer, from whom the tax office will get the details of their salary. Any extra earnings will also need to be recorded on the tax form, e.g. interest and dividends from investments. People whose work involves expenses can make claims for these to be allowed against tax so that they do not pay so much.

The amount of income tax paid depends on:

1. Income
2. Allowances

Everyone is given tax allowances depending on their status (including whether they are married or single, the size of their mortgage, whether they have dependent relatives at home, etc.). Each employee is given a tax code by the Inland Revenue. By looking at the 'free-pay' table issued by the Inland Revenue, the firm's wages department knows how much tax to deduct.

Rates of income tax in this country are progressive and go up in bands.

- A **progressive tax** is one where the more income a person earns, the greater the percentage of this income he or she pays in tax.
- A **constant tax** is one where tax paid is a constant proportion of income.
- A **regressive tax** is one where the more income a person earns, the smaller the percentage of this income he or she pays in tax.

See Fig. 6.5.

The amount of allowances and the tax bands change as time goes on, so it is best to illustrate the way in which income tax works by using a simple example based on imaginary figures.

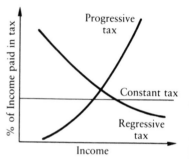

**Figure 6.5**  A diagram showing tax against income

Let us assume that single people are given a tax allowance of £2,000. The next £10,000 earned above this is taxed at 25p in the pound (25 per cent). The next £2,000 above this is taxed at 30 per cent and for each extra £2,000 earned tax goes up 5p in the pound, until it reaches a top rate of 50p in the pound.

Now let us assume that Prakesh Patel earns £12,000 a year and Balwinder Singh earns £20,000. The tax paid by Prakesh Patel is as follows:

| | |
|---|---|
| £2,000 at zero tax rate | 0 |
| £10,000 at 25p in the £ | £2,500 |
| Total tax | £2,500 |
| Pay after tax | £9,500 |

The tax paid by Balwinder Singh is as follows:

| | |
|---|---|
| £2,000 at zero tax rate | 0 |
| £10,000 at 25p in the £ | £2,500 |
| £2,000 at 30p in the £ | £600 |

| | |
|---|---|
| £2,000 at 35p in the £ | £700 |
| £2,000 at 40p in the £ | £800 |
| £2,000 at 45p in the £ | £900 |
| Total tax | £5,500 |
| Pay after tax | £14,500 |

We can see that the effect of this tax system is to reduce the difference in pay between Patel and Singh. Before tax, Singh earned £8,000 more than Patel. After tax, Singh earned only £5,000 more than Patel.

*Task*

Set out a spreadsheet to show the tax paid by four people in different income bands. Use the tax rates which have been used in the example above. The incomes of the four people are:

Bannister—£30,000
Hussein —£28,000
Peters    —£24,000
Gooch    —£16,000

(a)   What percentage of income does each pay in tax?
(b)   Use your spreadsheet to show the effect of an increase in income of 10 per cent for each of the four people.
(c)   What is the effect of a doubling of allowances?
(d)   How could the tax be made more steeply progressive?

When an employee leaves his or her job, the employer completes form P45. The P45 must then be given to the new employer who can then continue tax deductions with no complications.

At the end of the tax year an employee receives form P60, which is a summary of gross and net pay during the year. It must be kept safely as a record because an employee may want to apply for a mortgage on the basis of earnings, or claim sickness or unemployment benefit in the coming year and these benefits are earnings-related.

A person taking up work for the first time will probably not have a tax code or P45. Such people are normally taxed on an emergency code. If they are over-taxed they will be entitled to a tax rebate.

## National Insurance contributions

These are paid jointly by the employer and the employee, to the government. Contributions from National Insurance go into the National Insurance Fund, the National Health Service and the Redundancy Fund. These contributions pay for sickness and unemployment benefit, old age pensions and the National

Health Service. The employer's contribution makes up the greater part of the overall contribution. Contributions are not made by the unemployed or when an employee is claiming sickness benefit, provided a doctor's certificate is obtained.

The National Insurance Scheme was introduced as part of the overall scheme of the Welfare State. National Insurance provides a safety net for citizens who fall on hard times.

*Task*

You have been asked to advise young workers with problems at your place of work. What advice would you give in the following situations?

(a)   John rings you up to say that he will be away from work for a week with the flu.
(b)   Anne is leaving work to join another company at a higher rate of pay.
(c)   Sunil has just started work and is paying tax at a higher rate than he expected for his current wage.
(d)   Gloria is hoping to take out a mortgage on a flat. She wants proof of her earnings.
(e)   Gary feels that the government pension he will receive when he retires will not meet his needs.
(f)   Dave wants to know why he has to pay National Insurance contributions.

## Voluntary deductions from pay

Many employees also voluntarily pay out some of their wages for other purposes.

1.   *Superannuation/private pension schemes.* Many employees nowadays pay money into a private pension scheme to supplement their state pensions. For some workers this is a necessary condition of taking employment with a firm. The pension paid then depends on how much the employee contributes to the fund over the years.
2.   *Savings.* Some employees contract to pay a certain amount each month into a fund such as the government's Save-As-You-Earn scheme (SAYE). By saving regular sums, the worker is entitled to a lump sum with interest, after a given period of time.
3.   *Trade union contributions.* These can also be paid directly from wages.
4.   *Private medical scheme contributions.* An increasing number of people contract to make payments into a private medical scheme.
5.   *Contribution to the company social club.*
6.   *Contractual contributions to charity.*

## Statutory sick pay

The government has now made businesses largely responsible for paying sick pay to employees. This is called statutory sick pay (SSP). These payments are made if a worker is sick on normal working days.

## Computerization of wages

In large firms much of the work on wages is done by computers. This involves the calculation of wages, the printing of wage slips and the production of payment instructions to the bank. Data relating to the time an employee works is picked up by computer from magnetic tape, enabling the continuous recording of wages. Computers are able to handle a lot of work quickly and accurately.

One danger of using computers to calculate and record wages is the risk of losing information if something should happen to the wages program or disc. Therefore, firms will normally keep at least two 'back-up' copies of a disc which will be continually updated.

*Task—paying wages*

You work in the payroll department of a large company. You have been asked to take the pay packets of eight new employees to the department in which they work. Construct a database with seven fields and eight records relating to these workers. This database could then be added to a much larger database.

| Name | Department | Gross pay | Tax | National Ins. | Pension | Net pay |
|------|-----------|-----------|-----|---------------|---------|---------|
| Gregory | Sales | 120 | 24 | 12 | 10 | ? |
| Patel | Production | 150 | 30 | 15 | 10 | ? |
| Arnold | Office | 100 | 20 | 10 | 10 | ? |
| Minhas | Accounts | 200 | 40 | 20 | 10 | ? |
| George | Office | 20 | 0 | 2 | 0 | ? |
| Anthony | Sales | 120 | 24 | 12 | 10 | ? |
| O'Leary | Production | 240 | 48 | 24 | 20 | ? |
| Davis | Office | 40 | 0 | 4 | 10 | ? |

**Figure 6.6**  Payroll table

1. Print out an alphabetical list of all employees showing their gross and net pay.
2. Print out a list of the net pay of each employee and the department each employee works in.

3. Print out a list of employees that do not pay tax.
4. Print out a list of employees that are part of the company pension scheme and the department in which they work.
4. Print out a list of employees and the departments they work in. The list should be presented in descending order of gross pay.

## Making up a payroll

In order to make up a payroll, a firm must prepare a total outline of the workforce and the pay it is entitled to each week. Nowadays, firms encourage employees to open bank accounts because this simplifies the whole process of paying wages. When some employees are paid in cash, the wages department will make up a cash payroll. To do this, it has to calculate the amounts of bank notes and coins needed to make up the wage packets. The firm will make out a wage cash analysis in which it will use the minimum number of notes and coins to make up the wages (see Fig. 6.7 on page 112).

We can see that by making out a clear wage cash analysis, we get an accurate picture of how much needs to be paid out.

## Fringe benefits

Many jobs include a wide range of perks which do not appear directly in the pay packet. Railway employees and their families, for example, may benefit from free rail travel. Managerial jobs often include perks such as subsidized company cars and phone bills. Other fringe benefits include:

1. Subsidized canteen facilities.
2. Free training courses.
3. The right to buy the firm's product at discount prices.

### Case Study—Wages at Smith's Engineering

Smith's Engineering is a small firm producing lamiplate (plastic-coated metal items) for the motor vehicle industry. An example of one of its products is interior car panels. The firm employs a production line team of 42 manual workers, 5 supervisory and inspection workers, an office staff of 3 and a management team consisting of the managing director, who also handles personnel, a sales manager and a production manager. The company pays an outside accountant to supervise the books, which are kept on a daily basis by the office. The office also manages wages.

The manual workforce must clock in to work in the morning between 8.30 a.m. and 8.45 a.m. Workers lose pay if they clock in after

WAGE CASH ANALYSIS FOR RJP ELECTRONICS LTD

| CLOCK No. | NAME | WAGE | £10 | £5 | £1 | 50p | 20p | 10p | 5p | 2p | 1p |
|---|---|---|---|---|---|---|---|---|---|---|---|
| 001 | D. BYRNE | 120.00 | 12 | | | | | | | | |
| 005 | J. DAVIDSON | 100.53 | 10 | | | 1 | | | | 1 | 1 |
| 006 | C. DRAVSKY | 134.26 | 13 | | 4 | | 1 | | 1 | | 1 |
| 007 | D. GREEN | 107.32 | 10 | 1 | 2 | | 1 | 1 | | 1 | |
| 009 | B. MULLEN | 82.32 | 8 | | 2 | | 1 | 1 | | 1 | |
| 010 | S. MULLEN | 136.62 | 13 | 1 | 1 | 1 | | 1 | | 1 | |
| 012 | J. PATEL | 115.00 | 11 | 1 | | | | | | | |
| 017 | D. THOMAS | 137.21 | 13 | 1 | 2 | | 1 | | | | 1 |
| 036 | P. WHEELAN | 95.18 | 9 | 1 | | | | 1 | 1 | | 3 |
| 038 | G. WEST | 82.32 | 8 | | 2 | | 1 | 1 | | 1 | |
| | TOTAL | 1,110.76 | 107 | 5 | 13 | 2 | 5 | 5 | 2 | 5 | 6 |

SUMMARY OF CASH REQUIRED FROM BANK TO MAKE THE ABOVE PAYMENTS

|            |   | £ | p |
|---|---|---|---|
| 107 @ £10  | = | 1070 | 00 |
| 5 @ £5     | = | 25 | 00 |
| 13 @ £1    | = | 13 | 00 |
| 2 @ 50p    | = | 1 | 00 |
| 5 @ 20p    | = | 1 | 00 |
| 5 @ 10p    | = | | 50 |
| 2 @ 5p     | = | | 10 |
| 5 @ 2p     | = | | 10 |
| 6 @ 1p     | = | | 6 |
|            |   | 1110 | 76 |

**Figure 6.7**   Example of wage cash analysis

8.45 a.m. They are entitled to a 15 minute break in the morning and afternoon at set times. The lunch break is taken between 12.30 p.m. and 1.45 p.m., in two shifts. The afternoon session ends at 4.15 p.m.

Wage packets are handed out to workers on Friday afternoons. Employees have to work a 'week in hand', which means that the wages they receive are not for the current week but for the previous week.

The company also runs a bonus scheme, setting production targets for work. The bonus scheme sets three levels of bonus. The first is fairly easy for the workforce to achieve; the second is quite difficult; and the highest level of bonus has only been achieved once.

If orders for the firm's products are high, it will offer overtime to some workers. Overtime pay is one and a third times the normal rate. If workers work on Saturdays, they will get one and a half times the normal rate.

The supervisors, inspection and office workers sign in rather than clock in. The supervisory workers must sign in between 8.15 a.m. and 8.30 a.m. The office workers do not have to report for work until 9 a.m. Office workers are entitled to a fixed rate of salary. Supervisory and white-collar workers are not entitled to a bonus, but their rate of pay is higher than that of manual workers. Overtime is paid at time and a half. The office workers' day ends at 4 p.m.

The managerial staff have no fixed hours or method of recording hours worked. They also get fringe benefits in the form of a petrol allowance for mileage on company business. They can also include other expenses and their telephone bills are paid by the company.

Fringe benefits for all employees include a subsidized canteen and subsidized drinks and confectionery machines.

*Questions*

1. What method of checking hours worked is used for each of the following?
   (a) manual workers
   (b) office staff
   (c) management
2. Why do you think different methods of checking are used for these groups?
3. Who works longer hours—office workers or production staff? Explain your answer.
4. Do you think that it is fair that different groups of employees at Smith's are paid in different ways? Explain your answer. What alternative could you suggest?
5. Explain how the company bonus system works. Why do you think that it is structured in this way?
6. What is a 'fringe benefit'? List the different benefits received by different groups in the case study.
7. Explain what is meant by working a 'week in hand'.
8. Why is overtime pay higher than basic pay?

## Questions

1. Complete the following sentences using the terms below.

Gross pay
Net pay                          Time-sheets
Commission                       Wage cash analysis
Band time                        Statutory sick pay
Core time                        National Insurance
Flexitime                        Piece rate
Clock cards                      Time rate

(a) Salespeople often earn . . . . . . . . on the basis of the sales they make.

(b) When workers travel from one job to another, the supervisor will sign their . . . . . . . .

(c) Total pay before deductions are taken away is known as . . . . . . . .

(d) . . . . . . . . is the total working time of a business.

(e) The hours a worker can choose whether to work or not are known as . . . . . . . .

(f) The compulsory hours employees must work are known as . . . . . . . .

(g) The wages department will make up a . . . . . . . . when workers are paid in cash.

(h) . . . . . . . . is total pay minus deductions.

(i) An example of a statutory deduction from pay is . . . . . . . .

(j) . . . . . . . . are used by firms to check the number of hours employees work.

(k) One method of paying workers by results is by a . . . . . . . .

(l) One method of paying regular wages per hour is by a . . . . . . . .

(m) The employer has now taken over a major role in paying . . . . . . . .from the Department of Health and Social Security.

2. Read the pay slip in Fig. 6.8.

(a) How much is J. Summers's gross pay?

(b) How much is J. Summers's net pay?

(c) Explain the difference between gross and net pay.

| BASIC PAY | | DEDUCTIONS | |
|---|---|---|---|
| Basic pay | 800.00 | Tax | 150.00 |
| Overtime | 100.00 | Nat. Insurance | 70.00 |
| | | Superannuation | 50.00 |
| | | Union | 5.00 |
| PAY ADVICE: J. Summers | | | |
| SOUTHERN CHEMICALS | | | |

**Figure 6.8** Pay slip of J. Summers

3. Make out a wage cash analysis for Summerfield Confectionery, following the pattern in Fig. 6.7. The employees and their wages are shown next.

| Name | Wage |
|------|------|
| J. Arthur | £117.12 |
| B. Brown | £32.14 |
| C. Condery | £15.86 |
| D. Davis | £12.21 |
| S. Egerton | £48.92 |
| T. Fish | £112.19 |
| R. Grist | £135.73 |
| S. Haralambos | £86.32 |

4. The card in Fig. 6.9 appeared in a jobcentre in Reading.

> **JOBCENTRE**
>
> **JOB: Apprentice tool-maker**
>
> **AREA: Woodley**
>
> **WAGES: Starting at £85 per week. Fringe benefits**
>
> **HOURS: 38 hour week including flexitime**
>
> **DETAILS: School-leaver required with GCSEs in technical subjects**
>
> **Card no: 112**

**Figure 6.9** Jobcentre advertisement for an apprentice tool-maker

(a)  What is a jobcentre?

(b)  Who funds the jobcentres?

(c)  Why is it important for the jobcentre to make clear the location of the job?

(d)  Name a fringe benefit that may go with the job.

(e)  Explain what is meant by flexitime as advertised on the card.

(f)  What sort of training would you expect to go with the job?

5. Mullen Enterprise operates a bonus scheme to discourage absenteeism from work. The scheme covers the 7000 manual workers in three plants at Dunstable, Southampton and Liverpool. The firm agreed to pay a weekly bonus if plant absenteeism fell below 12 per cent on the following scale:

| Rate of absenteeism (%) | Bonus |
|-------------------------|-------|
| 11–12 | £0.50 |
| 10–11 | £1.35 |
| 9–10 | £2.25 |
| 8–9 | £3.40 |
| 7–8 | £4.25 |

|   |   |
|---|---|
| 6–7 | £5.10 |
| 5–6 | £6.00 |

(a)   What per cent bonus would workers at a plant receive if the rate of absenteeism was 6.5 per cent?

(b)   Julia Nash works at the Dunstable plant and earns £150 a week regularly. How much would her gross pay be in a week in which absenteeism was 9.5 per cent?

(c)   From the employer's point of view, what would be the advantage of operating the above scheme?

(d)   At what times of the year would the scheme be particularly effective?

6.   Below are some figures showing the extent to which the times at which employees start and finish work are formally checked. (*Source*: Workplace Industrial Relations Survey.)

|   | % |
|---|---|
| Manual workers checked in some way | 54 |
| Non-manual workers checked in some way | 13 |

*Methods of checking*

Clocked:

| | |
|---|---|
| Manual | 32 |
| Non-manual | 2 |

Checked in:

| | |
|---|---|
| Manual | 13 |
| Non-manual | 6 |

Sign in:

| | |
|---|---|
| Manual | 10 |
| Non-manual | 5 |

(a)   What percentage of manual workers are *not* checked in at work?

(b)   What percentage of non-manual workers are *not* checked in at work?

(c)   Give an example of a manual worker.

(d)   Give an example of a non-manual worker.

(e)   What is the most common way of checking in manual workers? Explain how this system operates.

(f)   Under what circumstances is signing in a suitable way of checking on workers?

7.

(a)   Compare time and piece rates as methods of payment.

(b)   Explain how statutory sick pay operates.

(c)   Describe in detail statutory and voluntary deductions from pay.

8.  Look at the pay slip which follows and answer the questions relating to it.

|  | £ | £ |
|---|---|---|
| Basic pay | i | |
| Commission | 120 | |
| | ——— | |
| | | 1220 |
| PAYE | 215 | |
| Superannuation | 70 | |
| National Insurance | ii | |
| | ——— | |
| NET PAY | iii | 370 |
| | ——— | |
| | | iv |

| Taxable pay this employment | 13375 |
|---|---|
| Tax this employment | 2575 |
| Superannuation | 850 |
| National Insurance | 980 |

Ref:       4-07-09851
Name:     T S Renrut
Address:  25 The Avenue
            West Winchley
            Ambleshire

(a)  What are the figures which are missing on the pay slip at (i), (ii), (iii) and (iv)?
(b)  What kind of job does Renrut have? Explain how you know this.
(c)  What is meant by (i) PAYE? (ii) National Insurance? (iii) Superannuation?
(d)  Why might Renrut receive less net pay than someone else with the same basic pay? (Give seven reasons.)

9.  Study the job advertisement below before answering the questions that follow:

**SOCIÉTÉ D'ASSURANCES-VIE**
NOISY-LE-GRAND (93)
*recherche*
**pour son service comptabilité**
**UN (E) EMPLOYÉ (E) TEMPORAIRE**
**(3 mois renouvelables)**
BAC G2 EXIGÉ
Avantages sociaux appréciables, horaires
variables et restaurant d'enterprise.
*Adresser lettre manuscrite accompagnée d'une photo
d'identité et d'un curriculum vitae précisant les
prétentions à:*
**R-B CARRIÈRES (n° 22)**
20, rue Fourcroy, 75017 PARIS
*qui transmettra.*

**Figure 6.10**  Job advertisement

(a) What type of company is offering the job?
(b) Where must applications be sent to?
(c) What do you need to send with the letter of application?
(d) What fringe benefits go with the job?
(e) Why does the advertisement state UN (E) EMPLOYÉ (E)?
(f) What do you understand by the terms (i) prétentions (ii) 3 mois renouvelables?
(g) What sort of job is being offered?
(h) Where is the job?

## Coursework

1. Why do wage rates vary for different jobs? Collect some job advertisements from a newspaper and investigate why these differences exist. Send a questionnaire to the firms concerned to try and get them to rank factors determining pay rates. What do employees think?
2. This class assignment on wages should be tackled in conjunction with the personnel department of a local firm. A class discussion should determine the range of suitable questions, for example:

(a) What wages system does the firm operate (piece rate, time rate, etc.)?
(b) How are the wages calculated?
(c) When are the wages paid?
(d) How are the wages negotiated?
(e) What system does the firm use to measure work?
(f) What are the chief problems encountered in organizing wages.
(g) Is it possible to identify needs for improvement?
(h) What suggestions can be made for improvements?
(i) How can these improvements be organized and evaluated?

Working in groups, the class should establish sets of related questions for tackling the assignment as groupwork. Each group should choose their own title question to investigate.

# 7

# Production

Throughout the world people are involved in identifying opportunities to create goods or provide services to match our needs and wants. In the first chapter we saw that the concern of production is to add value to things so that they become goods and services that people will want. Production involves occupations from primary, secondary and tertiary areas because everyone in each occupation helps to add a bit more value to something the user benefits from, improves the welfare of our society and provides us with the standard of living to which we have become accustomed. For example, the refuse collector helps to make the streets in the neighbourhood clean and tidy, the police force provides us with an environment in which crime is deterred, the childminder enables others to go to work or enjoy leisure, the factory worker helps us to enjoy manufactured goods and the teacher provides us with an opportunity to benefit from learning and all of the challenges that that brings.

Modern societies like the United Kingdom are said to be in their third wave of development. In their first wave most occupations were based upon agriculture; the second stage was dominated by manufacturing industry; in the third wave the service sector has become increasingly important and more people are employed in service occupations than in any other sector.

A society in which production takes place is therefore one based around the process of creating value—through both paid and unpaid activities in manufacturing, service and primary industries. The production activities, processes and principles outlined in this chapter are therefore capable of being applied to almost any industry or occupation.

## Research and development

A considerable amount of planning must take place before a product is released or a service is provided. This planning process involves extensive knowledge of the market and its constantly changing tastes and it links in with the research and development function. Setting up a production line or providing a new service can involve considerable cost. Careful work in the early stages will help to ensure that the launch will be successful and consumers receive the goods or services they require.

The decision making process will depend upon information received from the market. If it is felt that the changing wants and needs can be met and that they provide viable market opportunities, researchers can develop their ideas and generate a design. (See Fig. 7.1.)

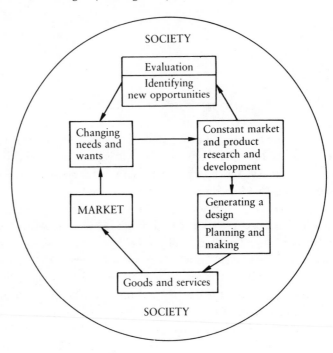

**Figure 7.1** The decision making process

The design must be attractive to consumers, functional and efficient. The researchers must also consider a host of questions such as those indicated in Fig. 7.2. An organization might be reluctant to change an earlier design, particularly if it provides some form of status or helps to portray the image of the organization, e.g. the radiator grill of a BMW. A designer must also bear in mind the treatment a product may receive; for example, toys have to be particularly durable. They may also wish to build into the design planned obsolescence so that the product will need replacing after a particular period; many cars, for example, are only built to last a limited number of years.

Once a design has been developed, the researchers will either build a prototype which can then be tested, or trial the service on offer. Many prototypes will be tried and then discarded, while others may be modified and improved. (See Fig. 7.3.)

In certain cases it may be worthwhile for an organization to apply for a *patent*, which is legal protection and provides the exclusive right to produce

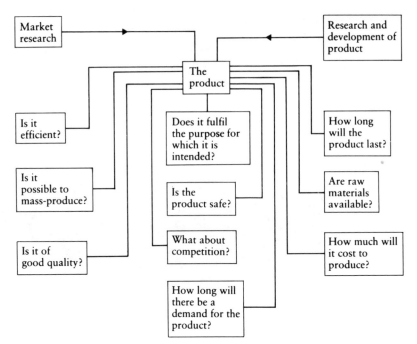

**Figure 7.2** Planning a new product

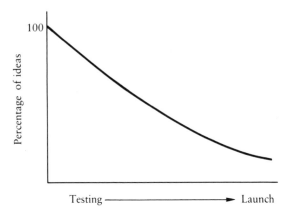

**Figure 7.3** Testing a product before a launch

and sell a given item. *Financial evaluation* of a product's potential is essential to assess the benefits it will ultimately provide. Sometimes it may be necessary to set up a *test market* which will be as near to the real situation as possible. The benefit of this is that it provides useful feedback which reduces the risks of a premature launch. The *launch* is the final process and involves presenting the product to the real market.

### Case Study—The Ford Oval

The Ford trademark of the script-in-oval is one of the best known corporate symbols in the world. The oval has been in regular use for over half a century and the script lettering dates back to the very beginning of the Ford Motor Company.

**Figure 7.4**   Ford logo

An important element in any product is the support provided by the producer's corporate identity. Such an identity helps to provide an image which communicates a message about the quality, reliability and safety of the good or service being provided. A strong supporting corporate identity may influence everyone who comes into contact with that organization such as customers, employees and communities and it may make them think they would rather deal with that organization than others in the same market.

The Ford oval is displayed both on the front and the back of each vehicle and also appears in the centre of the steering wheel. At the front it appears centrally on the bonnet or radiator grill and at the rear on the boot-lid or tailgate. The oval is viewed as an ambassador for the company.

*Questions*

1.  Make a list of logos from other organizations that you regularly come across. Draw as many as you can.
2.  Explain what is meant by a corporate identity. Give three reasons why a corporate identity is so important for many organizations.
3.  Choose the logo of another organization. Carry out a survey to find out how people react to that logo. Examine how far your chosen logo and the corporate identity it portrays reflect the nature of the products or services supplied by that organization.

4. What sort of image does your school or college portray? How far does this identity benefit your institution? Working in groups, suggest how far this image could be changed to reflect greater European awareness.

## What is production?

Production is the process concerned with mobilizing resources to add value to a product or a service so that consumer satisfaction can be created. With a manufacturing company this will involve buying in raw materials and then transforming them through a series of processes and stages into finished products which can then be distributed to the market. (See Fig. 7.5.) For an organization offering a service, their production function will involve organizing resources efficiently to offer the ultimate consumer the best possible value and quality.

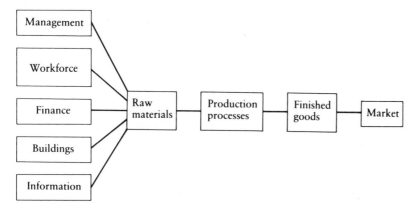

**Figure 7.5**   A manufacturing organization's production process

## Planning production

Organizations depend upon the management abilities of their production or operations team to carry out the production function in a way which satisfies the needs of their customers. Many would argue that this function is always 'the sharp end' of an organization's activities and the most difficult to manage successfully. Targets have to be met and standards have to be kept up. A failure to meet objectives or maintain efficiency may directly affect an organization's future credibility.

The production function usually involves the control and coordination of the bulk of an organization's resources such as capital, assets, labour and other factors. Organizations will operate some form of chain of command for dealing with production, as well as a schedule or timetable of activities mapping out the production processes. An efficient production process would:

- minimize costs
- maximize quality
- satisfy the requirements of customers
- maximize the use of plant
- minimize the inventory

All areas of an organization depend upon the production function running smoothly and to schedule.

## The plant

In order to add value to a product or service some sort of plant or base is necessary. The location and size (see Chapter 5), design, safety and layout of the plant are all of great importance for the production manager.

The design of a plant or of equipment in an organization should enable it to function efficiently. In setting out equipment in a plant, designers should aim to improve coordination, cut process time and also minimize costs.

### Case Study—Designing a car park

Designing a plant and all of the problems this involves of putting facilities in readily accessible places to save on time, space and cost, can be compared to the process a planner has to go through when designing a good car park. We probably all know of badly designed car parks!

Using a blown-up copy of the template provided (see Fig. 7.6), suggest locations for the following:

- lines of car parking spaces
- public toilets
- pay and display ticket machines × 4
- trolley parks × 4
- tourist information centre
- car wash

Put arrows into your diagram and design a suitable arrangement to avoid congestion and hold-ups. Compare your results with the results of others. Then answer the following questions.

#### Questions

1. Briefly explain why the problems you came across coordinating facilities for a car park, are similar to those that every organization which produces goods and services regularly encounters.

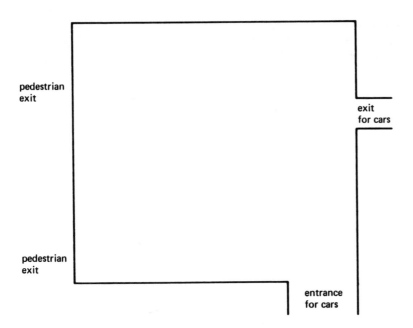

**Figure 7.6**  Car park template

2.  Make a list of places which you have visited which have:
    (a)  a badly designed layout
    (b)  a well designed layout
    Provide a reason for each answer.

*Maintaining* plant and equipment is essential to ensure the smooth and efficient operation of the organization. A maintenance department may include electricians, plumbers and joiners, as well as many other skilled workers. The effectiveness of a maintenance department may be judged by the number of breakdowns and the nature of accidents which take place at work. *Safety* is important and it is the duty of an employer to remove all possible causes of accident.

## The process

There are three main types of process: job, batch and flow production.
*Job production* is concerned with the production of single individual items such as a bridge or a ship. A firm might be producing several different jobs at the same time. The danger of this type of production is that when a particular job is finished, other orders may not be forthcoming and workers may be laid off and resources become idle. This has been a problem in the construction industry whenever a large building project or a motorway has been completed.
*Batch production* exists where batches of similar products are supplied when

orders are received. This type of production often takes place when a range of different products is being provided.

*Flow production* exists where production processes involve an uninterrupted sequence of stages from one process to another. Each stage adds a little more to the finished product.

Increases in the volume of goods manufactured or services provided may lead to some form of mass production. *Mass production* is the production of goods on a large scale and can be applied to job, batch or flow production. It will usually follow that the greater the volume of mass production, the greater the benefits of economies of scale as the firm moves towards it lowest unit cost size.

## Modern technology

Technology is the process of applying knowledge to the development of tools, products and processes for human purposes. For example, we might want to improve the production of chocolate bars so that one chocolate bar tastes like another with a given recipe. A technologist might work out a solution to this problem—machinery that provides a consistent taste.

A technique of production is concerned with the way in which labour, equipment and other means of production are combined to make a finished product. Therefore we can change the technique of production by altering the way we combine factors; for example, if we make a cake using an electric mixer rather than a spoon we will have changed the technique of production.

Technological change is concerned with adding new techniques of production to those which are already known. Today we live in a world in which technological change is very rapid and in which some industries are described as 'high-tech'.

How high is the 'high' in high-tech? This is a difficult question to answer. Most people when asked to define modern technology will mention things like microchips, computers and telecommunications equipment. High-technology products generally involve an 'above average' concentration of scientific and engineering skills.

Defintions of high-tech generally concentrate on the number of scientists and engineers involved in an industry or, the amount of money spent on research and development in a particular industry. If we take a broader view of modern technology, as involving rapid changes in techniques of production, we can see that this would apply to a wide range of businesses. Obvious areas of modern technology would include information processing in banking and insurance and the automated production lines in many factories. Today, even small businesses might employ a small business computer, a telephone answering machine and a fascsimile machine (fax).

### Case Study—Technology

It is easy to take for granted the vast range of technological products that we regularly use. These products often make a positive contribution to the way in which we lead our lives and help to provide us with a better standard of living.

*Questions*

1.  Make a list of products which you use in your household which you would describe as 'high-tech'.
2.  Explain how each of the products you have mentioned contributes to improving your way of life.

*Computer-aided design (CAD)* has improved the reliability and speed with which the design of complex structures such as aeroplanes, cars and bridges can take place. The system couples the electronic drawing board of a powerful computer system with a magnetic pen. The designer is able to use the computer to draw automatically sections of whatever he or she is working on. The computer will also make mathematical calculations and thus the designer is saved thousands of hours of background work.

As well as CAD, developments have also take place in machine tools and many are now controlled numerically (*Numerical Control—NC*) or controlled numerically by a computer (*Computer Numerical Control—CNC*). *CADCAM (Computer Aided Design/Computer Aided Manufacturing)* exists where data from the CAD system is used to drive machines and has therefore become involved in manufacturing processes. A more recent development in this process is called *Computer Integrated Manufacturing (CIM)*. This process goes further as not only is the product designed on a CAD system but, it also orders materials, drives CNC machine tools and has its own control system which provides data for purchasing, accounts, sales and other functions.

*Robots* are multi-purpose machines that can be programmed and reprogrammed. An industrial robot in a car factory may be able to be programmed to paint and then reprogrammed to weld pieces together, or to assemble parts. We can thus see that robots have the following advantages over human labour in doing simple repetitive tasks:

1.  They can work longer hours.
2.  They will not get bored.
3.  They can operate faster.
4.  They may be able to work more accurately.
5.  They are usually cheaper to run.

Robots in industry are now being fitted with vision recognition systems. This makes it possible for them to recognize objects by their shape and size and to fit items like car windscreens by measuring up and centring the screen.

### Case Study—Vehicle design

Over recent years motor vehicle design techniques have been revolutionized by modern technology and the availability of computer-literate designers. Today's designers demand a CAD environment because this is what they are used to.

Modern design techniques include the use of computers for 3D styling. Sometimes learning how to use such systems cannot take place overnight. Lengthy training periods, as well as high software and hardware costs, have to be justified. However, the benefits of such technology are evident in the provision of improved quality and faster turnaround to provide a more competitive edge in a rapidly changing marketplace. For example, computers will do fairly extensive modifications much more quickly. Though clay modelling will still continue in the motor industry, it will be used differently as clay models produced from computer data will be much more accurate than those produced by hand.

*Questions*

1.  List the benefits of 3D modelling systems in the motor vehicle industry.
2.  Briefly explain why investing in such a system would be important for a company wishing to stay competitive.

### The programme

Programming is essentially concerned with timetabling the vast resources used by the production department. Successfully filling orders to provide goods or services will depend on how staff plan and control activities such as schedules. These timetables will generate further organizational requirements in areas such as purchasing, stock control and quality control.

*Purchasing* involves procuring materials and is an important function when you consider that an average manufacturing company spend about one half of its income on supplies of raw materials and services. The purchasing department will aim for the best value for money at the lowest possible cost.

*Stock control* involves holding stocks of raw materials, work-in-progress, finished goods, consumables and plant and machinery spares. The aim of any stock control system is to provide stocks which cater for uncertainties but which are at minimum levels and so ensure that costs are kept low while, at the same time, not affecting the service to customers.

*Quality control* is a system designed to satisfy the customer as cheaply as possible with a product that can be delivered on time. Though quality control was viewed in the past as a sort of inspection department, it is seen today as a system which tries to coordinate groups in an organization to improve quality in a cost-effective way. It will involve looking at the features of the design and how these will satisfy customers, at the quality of product manufacture and at the quality of the final good or service produced.

## The people

The success of any production process will depend upon the people it involves. Just as with any othe resources, the quality of the labour force will relate to the amount invested in it. Training and education will be important. Management will seek to obtain the most from employees and yet will also nurture them as a valuable resource.

As the bulk of those working in an organization will tend to work in production and so directly add value to the final good or service, effective administration and human relations will be important.

*Work study* is concerned with analysing the efficiency of labour in order to maximize its use. A *method study* will examine the way in which a job is being undertaken and try to provide a better way of doing the job in order to reduce costs. *Work measurement* is the establishment of techniques to time workers, so that jobs can be carried out with a defined level of performance for the purpose of creating worker incentives, motivation and predictions of future performance. An essential feature of work study is the understanding of *ergonomics*. This is the study of the worker in his or her working environment and looks at the relationship of the worker to the machines and tries to understand how these relationships can affect performance. This enables the workplace to be designed around the capabilities of the operator.

### Case Study—Automation in a modern brewery

Mechanization involves the use of machinery. The machine is, however, controlled directly by the operator. Automation, on the other hand, involves the creation of a control unit to control the machine. Instructions are fed into the control unit which then controls operations. (See Fig. 7.7.)

In the UK today the beer and lager market is dominated by a few large breweries. These firms are able to produce high outputs at a low average cost per unit. The brewing process is controlled by a central computer which checks that the mixing of ingredients has taken place correctly and takes regular readings on temperatures and fermentation.

Bottles returned from public houses and other retail outlets will be returned on palettes containing several crates of bottles. The crates will be lifted off the palette automatically and a machine will pick up the

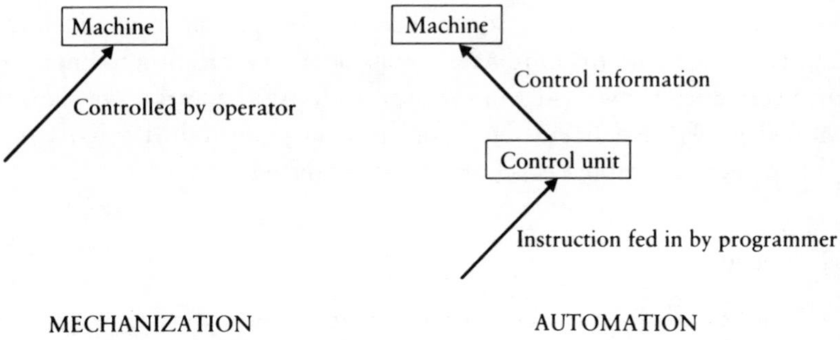

**Figure 7.7** Diagram showing the difference between mechanization and automation

bottles and they will pass down a line into a washing machine. The bottles will then be checked for faults by an electronic device that looks at the structure of the bottle. The bottles will be automatically filled and an electronic eye will check that the contents reach a certain level in the bottle. The machine line will then label and cap the bottles. They will be placed in crates and a number of crates will automatically be placed on a pallet, which is automatically stacked on an out-going lorry. The whole process has been pre-designed to eliminate the need for labour in the main line of production. Labour will only be required to supervise the computer and maintain the machinery.

*Questions*

1.   Why is the beer and lager market suitable for mass-production?
2.   What other production lines can you think of that are suitable for automated production?
3.   What types of production would be unsuitable for mass-production?
4.   Who benefits from automation?
5.   Who loses out as a result of automation?

## Case Study—Producing tin boxes at Huntley, Boorne and Stevens

The first stage of making a tin box is to find a customer. This is done by a salesperson who finds out exactly what the customer wants: the size, the materials required, the colours and a basic idea for a design. The salesperson then goes back to the designer who designs the tin box. They make up a model of the box in stiff cardboard. This model is then taken back to the customer and if it is acceptable and they can agree on a price the factory will go into production.

The purchasing department orders the tin plate and the ink, which is in four colours: red, blue, yellow and black. It also buys the extra parts that the production department needs to put on the firm's existing machines so that they can do the required job. The next stage is to paint the design on to the tin plate. The tin box is usually made up of a number of components. A square tin has three separate parts: the bottom, top and sides. A number of the same components are printed on one sheet of tin plate. The bottom is not always printed. The printing method used is offset lithography. This printing is not done straight on to the tin but on to a rubber blanket. The colours are printed as thousands of tiny dots; the closer they are together the darker the colour. The print is transferred from the rubber roller to the tin plate.

The first colour to be printed is blue, then yellow, followed by red and finally black, which gives an outline to the other colours. When the pieces have all been printed they are cut into individual bodies. The lids are pressed into shape by putting them in a power press. The sides of the box are folded into the right shape on a body form; the sharp edges are all folded in under the seams and rolled and pressed tightly. The bottom is placed with the body and the edges of both components are rolled up together. The lid is then put on and the box is finished. Different types of boxes are made in slightly different ways, but the process is basically the same. The machines are fitted differently for making each type of box.

*Questions*

1. Where does the process of manufacturing a tin box begin?
2. Identify six different occupations involved with the manufacture of a tin box.
3. How does the division of labour come into tin box manufacture?
4. How is specialization of machinery (rather than specialization of labour) involved at Huntley, Boorne and Stevens?
5. What is the most important stage in the production of a tin box?
6. From what you have read, would you say that Huntley, Boorne and Stevens use a job, batch or flow method of production?
7. In what way can the firm be said to be employing a technique of production?
8. In what ways might tin box manufacture be subject to technological change?
9. Would computer aided design be helpful to the firm? If so, why might it not be prepared to use it?
10. Why would Huntley, Boorne and Stevens use quality control inspection?

**Case Study—Moisturizing aftershave**

The following extract appears on the reverse side of a bottle of moisturizing aftershave:

'MODE D'EMPLOI: APPLIQUER UNE PETITE QUANTITE APRES LE RASAGE ET FAIRE PENETRER JUSQU'A SON ABSORPTION TOTALE. EVITER TOUT CONTACT AVEC LES YEUX.'

*Questions*

1. Translate the above extract.
2. Explain why products often have instructions printed on them in several languages. Have you ever come across products which have not had your language printed on them?
3. Produce some instructions of your own in French which would be suitable for a bottle of shampoo.

# Questions

1. Complete the following sentences using the terms below:

Research and development      Drawing office
Planned obsolescence          Production supervisors
Prototypes                    Break-even analysis
Purchasing manager            Ergonomics
Quality control               Automation

(a) Before going into production it is common to test several . . . . . . . . of a product.
(b) . . . . . . . . is essential to ensure that finished products meet the required standard.
(c) The . . . . . . . . has the responsibility of buying in the parts required for production.
(d) The . . . . . . . . is a place where manufacturing drawings are produced.
(e) Documents are issued to . . . . . . . to tell them what to produce.
(f) Manufacturers employ a process known as . . . . . . . . to check that resources are being used efficiently.
(g) . . . . . . . . involves setting up a control unit so that machines can run themselves.
(h) Many manufacturers build . . . . . . . . into their products so that consumers will have to replace them after a period.
(i) High technology industries involve a lot of . . . . . . . .
(j) . . . . . . . . highlights the amount of sales required to cover costs.

2. Would you classify each of the following as an example of job, batch or flow production?

   (a) Mars bars
   (b) Portrait photographs
   (c) A commemorative issue of tin boxes
   (d) An ocean liner
   (e) Tinned cat food
   (f) Insurance policies for households
   (g) Haircuts
   (h) A play
   (i) Electronic circuit boards
   (j) Cars
   (k) Wallpaper

3. In the second half of the 1980s the top ten high-tech sectors of the American economy in terms of money spent on research and development were:

   - Missiles and spacecraft
   - Electronics and telecommunications
   - Aircraft and parts
   - Office automation
   - Ordnance and accessories
   - Drugs and medicines
   - Inorganic chemicals
   - Professional and scientific instruments
   - Engines, turbines and parts
   - Plastics, rubber and synthetic fibres

   Try to divide the following 10 products into the above sectors:

   (a) Vaccines
   (b) Generators
   (c) Satellites
   (d) Non-military arms
   (e) Helicopters
   (g) Desk calculators
   (g) Telephone apparatus
   (h) Nitrogen
   (i) Optical instruments
   (j) Synthetic resins

4. Outline the considerations a manufacturer has to take into account before making a decision to produce a product. Describe the problems of research and development.

5. Select *one* example of a business which is known to you.

   (a) What is the business called?
   (b) What is the main activity of the business?
   (c) Is this business in the primary, secondary or tertiary sector of the economy?

   (*Source*: London and East Anglian Group)

6. 'Disabled Support' is a non-profit making charity. It employs disabled people and raises funds for them by selling Christmas decorations. The charity is considering using advanced technology in its design, manufacturing and administration processes. At the moment it uses the same equipment in the office and factory as it has for twenty years.

   (a) How would the aims of 'Disabled Support' differ from those of most businesses?
   (b) Explain what types of advanced technology 'Disabled Support' could employ in:

      (i)   Design
      (ii)  Manufacture
      (iii) Administration

(c) State the advantages and disadvantages of 'Disabled Support' introducing advanced technology, considering the implications for the workforce and the aims of the organization.

(*Source*: Midland Examining Group)

## Coursework

Why is different technology used in different circumstances?

The sealing of cans is the process of closing one end of the can with a lid. This process can be done by using two different methods of production technology.

The first way is to use a semi-automatic machine that makes one can at a time. Not much skill is required to operate the machine, but the quality is poor, and 5 per cent of the cans are rejected by quality control. As a result it is necessary to have a supervising officer at every fourth machine.

The second method is to use an automatic machine that seals four cans at a time. There is very little manual work involved except the control of the machine. The workers need to be skilled in operating the machine. The quality of the work is very high and there is less need for quality inspection.

Southworld, a multinational company, has canning factories in many countries throughout the world. All these canning plants were set up at the same time but in some countries the firm installed the semi-automatic machines and in others the automatic machines. As a group, discuss the reasons why the firm may have chosen to use different technology in different countries. You should then go on to ask the question whether advanced technology is most suitable in all circumstances.

## Questions

1. How is production organized in a local manufacturing or service business?
2. Contrast the production constraints in a service and a manufacturing business. How and why do they differ?
3. Pick a local firm and say why it has employed automated technology.
4. What is the purpose of work study?

# 8
# Marketing

## What is a market?

A market is a situation in which goods can be bought, sold or exchanged. The essential requirement are *buyers*, *sellers*, *goods* and *money*.

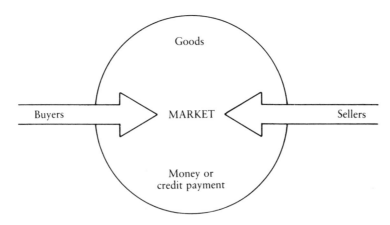

Figure 8.1  A market situation

In the early 1990s many people in Eastern Europe were confused when they heard the word 'market'. Some of them thought that it meant a 'street market' only. Of course, the term 'market' is much wider than that. A market process involves any form of exchange or transaction. So we can talk about the market for shoes, for bread, for insurance, for stocks and shares and for any other good or service. (Who are the buyers and sellers in the following markets: the housing market, the job market, the stock market, the supermarket and the market for international football stars?)

## The importance of the consumer

The consumer is the final user of a product. Any business that hopes to be successful needs to be aware of the needs and wishes of their customers. There

135

are many new products which consumers are willing to try once. However, they will not buy again unless the product satisfies them. Businesses therefore need to be *market conscious*. An example of a highly successful market conscious company is Pedigree Petfoods. In 1991 they set out their view of the market in the following way:

'We work constantly towards identifying and satisfying consumer needs. It is the activity from which all else springs. We never forget that we cannot influence millions of consumer choices until we have convinced first one, then a second and a third customer that our product is worthy of purchase. Our success is based on thorough research of the wide range of needs for pet animals and their owners. The knowledge which we gain is translated into a range of quality products which satisfy these needs better than any of our competitors.'

If you study the quote carefully, you will see that Pedigree Petfoods set out to know and understand their customers so well that their products fits them and then sells itself.

Of course, marketing petfood is more complicated than say, for example, chocolate, because animals cannot talk. However, all consumers provide feedback which determines their future buying patterns. If your dog refuses to eat his or her dinner you will not buy that brand of dog food again.

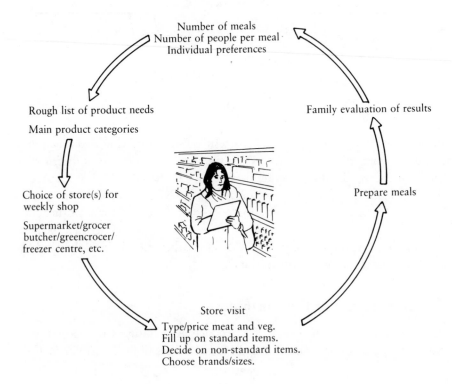

Number of meals
Number of people per meal
Individual preferences

Rough list of product needs

Main product categories

Choice of store(s) for weekly shop

Supermarket/grocer
butcher/greencrocer/
freezer centre, etc.

Family evaluation of results

Prepare meals

Store visit
Type/price meat and veg.
Fill up on standard items.
Decide on non-standard items.
Choose brands/sizes.

**Figure 8.2**  Rough meal plan for a week

A survey carried out by the magazine *Marketing* in 1990, showed the importance of consumer feedback from one week to another in determining family buying patterns. The survey looked at 'Why do shoppers buy?'

The survey revealed a cycle of identifying shopping needs, designing a shopping list, planning and making store visits to make purchases, preparation of meals, evaluation of the results by family members, leading round once again to the design of a rough plan for the following week (see Fig. 8.2).

## What is marketing?

Marketing is a strategic planning process. In its simplest form marketing answers the question: *What does the customer want to buy?*

The aim of the marketing process is to discover what customers require and to plan and organize ways of meeting these requirements in such a way as to make profits.

As a strategic planning process, marketing should investigate and provide answers as to:

*What* should be produced?
*Why* it should be produced?
*How* it should be produced?
*When* it should be produced?

The 'what?, why?, how? and when?' does not just relate to the products. Marketing should also coordinate all the other important areas of market research, advertising, promotion and other areas that are considered in this chapter.

### Marketing and marketing services

To carry out marketing (the strategic planning process described above) you will need marketing services (see Fig. 8.3). Marketing services will include advertising, public relations, trade and consumer promotions, point-of-sale materials, publicity and sales literature.

The marketing process involves identifying needs and opportunities, designing ways of meeting these needs and opportunities, planning (advertising campaigns, strategic plans, market research questionnaires) and making outputs to meet these requirements and evaluating these outputs in order to identify further needs and opportunities.

*Task*

You work in the marketing department of a well known soap powder manufacturer. A rival company has recently developed a new powder, which

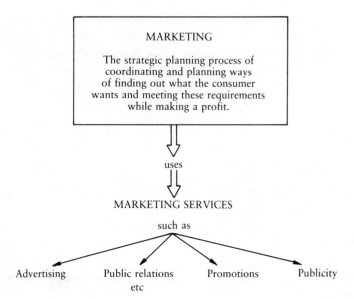

**Figure 8.3**   Marketing processes

they claim 'washes whiter than any other powder'. You feel that your existing brand is more effective.

(a)   Design a poster campaign to combat their advertising. You will need to produce a set of at least three different posters and a report to your marketing manager to explain the theme behind the campaign and where the posters will be located.

(b)   Explain how the development of your campaign relates to the process diagram shown in Fig. 8.4. (You will need to complete the diagram yourself by putting in descriptions at a, b and c.)

## Marketing steps

Two major ingredients should be blended together in the preparation of a good or service for the market:

1.   *Market research*: Finding out, recording and then making sense of the views of consumers. For example, you want to find out how many people will buy a new chocolate bar which is wrapped in pink paper and costs 20p. How will you find out this information? Perhaps you will ask every tenth shopper in the high street on a Saturday afternoon. You could invite a selected audience to your premises to chat about their views. How will you record what they say? Will you tick off the boxes on a record sheet, or maybe take detailed notes of what they say? How will you make sense of this information? Will you add a list of ticks together under headings such as very good, good, poor and so on, or will you try to get a general impression of peoples' views?

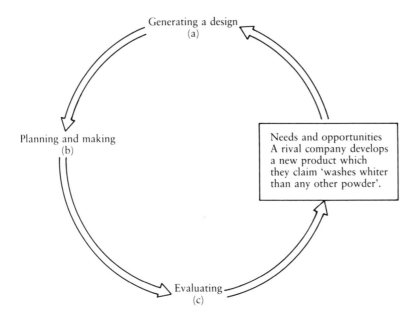

**Figure 8.4**  Marketing process

2. *Product research*: Involves developing new products in line with your market research to meet the needs of consumers. The production department of a company constantly comes up with ideas for new products and changes to existing ones. However, there is no point in making changes if customers do not want them, or if the extra cost will be greater than the extra revenue. Product development and market research must therefore go hand-in-hand. (See Fig. 8.5 overleaf.)

## The life cycle of a product

The collection of information about the market provides management with a degree of safety. For example, research will show whether a product is likely to be successful.

An important part of marketing is the understanding of a product's life cycle. When a product is launched, its sales are likely to be low and promotion will be expensive. If the product is successful, sales will increase until they reach their peak. Eventually new products will come on to the market and the sales of existing products will decline. When we look at the curve in Fig. 8.6, we must bear in mind that the time period for the cycle will vary between products. For example, the sales of Mars bars are still, after many years, only somewhere between boom and peak. Other products, such as fashion clothes and products that only catch the public imagination for a short while, have much shorter product lives.

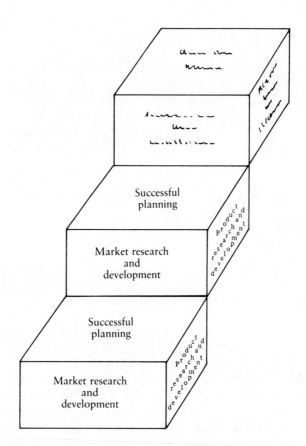

**Figure 8.5**   Steps to success, combining market/product research and development

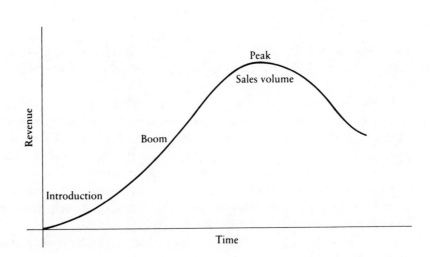

**Figure 8.6**   A product only has a certain lifespan

## Case Study—Products to eliminate home chores

Robot vacuum cleaners, microwaves that know what is in them, irons that sense what fabric they are pressing, food mixers which bake cakes! These are some of the products being developed in research laboratories across Europe, the US and in the Far East for launch before 1995. (See Fig. 8.7.)

**Figure 8.7**  Living a better life

With more than £6 billion at stake in the European market alone, it is hardly surprising that companies are rushing to get their products on to the market. There is so much activity in the market that companies are fast making obsolete their own inventions and product life cycles are constantly falling. A vacuum cleaner used to last 20 years and an iron 7, but now people replace vacuums every 7 years and irons every 3 years.

*Questions*

1.  Why is so much activity taking place in the market for domestic appliances?
2.  How will the new products mentioned in the case study help us to improve our lifestyles?
3.  What is happening to product life cycles as a result of all of this activity?
4.  Choose a domestic commodity. Survey family and friends to find out how long the life cycles are for commodities of this type.

An understanding of the lifespan of a product will enable the marketing manager to plan his or her activities. From time to time, market research will indicate that fresh life will need to be injected into a product. Having identified this need, it will be necessary to design, plan and make changes to a product in order to extend the growth period of the product life cycle.

## The marketing mix

The marketing mix is often referred to as the '4 Ps', i.e. product, price, place and promotion. To meet customers' needs a business must develop *products* to satisfy them, charge the right *price*, get the goods to the right *place* and it must make the existence of the goods known through *promotion*. (See Fig. 8.8.)

**Figure 8.8**    The marketing mix

'Mix' is an appropriate word to describe this part of the marketing process. A mix is a blend of ingredients designed to achieve a common purpose. Each is vitally important and depends upon the others for its success. As with a cake, each ingredient is not really satisfying on its own, but with these blended together it is possible to produce something really special. In the same way that there are a variety of cakes to suit various tastes, the marketing mix can be specially designed to suit the precise requirements of the market.

The correct combination of such elements will enable a company to fulfil its role. Elements of the mix will vary in emphasis from one product to another. Figure 8.9 compares the marketing mix for two different products.

The perfect mix is one in which:

(a)  The *product* has the right features. For example, it must look good and work well.

(b)  The *price* is set at an attractive level. Consumers will buy in large quantities to produce a healthy profit.

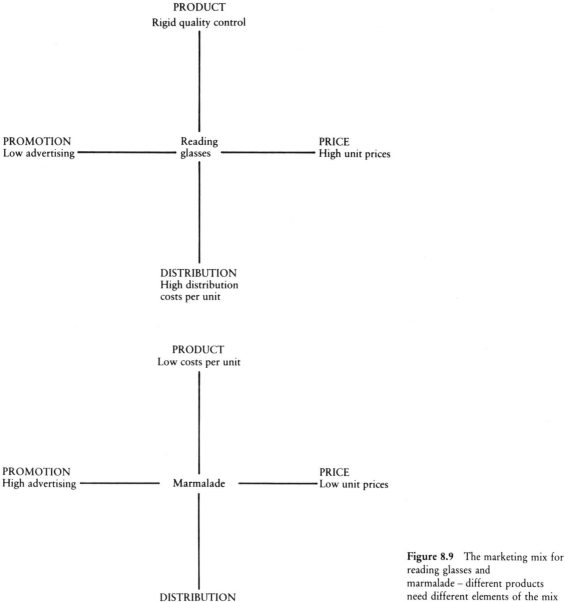

PRODUCT
Rigid quality control

PROMOTION
Low advertising —————— Reading glasses —————— PRICE
High unit prices

DISTRIBUTION
High distribution
costs per unit

PRODUCT
Low costs per unit

PROMOTION
High advertising —————— Marmalade —————— PRICE
Low unit prices

DISTRIBUTION
Low distribution costs per unit

**Figure 8.9** The marketing mix for reading glasses and marmalade – different products need different elements of the mix to be emphasized

(c)  The goods get to the *right place*. Making sure that the goods arrive when they are wanted and where they are wanted is an important operation.

(d)  The target group needs to be made aware of the existence and availability of the product through *promotion*. Successful advertising helps a firm to spread costs over a larger output.

*Task*

Think of a product which you buy regularly such as, an item of confectionery (e.g., a Mars bar) or a teenage magazine (*Just Seventeen*). How effective are the ingredients of the marketing mix for this product?

Does the *product* meet consumer requirements?
Is the *price* right?
Can consumers always get it and at the *place* they want it?
What about *promotion*? What do the consumers think of it?

Before you start the exercise make sure you know who the product is supposed to sell to. Is the intended market teenagers? Male or female? Now choose a sample of 30 people to interview from the appropriate group, e.g. females in the age range 13–18.

- The **target market**. Your target market is the particular group of people who you feel will be particularly interested in the product and who have the money to spend on it. Once you are aware of the identity of your target market, you direct your marketing mix at this group.

Ask your sample to compare your selected product with three or four rival products. Rule up a table similar to the one below and then compare the brand you use with its alternatives.

| Product A | Very good | Good | Average | Poor | Very Poor | Comment |
|-----------|-----------|------|---------|------|-----------|---------|
| Place     |           |      |         |      |           |         |
| Promotion |           |      |         |      |           |         |
| Price     |           |      |         |      |           |         |
| Product   |           |      |         |      |           |         |
| *Product B* |         |      |         |      |           |         |
| etc.      |           |      |         |      |           |         |

Now suggest how the marketing mix could be improved for the product you buy.

The marketing mix will comprise a series of strategies which can be used to position a product to appeal to a particular market segment. For example, British Rail identified three segments in their InterCity market—business travel, leisure travel and obligatory travel. They then promoted the InterCity Business Theme to reposition InterCity at the quality end of the business market.

## Case Study—Arby's to fight in the fast food market

A US fast food chain famous for roast beef sandwiches is to make an aggressive attempt to take on fast food giants like McDonald's and Burger King in the UK.

Arby's outlets will sell roast beef sandwiches and also a variety of chicken and turkey sandwiches, as well as salads, potatoes and drinks such as Jamocha (coffee and chocolate) milkshakes.

Aggressive promotion is the key to Arby's bid and they recognize that a minimum of 4 per cent of sales must be spent on advertising which will give a worldwide budget of $48 million.

Plans are for a first unit trading by the end of 1991 expanding to a chain of 200–300 within 5 to 7 years.

Prices will be competitive, such as £1.50 for a roast beef sandwich.

### Question

Working in groups comment on the four elements of Arby's marketing mix highlighted in the case study. Consider who the mix is directed at and then decide upon whether you think Arby's attempt to enter the UK fast food market is going to be successful.

# Market research

Today, many modern companies feel that their major purpose is to satisfy consumer needs. Marketing has become their *total business philosophy*. Instead of having to use hard selling techniques to get the customer to buy goods, these market-led companies sell goods easily because they produce what the customer wants. To find out what the customer wants, a wide variety of market research techniques are used to answer questions such as:

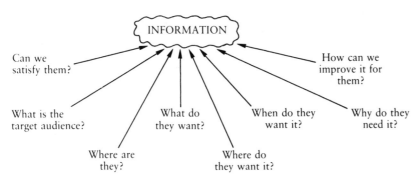

**Figure 8.10**  Market research

Market research information must be obtained and then analysed so that all the options are revealed. (See Fig. 8.10.)

Data collected can be either *primary* data or *secondary* data. Primary data is gathered first-hand by research in the 'field', while secondary data is the use of data already gathered by somebody else.

Primary data is usually gathered by conducting a survey in which information is obtained by interviewing a sample of the population being investigated. It is usual to use a questionnaire, which should be made with care. The questions should be simple and clear, should not be open-ended and thus difficult to analyse and wherever possible should be pre-tested.

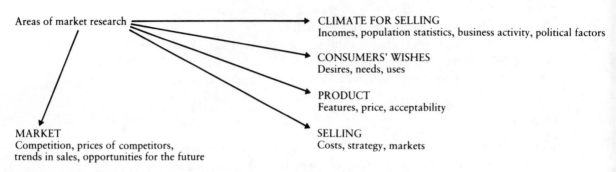

**Figure 8.11** Market research considers many different factors

Information may be gathered in the following ways:

1. By personal interviews with an experienced interviewer.
2. By post, though postal surveys tend to lead to slow results and the response rate is low.
3. By telephone, which is speedy and easy to administer, particularly for industrial markets.

Sampling might be random, with each member of the population having an equal chance of being picked; or it could be systematic, including, for example, every tenth member of the population; or an interviewer may have selected people to interview (e.g., the 100 best dressed people in Grantham).

Data must be processed and organized into an easily understood format so that trends or patterns can be detected (see the notes on presenting information in Chapter 1). Information may be represented in the form of pie charts, bar charts or pictures and statistical analysis may take place. Once the data has been analysed, a series of plans will be required and marketing managers will use the information to develop both their short-term and long-term strategies.

*Task*

Prepare a simple market research questionnaire to find out what types of hot and cold drinks a random sample of 100 people drink. Enter the information into a database. How will you construct your database? How easy is it to extract information rapidly from your database? Is it easy to make sense of the results? (Although you are only working from a small sample, the ease with which you can assess data will indicate whether your database would have been effective with a much larger sample.)

## Advertising

Most people understand advertising to be sellers publicizing their goods to customers. In fact, any type of publicity is advertising. In the UK, the body that spends most money on advertising is the government, which has all sorts of messages to put over to the public (see Fig. 8.12).

**Figure 8.12**  An example of the sort of message that the government may try to put over through advertising

The government rarely tries to sell things to people. More often it tries to inform them of their rights. This passing on of information is a very important part of advertising.

Most adverts, however, are not just there to inform the public—you do not see a soap powder advert that simply gives information about the powder. The advert goes further and contains a persuasive message. Most firms that try to sell goods will use *persuasive advertising*.

A persuasive selling message is one that promises to the people to whom it is addressed, a desirable and believable benefit.

There are many different types of advert that can be used to persuade, including the following:

1. Adverts showing a famous personality using the product.
2. Adverts comparing one product with other products.
3. Adverts using sex appeal.

Many firms aim to develop strong brand images for their products. A brand is the name of a company's product such as 'Frosties', 'Smarties', and 'Fairy Liquid'. If people associate a brand name with a product then this might help create loyalty for the brand. The creation of a good brand image will depend upon the marketing mix.

## Advertising agencies

If you were advertising the village dance you could simply make out some posters and place them around the village where they would attract most attention. However, firms risking a lot of money on an advertising campaign must make sure that their advertising is in safe hands. Generally firms will therefore employ an advertising agency to carry out the campaign.

For advertising to be successful it must do the following:

1. Reach the right audience.
2. Be attractive and appealing.
3. Cost little in relation to the extra sales made.

## Reaching the right audience

An advertising agency will know the best way to reach the right audience. It will have several media available for use and the choice will depend upon the size of audience the client wishes their product to reach. (See Fig. 8.13.)

The advertising agency will be in a good position to advise on the best media to use. Perhaps if a firm wants to produce a new biscuit or bar of chocolate it will be advised to use television advertising. People in Britain watch a lot of television and firms showing their adverts during popular programmes, like the Australian soaps, can reach millions of people.

Recently, television advertising has been threatened by television gadgetry. More and more families have push-button remote control units for their televisions, allowing them to switch over during the adverts without leaving their seats. In the US, people have automatic switch over controls on their televisions so that when the adverts come on, the television switches over to another station until the adverts are over.

Obviously, if a firm is selling a specialized product, like expensive fur coats, then the advertising agency will suggest that it uses a specialist medium like an exclusive womens' magazine.

**Figure 8.13** Advertising must be directed at the right audience

**Figure 8.14** 'The Gold Blend soap opera' (Source: The Nestlé Company Ltd)

### Case Study—Advertisment recall

Whether advertisements have communicated a message effectively or not largely depends upon whether the consumer is either influenced by the message or can recall the message at a later point in time. However the advertisements are conveyed, they need to leave an impression if they are to work. Some of the more noted campaigns over recent years have included 'the Gold Blend soap opera' (see Fig. 8.14), the 'Tetley Teafolk', 'Carling Black Label and I bet he drinks . . .', 'British Telecom and Maureen Lipman' and 'Coca-Cola showing young people enjoying themselves'.

*Question*

Working in pairs, put together a table of the *top ten* adverts at this moment in time. Survey a group of people and find out what adverts they spontaneously recall. Having made a list of the top ten adverts explain why you think they effectively communicate their message.

## Attractive and appealing advertising

The advertising agency will have experience in planning the layout of campaigns. Sometimes the firm selling the goods will have a big say in what goes into the advert and sometimes the advertising agency will decide alone how the advertising should be done.

## Cost in relation to the extra sales made

The extra sales made as a result of an advertising campaign are expected to bring in far more money than the cost of that advertising. However, measuring the extra sales made as a result of an advertising campaign can be very difficult.

Sometimes when a new product is being marketed it will be given a trial run in a selected area of the country. Usually this will be in a particular Independent Television (ITV) region. For example, a crisp company brings out a new star-shaped crisp. Its advertising agency might then advertise the crisp in the Tyne-Tees region. The results of this test-market in the north-east of England will determine whether or not it will then be launched nationally. By carrying out a pilot scheme the company will not lose a lot of money if the product does not sell well.

# Control over advertising in the United Kingdom

Advertisers cannot just say anything they like when preparing an advert.

1. They must keep within the law. For instance, the Trades' Description Act lays down that goods put up for sale must be as they are described (e.g., a waterproof watch must be waterproof).
2. The advertising industry has its own code of practice which advertisers must obey.

## *The British Code of Advertising Practice*

This is a voluntary agreement entered into by firms in the advertising industry to keep their adverts up to certain standards. For instance, when advertising slimming products, like slimming pills and biscuits, the advertiser must say that these should be taken in addition to a balanced diet. In other words, the advertiser should not suggest that a person can slim by simply eating biscuits—this would obviously be dangerous to health. The British Code of Advertising Practice covers newspapers, magazines, cinema adverts, leaflets, brochures, posters and commercials on video tape, but not on TV and radio.

**Figure 8.15** The Advertising Standards Authority uses advertisements like this one to put its own message across

*The Advertising Standards Authority (ASA)*

The ASA is responsible for supervising the British Code of Advertising Practice, except for Independent Television. You might have seen an advert that appears in national newspapers and magazines, part of which looks like Fig. 8.15. The advert goes on to say that if you have any complaints about adverts in the paper you should write to the ASA which will take up your complaint. Of course, some of the complaints received by the ASA are frivolous, like the man who complained that he had poured Heineken lager on his pot plant and it had died.

However, if the ASA feels that an advert is indecent or untrue it will ask the advertising agency that produced the advert to change it. The advertising agency will then change the advert because they know the ASA can ask the media to stop printing adverts by that agency.

*The Independent Television Commission*

Following the 1990 Broadcasting Act, the Independent Television Commission (ITC) was set up to replace the Independent Broadcasting Authority (IBA). In doing so it now exercises control over television advertising.

## Sales

This is an area of great importance for the success of a business. Selling involves getting the customer to purchase a company's products. The salesforce must have a good understanding of the product it is selling and must know the market well enough to know the customer's desires. A salesperson's job requires persistence and energy and can be one of the most difficult in industry. The salaries of sales personnel are often linked to sales, through commission.

Any salesforce must cover as many areas of a market as possible and often sales representatives are each allocated a territory which comes under the supervision of an area sales manager. Salespeople can provide a close link with customers and often establish such a good relationship that repeat orders are made. They are often involved with the promotion of new products, providing displays and demonstrations as well as helping at exhibitions. Sales relate directly to profits and targets are often set for the salesforce. Export orders are often fundamental to the success of the business and overseas operations are quite common.

*Task*

List the qualities someone would need for a career in selling.

### After-sales service

After-sales service usually applies to durable goods such as washing machines, central heating systems, electric cookers and other items of equipment. A business must decide whether it is going to offer its services for a period of time after the sale has been made. After-sales service helps to create loyalty. For example, some electricity companies work on the principle that a customer is for life and the selling of an applicance is the start of a business relationship. Another aspect of after-sales service is the handling of enquiries and complaints from customers. Some firms will actually send out circulars to customers encouraging comment, whereas others will respond to customers as and when required.

Offers of after-sales service may be an important part of the promotion of the product. An example of this would be where a car sales firm offers a free service after a given number of miles.

## Distribution

The *channel of distribution* is the route which products follow from the manufacturer to the consumer. Market research will often reveal channels of distribution used by competitors.

The traditional way of distributing goods from a manufacturer to a market is through a small number of wholesalers, who then sell the goods to a larger number of retailers. (See Fig. 8.16.)

In this way, a wholesaler is a go-between who buys in bulk from manufacturers and breaks the bulk down into small units for retailers. Wholesalers often provide a variety of services which benefit both manufacturers and retailers such as, warehousing, credit, transport and packaging. However, the existence of wholesalers adds to the selling price and wholesalers cannot be expected to concentrate on any one manufacturer's goods.

If a manufacturer sells direct to a retailer it can exert greater control over its sales and the manufacturer and the retailer can work together on sales

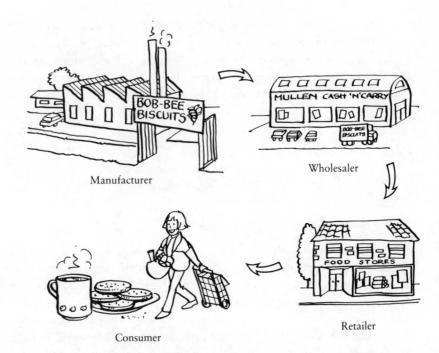

**Figure 8.16** The traditional route from manufacturer to consumer – via a wholesaler and a retailer

Manufacturer

Wholesaler

Consumer

Retailer

promotion schemes. Selling direct to retailers involves a larger salesforce and increased transport charges when sending smaller consignments. If circumstances allow, it can be possible for manufacturers to sell directly to consumers, particularly if the product is a high-cost one and has a good reputation within the market. (See Fig. 8.17.)

The manufacturer has to think carefully about choices of distribution and aim to minimize selling costs and maximize sales.

Retailers are in direct contact with consumers and are therefore in the best position to understand individual consumers' desires. An efficient system of retailing is essential if the types of commodities made by producers are to relate closely to consumers' desires. A retailer is the outlet through which goods are sold to consumers and may exist in a variety of forms, for example, single unit shops, chain stores or multiples, supermarkets, department stores and hypermarkets.

**Figure 8.17** Sometimes a manufacturer will sell direct to a retailer, missing out the wholesaler; and sometimes even the retailer will be missed out when a manufacturer sells direct to the consumer

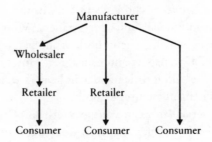

# The role of microelectronics

Over recent years, technology has played an increasing role in marketing. For example, market research information will be stored, sorted and analysed from a computer *database*. Information can be displayed using *graphics*. It is not just the products which are designed by *Computer Aided Design*. The packaging, promotional material and advertising can also be designed using CAD.

*Stock control* is a vital ingredient to get the goods to where consumers require them at the right time. By keeping too much stock a company will unnecessarily tie up money and space which could be put to better use. Keeping too little means that customers may be frustrated. In a modern company, an effective communications system is needed to link the distribution network, so that needs can be communicated to suppliers. A computerized stock control system will record and monitor the movement of stock and also advise when it is necessary to re-order.

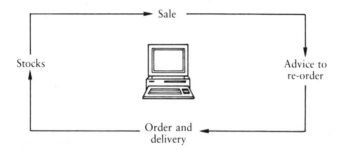

Figure 8.18 Computerized stock control system

### Case Study—Supermarkets

Supermarkets deal with thousands of items of stock. Holding information on these items is essential to ensure that shelves and backing stores do not empty. Information can be obtained either by:

(a) counting stocks on shelves

*or*

(b) recording details at the checkout.

*Hand counting* might be used to count stocks on shelves. Such a simple method would be far too slow and unreliable for a large supermarket.

*Mark sense documents* might be available. A computer prints out a list of the range of goods sold, alongside which are a number of clock marks. By shading in these marks while checking the shelves, information can then be passed on to the computer, which will read and process the information before re-ordering where necessary.

*Bar codes* are a pattern of thin and thick lines used to identify details of a product. Every product has a unique pattern of lines. A bar code appears on most products and contains information about the product.

*Shelf marking bar codes* can be placed under the shelf of each good so that supermarket staff can use a *portable data entry terminal* (PDET). Staff pass a light pen over the bar coded shelf labels of goods which need to be re-ordered and then use the PDET keypad to type in the number required. This information is then sent through a telephone line to a central computer.

*Kimball tags* are often used at the checkouts, particularly in clothes stores. Tags are collected and then sent in batches to a computer centre for processing. The more modern method is through *Electronic Point of Sale terminals* (EPOS). These are computer-based 'intelligent tills', where operators enter the bar code number of each item, either by typing in the number using a reader or scanner. The EPOS terminal registers the code and displays the price.

*Questions*

1. Explain why a stock control system is so important for a super-market.
2. Working in groups, share your experiences of town and city retail outlets. Make a list of stores and indicate what stock control systems you feel each uses.
3. Produce a table showing the:
   (a) advantages and
   (b) disadvantages of bar codes.

*EFT-POS* is a system designed to take EPOS even further. It stands for *Electronic Funds Transfer at the Point of Sale* and is a new method of payment which will become the basis for a national electronic shopping system.

EFT-POS will link retail tills using BT lines with the computers of banks that hold retailers' and shoppers' accounts. Electronic information will be contained in a customer's debit card. When a transaction takes place, the retailer's bank will receive information of funds due and the customer's bank will confirm the transaction and debit the customer's account. The payment procedure is a simple one:

Stage 1—The customer hands the card over to a cashier who passes (SWIPES) the card through a reader.
Stage 2—The cashier enters the amount to be paid in the terminal.
Stage 3—The customer will sign a receipt or enter an identification number.
Stage 4—The transaction is checked and authorized and a receipt is issued.
Stage 5—The cashier returns the card, together with a receipt.

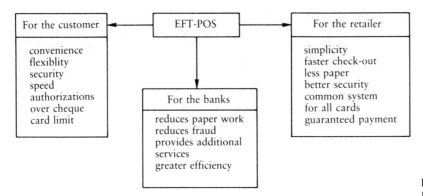

**Figure 8.19** Advantages of EFT-POS

# Transport

The location of a firm will influence its costs. A transport department will not just provide transport for raw materials and finished goods, but will also provide a fleet of vehicles to assist the organization's sales and management functions. One important decision will be whether to purchase a fleet of vehicles, use private carriers or lease vehicles.

## Major forms of transport

### Road

The major benefit of road transport is that it can deliver door-to-door and this cuts out intermediate handling. However, congestion is a major problem.

### Rail

Railways help to keep traffic away from the roads and their major benefit is for bulk loads over long distances.

### Sea

Shipping often provides the most suitable method of transport for low value, bulky goods, as well as containers.

### Air

The major advantage of air transport is its speed, but it does tend to be used for cargoes which are expensive in relation to their weight, for items which are needed urgently and for perishable items which have a short shelf-life.

## Case Study—Ungaro goes down market

For the past 25 years, Emanuel Ungaro has been designing highly individual clothes for the happy few. Today he is seeking to reach a much larger group of consumers. It has been reported that he is looking for a partner in order to create middle-level lines and to open new shops.

Mr Ungaro has always been one of Paris' most controversial designers. His florid, brightly coloured creations always arouse strong emotions—and also fetch high prices. *Haute couture* suits average at more than $20,000.

By going down market Mr Ungaro will be following the example of designers like Yves St Laurent, who have set up increasingly successful luxury good groups. Analysts feel that Mr Ungaro seems to be making the right move at the right time and that his sales could rise rapidly.

*Questions*

1. Explain what 'Ungaro goes down market' means.
2. Why do you feel Mr Ungaro is trying to make his products reach a wider base of consumers.
3. Form small groups to discuss how Mr Ungaro should adjust his marketing mix to cater for a significantly larger group of consumers. Report your conclusions back to the group.

## Case Study—Living in an electronic marketplace

The electronic marketplace could change the way in which people buy and sell goods and services over the next few years. The bargaining of the future will be electronic and markets could be global.

Electronic marketing is already well-established. For example, IT is used to target customers through computerized databases.

Database marketing has led to customized products and packages and direct mail specifically directed to the specific needs of each customer.

Electronic purchasing is less common. However, this will grow as suppliers deal with their customers through electronic interchange. Electronic purchasing will enable a buyer to compare prices between suppliers.

Electronic marketing therefore benefits *sellers*, enabling suppliers to reach more customers with a better targeted product. Electronic purchasing benefits *buyers* who can compare the prices of suppliers. In the true electronic marketplace buyers and sellers will come together

Suppliers                                                    Customers

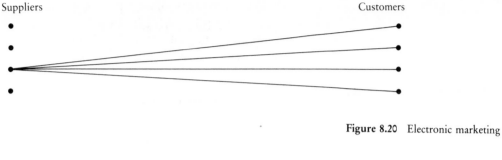

**Figure 8.20**   Electronic marketing

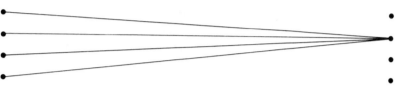

**Figure 8.21**   Electronic purchasing

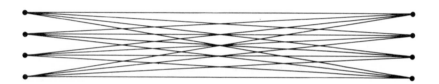

**Figure 8.22**   An electronic marketplace

rather like the stock market. This will allow round the clock trading on a global scale. Both buyers and sellers will be assured of the best possible deal.

*Questions*

1.  Explain the meaning of:
    (a)   electronic marketing
    (b)   electronic purchasing.
2.  How will this benefit buyers and sellers?

## Case Study—Renault 25

Read the advertisement and then answer the questions in English.

# NOUVELLE RENAULT 25

La nouvelle Renault 25 réalise l'union de toutes les exigences: l'intelligence et le confort, le plaisir de conduire et la sérénité, la puissance et la sécurité, l'économie et la garantie de pièces partout disponibles.
Encore plus silencieuse, encore plus confortable, encore plus accueillante, la nouvelle Renault 25 est un véritable salon.
Direction assistée et conditionnement d'air, chaîne stéréo 4 x 20 W et habillage en cuir sur demande... ceux dont l'exigence guide la vie, vont enfin trouver avec la nouvelle Renault 25, une voiture à leur mesure.

**Figure 8.23**   Nouvelle Renault 25 advertisement

*Questions*

1.   Describe the benefits of the Renault 25.
2.   What evidence in the advert indicates that Renault is a market conscious company?

## Question

1.   Complete the following sentences using the terms below:

Direct mailing
Mass media
Advertising agency
Informative advert
Trade journal
Persuasive advert
Market research

(a)   An advert just giving the plain 'hard facts' about an item for sale would be an example of an ..............

(b)   An advert which tries to entice somebody into buying an item through subtle techniques is an example of ..............

(c)   A firm specializing in helping people to advertise their products is called an ..............

(d)   National newspapers, television, the radio and cinema are collectively called the ..............

(e)   A magazine providing specialist information about a particular line of business is called a ..............

**Figure 8.24** Ramesh Gehlot and his greengrocer's business (Source: Kim Hooper, Reading)

(f)  Before firms market a product, they will normally carry out a ...............

(g)  Advertising by posting leaflets direct to potential customers is known as ...............

2  Ramesh Gehlot (see Fig. 8.24) has just opened a new greengrocery business and decides to spend £500 launching the business by advertising.

(a)  Suggest four ways in which this advertising budget could be spent.

(b)  Explain three motives the advertising could appeal to.

(c)  Describe two other ways, other than advertising, in which Ramesh could promote his sales.

(d)  Which of the methods of sales promotion you have given in answer to (c) would you expect to be the most effective?

(e)  Explain, with reasons, whether you think it is worth promoting a new greengrocery business.

3.  You are the marketing manager for a well known national supplier of sporting equipment. In recent months your rivals have started marketing inferior imitations of your football boots. The managing director has called you into her office and told you that you can have an extra sum of advertising money to win back customers. What methods of marketing would you employ?

4.  Study the adverts in a teenage magazine. Which products would you expect to have long life cycles and which ones short life cycles?

5.  Explain how the marketing mix will vary for the following products:

(a)  Chocolate

(b)  Newspapers

(c)   Rulers
(d)   Electric blankets
(e)   New houses

6. Sylvia Whitbread, who owns a manufacturing business, decides to acquire her own delivery fleet instead of using haulage contractors. What are the benefits of making such a decision?

7. Hobbs and James plc are a long-established manufacturer of sweets. Although they are a public limited company the majority of shares are owned by members of the James family. The James family hold the main positions on the company's board. The firm produces a range of well known products but, sales have declined in recent years as newer products have entered the market. For many years the firm's best seller has been 'Fruit Ovals' a very popular variety of hard sweets. It is this brand which has suffered the largest fall in sales.

As a result, younger members of the family have put pressure on the chairman, Sir Harold James, to react to changes in the sweet market and, at last, he has accepted their advice.

(a)   Why do you think the James family wish to own over half the company's shares?
(b)   Draw a diagram to illustrate the life cycle of a typical product and clearly illustrate the point of the cycle which 'Fruit Ovals' may have reached.
(c)   Before introducing new products, Hobbs and James have to research their market.
  (i)   List *three* ways by which Hobbs and James may carry out market research.
  (ii)  Researching a market to discover customers' opinions is expensive. Why, then, do firms spend money on such research?
(d)   What evidence would show that a company was, perhaps, being badly managed?
(*Source*: Southern Examining Group)

8. Compare the marketing mix of manufacturing firms and service industries.

9. Explain what is meant by market research. How would you carry out a market research campaign for a new type of crisp?

10. What is the function of the wholesaler in the chain of distribution? In what situations is the wholesaler eliminated from distribution?

## Coursework

1. Margaret Greaves was going to open up a dress agency in Castlegate, Grantham. The dress agency was to deal in good quality, nearly new clothes. She had learnt on a business studies course that the Post Office

CAROUSEL

*13 Castlegate*
*Grantham*
*Lincs*
*NG31 6SE*

*Telephone: (0476) 79983*

Dear

On Monday 7th April the "Carousel" Dress Agency will open
at 13 Castlegate, Grantham.

I am approaching a very select clientele who have good dress
sense and taste, in the hope that we may be of help to one
another.

In your wardrobe you possibly have a range of good clothes which
you may simply have tired of, dislike, or which represent a
mistake (which of us hasn't!). My service may help to recoup
some of the considerable outlay of those purchases.

Carousel will sell for you ladies' and childrens' clothing on a
commission basis of 60% to the client and 40% to Agency, plus a
10p per item handling charge (maximum 50p). Naturally all items
must be in excellent condition and seasonal.

It is my intention that the Agency will provide quality
merchandise, personal service and the guarantee of a confidential
retlationship with my clients.

In addition I will stock some select new clothing - hand
knitteds, fashions made exclusively for Carousel, and a range of
inexpensive, pretty gifts.

I look forward to hearing from you on either my business or home
telephone number (Grantham 79391).

Sincerely yours,

M. Greaves

**Figure 8.25** Letter produced by
Margaret Greaves for her mail shot

provides a free service of up to 1000 first class mail shots for any business
just starting up. She decided that this would be the best way of telling the
sort of people she wanted to come to her shop how to find her and what
she had to offer. She thought that any other form of advertising would not
be sufficient because it would not target the right audience. The letter that
Margaret prepared for her mail shot is shown in Fig. 8.25.

(a)  Put yourself in Margaret's position—you have 1000 mail shots to send
     out. How are you going to decide who to send the mail shots to and
     how will you go about the task?

(b)    The dress agency was going to open on Monday, 7 April. Margaret decided to send out a small poster on an A4 sheet of paper just giving the important details about the opening and the business on it. She decided to have the picture of the carousel in the centre of the poster. Draw the poster putting in the details which you would regard as important.

(c)    Why do you think that the Post Office is prepared to offer new businesses a free mail shot of 1000 letters?

(d)    Once the business was under way would Margaret need to carry out any follow-up marketing? Explain your answer.

2.    How do mail-order firms advertise? This would be a suitable coursework topic for all students.

3.    A high street bank is considering the development of a new cash-dispensing machine. How would it go about carrying out this decision. You should try to think up suitable questions to investigate. The class could then be split into groups each of which is to investigate a particular topic area. Possible questions might be:

(a)    What type of market research should be carried out?

(b)    What questions should be asked in the market research?

(c)    Who will be the bank's competitors?

(d)    What should be the design of the cash dispenser?

(e)    What should the service be called?

(f)    How much would it cost to produce and install?

(g)    How could the dispenser be promoted?

(h)    How should charges be made for using the service?

(i)    How will the scheme be financed?

(j)    Who will organize the project?

(k)    How will the bank decide whether the scheme is a success?

# 9

# Communication

Communication is the passing on of ideas and information. In business we need good, clear communications. The contact may be between people, places or organizations and can be in a number of forms such as *gestures*, *actions*, *speech*, *writing* and the use of *technological media*. Each of these forms of communicating requires special skills in order to achieve the desired result. For example, some people are very good at expressing their ideas orally, others are good at presenting things on paper and, increasingly today, many people develop information processing skills with electronic media.

Communication skills can be learnt and developed in the same way as manual skills. As businesses exist in a constantly changing environment these skills have to be constantly refined and developed.

### Case Study—Communication exercise

1. Select a volunteer from the group.
2. Give him or her the pattern sheet (Fig. 9.1). The volunteer must now describe the patterns to the rest of the group.
3. The rest of the class should try to draw the shapes described by the person with the pattern sheet.

The aim of this exercise is to show how difficult it is to communicate even simple shapes. Discuss the answers to the following questions.

*Questions*

1. How easy was it to understand the instructions given?
2. Why is it easier to draw some of the shapes than others?
3. Communication problems arise when one of the following is the case:
   (a) The language is not fully understood.
   (b) The method used for passing on the message is poor.

**Figure 9.1** Shapes for the describing exercise

(c)   There are too many steps in communicating the message. What other barriers to communication can you think of?

4.   What signs do people use when communicating with each other?

## Basic communication inside a business

The passage of information can be seen as a flow from the sender to the receiver (see Fig. 9.2).

### Spoken communication

The most frequent type of communication within a business will be spoken communication as a result of face-to-face contact. Much of this communication will be in the form of ordinary conversation with colleagues. The nature of the conversation will, however, vary according to various characteristics of the

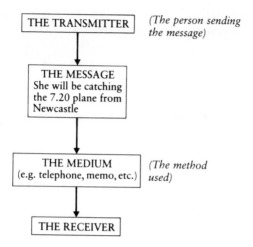

**Figure 9.2**  The flow of information from sender to receiver

listener. For example, in the same way that we would speak differently to a five year old, a parent, a friend or bank manager, we also vary our verbal communication according to the status or position of the person we are communicating with at work. Whether verbal communication is being directed upwards or downwards, it allows detailed and technical expertise to be communicated efficiently. Verbal communication can involve speaking to the public, making a contribution in meetings or even addressing a conference.

## Taking and giving telephone messages

One of the most important communication skills to develop in business is being able to use the telephone and, by doing so, being able to convey a clear and professional image of the organization you work for. When answering the phone this will involve answering it promptly, giving the name and number of the firm and keeping a message pad handy. If you ask the caller to hold, if they are either waiting for someone or for some information, constantly check with them to tell them what is happening. Offering to help and asking appropriate questions are important in order to clarify understanding. When making a telephone call you need to make sure that you have the correct code and number before you dial. If you are giving a message it is useful to put it on paper beforehand to ensure that you communicate it accurately. Always be prepared to leave the telephone message on an answering machine.

### Task

Imagine that you work for Bulco Ltd and have to phone someone to say that your employer has been delayed and will be 15 minutes late for their appointment. Compose a message and then put it on a cassette. Play the message back to other members of the class. Comment on how the message was communicated, e.g. clarity, information provided, speed, etc.

## Business meetings

A meeting is the name given to a gathering of two or more people who decide to meet together for a particular purpose. The aims of a meeting may be to do any of the following:

1.  Make plans
2.  Pass on information
3.  Discuss issues
4.  Iron out problems
5.  Motivate people

In order to take an active part in meetings you have to both listen and speak to others. When listening to others you need to:

*   take in to account the background and position of the speaker.
*   think about the implications of whatever they are saying.
*   make notes so that you can recall information.

When making a contribution to a meeting:

*   prepare what to say, making notes if necessary.
*   watch for the reactions of listeners.
*   vary the tone of your voice and look at the group.

Meetings in most organizations tend to follow a standard pattern. Before the meeting takes place, an *agenda* will be circulated to the people taking part. A formal meeting will usually take the following form:

1.  *Apologies.* A list of the people who are not able to attend is read out.
2.  *Minutes.* The notes from the last meeting are read out. Sometimes people might question the accuracy of these minutes.
3.  *Matters arising* (from the minutes). This will be a discussion on decisions made at the last meeting and their follow-up.
4.  *Correspondence.* This will be a discussion on relevant letters received since the last meeting.
5.  *Reports.* Some members may have been asked to make a report for the meeting. These reports will be read and discussed.
6.  *The meeting itself.* This involves a discussion of issues which might require a vote to be taken on policy.
7.  *Planning the next meeting.* A date, place and time are chosen for the next meeting.
8.  *Any other business.* If there is still time it may be possible to raise issues not on the original agenda.

The chairperson runs the meeting and all remarks must be made 'through the chair' (see Fig. 9.3). The secretary sets out the agenda for the meeting, informs the members of the agenda and takes the notes (minutes). Though most meetings are small affairs with jut a few present, businesses with shareholders are obliged to have general meetings open to all shareholders to attend. Some are held on a regular basis, e.g. the Annual General Meeting (AGM). However, an Extraordinary General Meeting may be called to deal with a special event.

**Figure 9.3**  Chairperson Anne Macdonald runs the meeting (Source: Kim Hooper, Reading)

## Written communication

This varies from the very simple to the very complex. It tends to be used:

- where the receiver of the information is remote from the sender.
- where the information is complex.
- where the information needs to be constantly referred to.
- where the sender wishes to address a group of people without seeing them face-to-face.

One of the most frequently used forms of written communication is the *memorandum*. The word 'memorandum' derives from the Latin word memorare and means a 'thing to be remembered'. Today, memos are more than just memory aids and have become a way of communicating with others within the business.

As memos are internal they are different from letters. The organization's name will not appear on the memo and there will be no salutation or complimentary close. Memos should be as brief and straightforward as possible. They will often be distributed to a number of people. (See Fig. 9.4).

```
MEMO from the Safety Officer

    To: all staff  ........

Please make sure that cars are not
parked across the fire exit.
```

**Figure 9.4** Example of a brief, straightforward memo

*Task*

Write a brief memo to your business studies teachers telling them how you are getting on with your business studies coursework.

Another form of internal communication is a *report*. A report is simply a written communication *from* someone who has collected and studied some facts *to* a person who has asked for the report because he or she needs it for a particular purpose. A report may form the basis for a particular decision. It may be used to:

1. supply information for legal purposes
2. present the results of some research
3. assess the possibility of some change in policy.

*Informal reports* might be written on a report form or on a memo. They will contain:

1. Title
2. Introduction
3. Body of report (complete with findings)
4. Recommendations
5. Action required

A *formal report* will have:

1. A title page
2. Table of contents/index
3. Terms of reference (explaining the reason for the report)
4. Procedure (how the task was completed)
5. Findings
6. Conclusion (summary of findings)
7. Recommendations
8. Signature of writer and date

*Notices* are another form of internal business communication and can be placed in prominent places to provide useful information.

Often the only direct communication that people have with a company is through the *business letter*. A good business letter not only communicates information but also looks good and helps to generate goodwill. Letters are the most frequently used form of external business communication and provide a written record which can be used to send almost any type of business information. Their greatest benefit is their reasonable cost.

Business letters are usually on headed paper. Fully blocked layout is the most common form of display. (See Fig. 9.5).

**McGraw-Hill Book Company Europe**

Shoppenhangers Road
Maidenhead, Berkshire, England SL6 2QL
Telephone Maidenhead (0628) 23432
Cables MCGRAWHILL MAIDENHEAD Telex 848484
Faxes (0628) 770224 *Editorial, Marketing, Financial*
35895 *Customer Services* 777342 *Export, Distribution*
777891 *Production, Credit Control*

Our Ref DN/RD

6th May 1992

Mr A Field
White Horse Ltd
Gate Lane
REETH
North Yorshire
DL10 8NN

Dear Mr Field

<u>Completed manuscript - How to become a vet</u>

Thank you for sending me the manuscript so promptly.  Having
read it over the weekend I have been impressed by it's content
but have made some notes on a few areas which need minor
amendment.

I suggest that we meet to discuss these areas.  Perhaps you
would like to suggest a date early in June.  Also, if you have
any photographs to support your work, we would certainly be
interested in using them.

Yours sincerely

Charles Bull
Editor - Rural Studies

McGraw-Hill International (UK) Ltd.   Registered no. 64070 England   Registered office: as above

**Figure 9.5**   Example of a brief business letter

Business letters present information logically and in a form which can be readily understood by the reader. A good letter will be written in the style most appropriate for the recipient, this will enable it to have the greatest impact.

**Case Study—Applying to go on a course**

You have recently seen the following:

---

*Short Course for BUSINESS ADMINISTRATORS*

Bell View Hotel, SUTTON COLDFIELD

June 7/8th 1992                                                      £200

---

**Figure 9.6**   Advertisement

Using a word processor complete the following tasks. Justify the text and save and print.

*Tasks*

1.  Create a file MEMO 1. Write a memo to your office supervisor asking if you could attend the course and enquiring whether your firm is prepared to pay the fee.
2.  Create a file LETTER 1. Write a letter to the Short Course Organizer at the Bell View Hotel asking them to reserve you a place on the course. You are a vegetarian. Indicate your special dietary requirements.

# The electronic office

Nearly all organizations have offices to *handle information* necessary to run the workplace. For example, the offices in your school or college will have to deal with finances, student records, examination information, staff records, managing resources and other key areas. Just imagine how all of this information might be managed in the future. In the world of tomorrow the modern excutive will probably sit at a console surrounded by touch sensitive switches allowing communication with people and organizations around the world. The manager will probably also be able to converse with the system, address commands to it and use it to plan the various outcomes of any decisions which have to be made.

The office lies at the very heart of a business organization. Information is received in the office, processed and stored and then processed again before being set out. (See Fig. 9.8.)

Microelectronics and computers have changed the ways in which this information is handled. They are able to process words, numbers, pictures and

**Figure 9.7**  Dealing with operator error!

even sound—any kind of information which needs to be stored, transmitted, analysed or reproduced. In the past, machines in the office were traditional self-contained pieces of equipment which used paper to transfer information. Today much of this equipment does not use paper at all. We have moved towards the age of the *paperless office*.

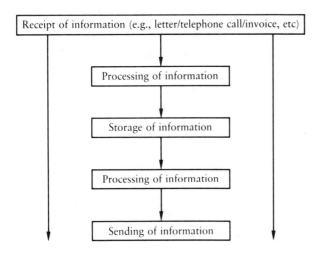

**Figure 9.8**  The flow of information in an office

### Case Study—Electronic Data Interchange (EDI)

EDI has the objective of simplifying and speeding up transactions between trading partners. It does this by enabling data, messages or documents to be transferred directly from the computer of one organization to the computer of another.

The clear advantages of such a system are considerable savings on paperwork, time and the need to re-enter information. The more business a company handles, the greater the benefits of this form of electronic trading.

When a major manufacturer moves to EDI all of its suppliers have to adapt to such a system. For example, the Rover Group has been an early pioneer of EDI. Apart from the massive clerical and administrative savings it has been able to make, it has also enabled it to reduce its stock levels and gear its plants more closely to the changing needs of market demand.

*Questions*

1. Explain how EDI reduces the need for paper in an office.
2. How has EDI helped the Rover Group to reduce its stock levels and enabled it to respond more closely to the changing needs of its customers?

## Sending and receiving information

In the past, the most common form of communication was by using paper. Information was written down and then sent off through the *post* and dealt with several days later. For many services this has been taken over by the *telephone*. Modern telephone systems are based upon microelectronics. Digital telephone systems offer:

- instant dialling of frequently used numbers
- re-direction of calls
- three-way conversations
- dialling without lifting handset
- indication of call waiting
- automatic redialling

As the case study on EDI illustrated, computers are often linked over the telephone network through a *modem*. Improvements in the telephone network to provide a fully digital system have resulted in a network for computers enabling them to communicate with each other, pass on information, save time and cut costs.

A rapidly increasing form of communication between organizations is the use of *facsimile transmission*. These machines allow the transmission of images from one 'fax' machine to another. Paper communications can be sent in a matter of seconds. In fact it is possible to send a page of text or graphics to the other side of the world in around about a minute. Some of the modern fax machines even combine functions. Amstrad feature a fax, answer machine, phone and copier all in one unit.

Another alternative to the post is a system of electronic mail. The 'mail-box' is a computer terminal linked to the telephone network: it can put messages into the system and store messages that have been sent through the system. Every user has a 'password' to allow him or her to use the system. A message can be sent to several mail-boxes at once and so the system can be used for internal memos in a company with several branches. The message will be stored in a terminal's memory until the mail-box is opened.

*Prestel* takes the mail-box communications service even further. It uses the telephone lines at home or in an office to provide a vast range of information and services. Using a simple keypad, the size of a calculator, users can call up information from hundreds of different sources, as well as using it as a confidential communications system.

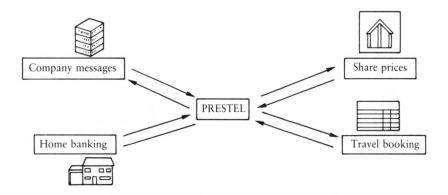

**Figure 9.9** Two-way communication provided with services from Prestel

### Case Study—Campus 2000

Campus 2000 is a specialist service provided for educational institutions. A telephone line and computer provide subscribers with access to the system. The Times Network Systems Ltd and Prestel have collaborated to provide this network. There are two main elements:

- *Databases*—which hold vast libraries of diverse information.
- *Electronic mail*—which provides efficient contact among users.

Campus 2000 already links most secondary schools and institutions in the further and higher education sector and a rapidly increasing number of primary schools are using the system.

Campus 2000 provides:

- a large network
- cheaper and faster communication
- communication at the price of a telephone call
- replacement of paper-based systems
- instant availability of the latest information
- a range of uses for the classroom

**Figure 9.10**   Campus 2000 logo

*Questions*

1. Explain how Campus 2000 might benefit schools and colleges.
2. Find out if your school or college has Campus 2000. If it has, ask your teacher to demonstrate how it works. Who uses the system and what benefits does it provide?

*Videoconferencing*

Videoconferencing is another way of sending and receiving information. Through a live video link BT videoconferencing provides groups of people at two or more locations, nationally and internationally, with the opportunity to hold face-to-face meetings. All of the participants can see what is going on and can contribute to the conversation. Videoconferencing also enables speakers to address a large conference at almost any location. For example, at Ford videoconferencing links have been used for international meetings for some time. Before videoconferencing, scheduling meetings of managers across the world would have been virtually impossible. Senior managers need now only spend a couple of hours at a meeting instead of having their valuable time used up travelling. The service also helps its users to make quicker decisions.

## Dealing with information

Any information received in an office has to be changed, processed or dealt with in some way. Offices will have to process *text* information based upon documents or forms, *numerical* information such as accounting items, or *image* information based upon graphics, diagrams or pictures.

The use of the word processor has greatly changed the workings of an office. Word processors are microelectronic machines which allow information to be typed in and changed or edited on screen before it is printed on to paper. They also allow the storage and retrieval of text from a memory store. They comprise five parts:

- a central processing unit with memory
- an input keyboard
- a monitor
- a disc drive
- a printer

**Figure 9.11** Word processing
(Source: Kim Hooper, Reading)

The word processor operator can produce many more finished pages than the typist, particularly if standard documents are being produced. For example, the Prudent Insurance Company want to interview the following people:

1. Mr Alberts at 9 a.m.
2. Ms Anees at 10 a.m.
3. Mr Cook at 11 a.m.
4. Ms Davis at 12 noon.

The letters inviting them for interview will be identical except for the names and times. Word processing means that the letter need only be typed once. Text can then be changed for each applicant.

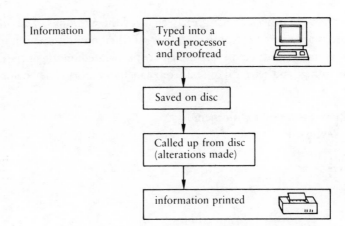

**Figure 9.12**    Word processing
stages

The letter below is a standard reply to an enquiry about prices:

                        Woodfield Natural Cosmetics Ltd
                                  Gate Lane
                                  DRIFFIELD
                              North Humberside


    Tel: 0876 45632                              6th June 1992

    Mr R Cram
    Albany Street
    Hook
    Hampshire


    Dear Mr Cram

    Following your enquiry of 1st June we are able to supply you
    with the following information:

    Stawberry soap        Ref 123/OH      £3.50 per doz
    Lemon conditioner     Ref 321/KL      £1.89 per doz

    Delivery is within 1 week of receipt of order.  Terms are 2.50%
    if payment is received within 30 days.

    Yours sincerely




    Roger Cook
    Sales Manager

**Figure 9.13**    Word processed letter

*Task*

1.  LOAD a word processing package into a computer.
2.  ENTER the letter shown above.
3.  Make CHANGES to the letter.
4.  SAVE the changed letter.
5.  PRINT out the letter.

In an office, information is stored and then retrieved for use by a variety of people for a range of purposes. A *database* is a collection of information or data stored in an organized way so that it can be retrieved. The information can be accessed from the computer, examined or searched and then assembled in a particular way such as alphabetically or numerically. For example, a bank or a building society will store information on the state of all accounts. If someone requests a balance enquiry, the computer can quickly be accessed to find the appropriate information.

*Task*

Ask a number of people to answer the following questions:

1.  Can you swim?
2.  Have you got blue eyes?
3.  Do you play tennis?
4.  Do you like discos?
5.  Do you like Monopoly?
6.  Have you ever been abroad?

You will need a postcard or index card for each person. Cut the top right hand corner off the card. Draw a line 1 cm down from the top of the card and mark intervals of 1 cm from the left edge to match the six questions you have asked. Use a hole punch to put holes in the markings. Number each hole from the left edge. Write down the name of each person on each card and, referring to their answers, clip the relevant hole with scissors if the answer is 'yes', or leave it if the answer is 'no'. (See Fig. 9.14.)

   You have now *created your own database*. Using a knitting needle, you could find out how many people play tennis. By lifting the needle in the hole of the relevant question all of those cards with 'yes' answers will drop out. 'No' answers will remain on the needle. You can ask two questions such as, how many people with blue eyes play tennis, by inserting the needle firstly into the hole matching one question and then into the hole matching the other question from those cards which have dropped out.

   Many issues cause people to worry about the nature of information held on computers. For example, is this information accurate, could it be used against you, has it been mixed up with the information of someone else? The effects

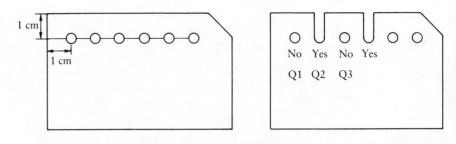

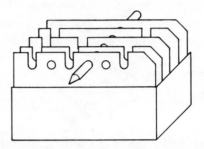

**Figure 9.14**  Create your own database?

could be serious and influence whether someone gets a job, is able to obtain a mortgage or might even lead to someone being wrongfully arrested!

The Data Protection Act serves to calm many of these fears. Under the provisions of the Act, companies wishing to store information on a computer system must register with the (government appointed) Data Protection Officer and indicate the type of data they are storing and the use they make of it. Any individual has the right to request (on payment of a small fee) details of any information held about them by the firm and to require any mistakes to be corrected.

**Figure 9.15**  Data protection act

With modern technology information from databases can be used to create spreadsheets or graphics.

A *spreadsheet* is a table of numbers which comprises a grid going across the page/screen and down the page/screen. A spreadsheet is used for making forecasts and calculations—the computer does the work for you. Every spreadsheet has the ability to perform the normal arithmetical operations of adding, subtracting, multiplying, dividing and raising a number to a power. For instance, a firm could make a forecast of all the money that will come in and go out over a 12-month period. (See Fig. 9.16.)

| | JAN | FEB | MAR | APR | MAY | JUN | JUL | AUG | SEP | OCT | NOV | DEC |
|---|---|---|---|---|---|---|---|---|---|---|---|---|
| REVENUE | 200 | 200 | 300 | 400 | 400 | 400 | 500 | 500 | 500 | 500 | 500 | 500 |
| COSTS | | | | | | | | | | | | |
| Heat | 20 | 20 | 20 | 20 | 20 | 20 | 20 | 20 | 20 | 20 | 20 | 20 |
| Fuel | 20 | 20 | 20 | 20 | 20 | 20 | 20 | 20 | 20 | 20 | 20 | 20 |
| Labour | 50 | 50 | 60 | 70 | 70 | 70 | 80 | 80 | 80 | 80 | 80 | 80 |
| Materials | 50 | 50 | 60 | 70 | 70 | 70 | 80 | 80 | 80 | 80 | 80 | 80 |
| TOTAL COSTS | 140 | 140 | 160 | 180 | 180 | 180 | 200 | 200 | 200 | 200 | 200 | 200 |
| PROFIT | 60 | 60 | 140 | 220 | 220 | 220 | 300 | 300 | 300 | 300 | 300 | 300 |

TOTAL PROFITS: 2720

**Figure 9.16** Spreadsheet of a firm's forecast income and outgoings for a year

Once a spreadsheet has been created, a change in any one of the entries can cause the entire sheet to be recalculated. For example, if the heating bill is lowered by a certain amount each month, the computer will automatically recalculate the columns to change the heating figures, total cost figures and profits for each month. It will also recalculate the total profit figure. Spreadsheets are becoming of increasing use for a whole range of business functions for a wide variety of managers.

*Tasks*

1. LOAD a spreadsheet package.
2. ENTER the details below onto a spreadsheet.

| Item | Annual sales | Selling price | Sales value | Unit cost | Cost of sales | Annual profit |
|---|---|---|---|---|---|---|
| 1 | 200 | 3.50 | 700 | 3.00 | 600 | 100 |
| 2 | 300 | 2.80 | 840 | 2.50 | 750 | 90 |
| 3 | 120 | 4.20 | | 3.50 | | |
| 4 | 200 | 3.70 | | 2.50 | | |

Annual sales is the number of items sold each year. Selling price is the price each item is sold for. Sales value is Annual sales × Selling price. Unit cost is the cost of each item from the manufacturer. Cost of sales is Annual sales multiplied by Unit cost. Annual profit is Sales value minus Cost of sales.

3.  CALCULATE the missing figures.
4.  Use a formula to generate total annual profit for the four items.
5.  SAVE and PRINT.

Drawings or pictures stored in a computer are known as *graphics*. Graphics programs might be able to show how a 3-dimensional shape could be drawn at different points on the screen, how to draw and fix a line, as well as reduce and enlarge an image. Some programs allow text to be drawn sideways as well as bar charts, pie charts, graphs and characters to be built from individual pixels. (See Figs. 9.17–9.20.)

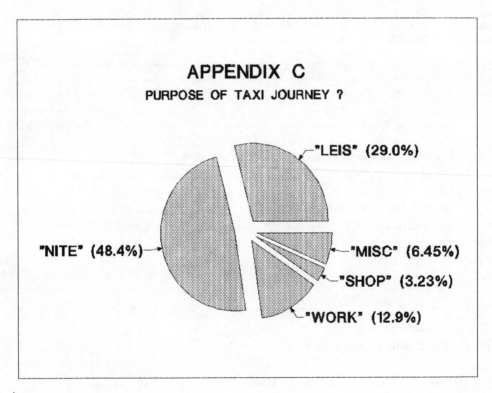

**Figure 9.17**   Pie chart

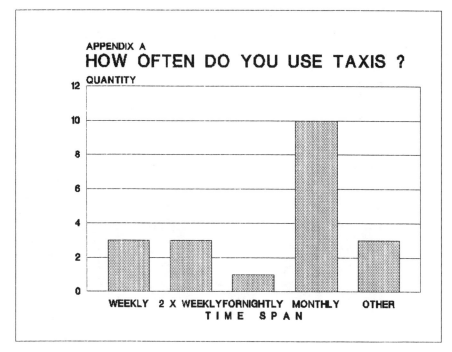

Figure 9.18    Bar chart

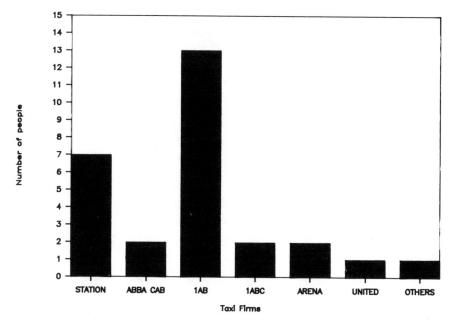

Figure 9.19    Bar chart (1)

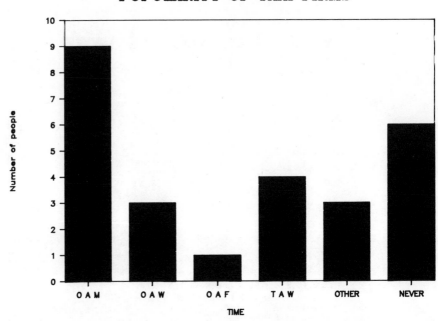

## POPULARITY OF TAXI FIRMS

**Figure 9.20**   Bar chart (2)

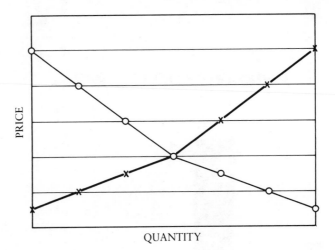

**Figure 9.21**   The results of an investigation into taxi use and pricing strategies in Darlington displayed using graphics packages by students at Darlington College of Technology

### Storage of information

All offices keep records of information. In the past most information has been stored on paper. Methods such as card indexes and filing cabinets were used to keep records in such a way that information could be retrieved. Traditional paper records, however, take up space and take time to sift through and sort out. To replace these large amounts of paper, information can now be stored using *magnetic storage* such as a tape or disc or *microform*. Microform is a term which covers all ways of reproducing documents reduced in size on microfilm.

In the office of the future, microelectronic machines will include:

- word processors
- computers
- facsimile machines
- digital telephones and exchanges
- magnetic storage
- computer-aided microform retrieval
- near-perfect quality printers and copiers

In this paperless office, these machines will be able to communicate electronically using a data network transferring digital information.

## Communication and language

Over the past decade we have seen massive changes covering social and cultural aspects of our lives, which have indicated that we are drawing closer together with our European counterparts. Today around half of our trade is with European Community countries. The finishing of the channel tunnel, the popularizing of satellite broadcasting and cheaper travel will make us further aware of the Single European Market.

We live in a world of words where to understand each other we need to understand each others' language. In this changing European existence, employers are becoming increasingly aware of the need to recruit staff with language skills. More and more job advertisements mention languages and we are seeing the beginnings of a truly European labour market, where adverts for jobs appear simultaneously in both the British and continental press.

With the developing of the Single European Market we are likely to see greater labour mobility. Harmonization of qualifications is going to provide you with a job market across the boundaries of many countries. The newly mobile Euro-manager will have to be capable of contending with language barriers. The worry of many is that many top jobs may go to those from countries where languages have been higher on the agenda than in Britain, such as those from Denmark and the Netherlands. There is also concern that language skills are needed to understand the technical jargon of one's trade. As a result, many vocational courses and materials today, including this book, involve a link with languages.

### Case Study—Technical terms

Knowledge of a language can help to support practical business situations. These might include making a telephone call, writing or replying to letters, entertaining visitors and any situation which may occur in the course of everyday business.

*Questions*

1. Explain how you would try to put at ease a foreign visitor to your firm. Indicate what language skills you possess and how you would use them in this situation.
2. Translate the following technical terms:

| | |
|---|---|
| Usine | Concession |
| Fabriquant | Alliance |
| Commerce | Promotion |
| Marque | Consommateur |
| Formule de marketing | Produit |
| Ventes | Comptes |
| Fonds | Actions |
| Annonce | Patron |
| Salaire | Syndicat ouvrier |

## Case Study—Communications

Patricia Perry was appointed office manager of a small engineering firm in Derby that was going through a phase of reorganization and modernization. Pat was instructed to bring the office into the twenty-first century. The firm employed 250 manual operatives, a salesforce of 6, 10 office workers, and 3 management staff. The office staff worked with manual typewriters and there was one switchboard operator using old-fashioned equipment. Pat's brief was to prepare a report which could be presented at the next board meeting, in which she should set out a list of priorities for modernization and cost the changes required, bearing in mind that the firm was keen to spend anything up to £100,000 on the venture.

*Question*

Imagine you are Pat. Set out the report that you would present.

# Questions

1. Complete the following sentences using the terms below. In each case give what you consider to be the best answer.

| | |
|---|---|
| fax | headed paper |
| database | minutes |
| electronic mail | memo |
| word processors | agenda |
| videoconferencing | floppy disc |

(a)    . . . . . . . makes it possible to link up, visually, people in different parts of the world.

(b)    Word-processed information can be stored on a . . . . . . .

(c)    The . . . . . . . of a meeting sets out the matters to be discussed.

(d)    A . . . . . . . can be used to store information.

(e)    An internal . . . . . . . is an effective way of communicating within a firm.

(f)    A . . . . . . . machine enables the electronic communication of maps, diagrams and documents.

(g)    The . . . . . . . of a meeting record the main points discussed.

(h)    . . . . . . . is used for business letters.

(i)    An alternative to the post is . . . . . . .

(j)    . . . . . . . have revolutionized the handling of information.

2.   What sort of electronic methods could be used for the following:

(a)    Sending an internal memo within an organization.

(b)    Sending a document required urgently overseas.

(c)    Visually linking up three groups of people in various parts of the world.

(d)    Typing out a standard letter.

(e)    Leaving a verbal message for someone to contact you.

3.   What do the following stand for?

| | | | |
|---|---|---|---|
| (a) | VDU | (d) | RSVP |
| (b) | AGM | (e) | ASAP |
| (c) | AOB | (f) | CPU |

4.   Argue the case for the electronic office.

5.   At a board meeting, concern was expressed about how Tasties Ltd and Les Gourmandises would communicate between the offices in Britain and France.

The data processing manager of Tasties Ltd, Mr Piers McBride, was invited to meet M. Hervé Scuiller, his opposite number in Calais, to look at current technology and jointly produce a report for their companies.

Using any keyboard, prepare a report, ready for translation, outlining the following:

(a)    ONE department of Tasties Ltd, other than marketing, where communications will be essential with the French counterpart. Give ONE reason for your choice.

(b)    THREE factors, other than the one given, which the English marketing team may have to take into consideration when introducing their products into a European market (e.g., package weights—litres of beer instead of pints of beer).

(c)    (i)    The methods of communication available to each department;

(ii)   Any constraints or limitations in the use of these communications.

(Source: London East Anglian Group)

6.   Read the following extract from the minutes of a board meeting of Belmar Ltd and then answer the questions which follow.

> INTRODUCTION OF NEW TECHNOLOGY The Board approved the proposal that the company should forge ahead with the introduction of new technology, both in production and administration, which it is hoped will result in increased efficiency for the company.

(a) Name two ways in which this information may have been communicated to the workers.

(b) How might Belmar Ltd benefit from the introduction of new technology?

(c) In what ways do you think the workers might react to the introduction of new technology?

(*Source*: Northern Ireland Schools Examinations and Assessment Council)

7.  How would you set up a database recording the following?

(a) The particulars of members of a firm.

(b) The different methods of telecommunication.

8.  Try to finish this exercise in two minutes.

(a) Read all instructions carefully.

(b) Pick up your pen.

(c) Write your name at the top of the paper.

(d) Underline your name.

(e) Rule a margin on the left-hand side of the page.

(f) Number the next 20 lines 1–20.

(g) Starting on the top line, draw an arrow going to the right-hand side of the page, but stopping *half an inch* short of it.

(h) Now draw a diagonal line going to the bottom left-hand side of the page.

(i) Draw a box in the left-hand corner of your page, *2 cm high and 15 cm long*.

(j) Write in it 'I must read instructions carefully'.

(k) Do none of the above.

From doing this exercise you should be able to appreciate the need to read carefully instructions communicated to you.


## Coursework

1. Should a large firm run a crèche so that the skills of people with small children to look after are not wasted?

   This is the only item on the agenda of a class meeting. The discussion will take place in class and every student must keep minutes of the meeting. When the minutes are copied up they should be compared in order to find the most efficient way of making minutes. (Frequently the minute-taker at a meeting will also participate in discussion.)

2. Pick a local firm and say what methods of internal communication it uses.

3. Write your own case study on the use of information technology and its effects upon improving communications within your school or college.

# 10

# Business documentation

Paper documents are an essential part of business life. At one time people talked about the 'paperless office', expecting that one day all records and documents would be stored on computer files. Unfortunately (or perhaps fortunately), this day has not yet arrived. In fact, businesses today store far more paper than ever before. However, most records are kept both on computer file and may also be stored on paper. The big advantage of computer records is the ease with which they can be called up. For example, if a customer rings up to find out why their order has not arrived it is a simple operation to call up the information on a computer screen showing delivery schedules. If a customer queries a bill, the information can be retrieved within seconds simply by keying-in the appropriate account number. Computer records will be kept in a simple and logical format so that they can be quickly accessed.

Although most records are now kept on computer databases it is important for us to know the types of documents which records relate to. These business documents are detailed in the notes below. Not all of these documents will be used in dealings between companies. However, most of them will be, in most sets of transactions.

We should not underestimate the importance of documents. If they are made out and sent out in a clear and organized fashion this will greatly improve business efficiency. If they are not, then all sorts of confusion can arise. How would you feel about a business:

- That sent your goods to the wrong place.
- Whose goods arrived late.
- That sent the wrong things.
- That failed to pay when requested.
- That sent out the wrong bills.
- That dropped other clangers.

# Types of document

There are many different types of business document. Documents are:

- necessary as proof of business dealings.
- a way of checking goods ordered and received.
- a record for bookkeeping.

Most transactions today are on credit and documents show who owes what and to whom. (See Fig. 10.1.)

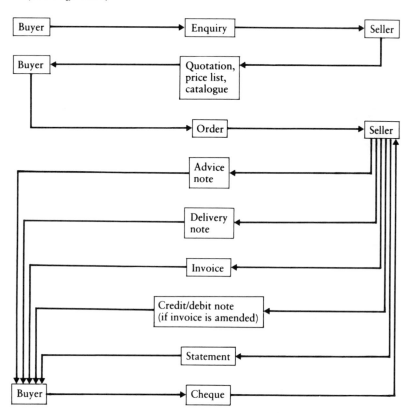

Figure 10.1   Diagram showing the documents that may be needed for a business transaction

Trading documents are normally headed with the name of the organization and can be used to promote that business. Most large and medium size organizations use computer records and documents will be printed (rather than handwritten). With the development of Desk Top Publishing, many smaller organizations have started to print their own stationery and documents.

## Letter of enquiry

A letter of enquiry will be sent to suppliers to find out what they can offer. Enquiries will often be sent to several suppliers so that different offers can be compared. A buyer may want to find out several things before placing an order. These details will include:

1.  Prices
2.  Details of goods
3.  Delivery dates and details of how goods will be carried
4.  Discounts

An enquiry may be a written letter, or the firm may use its own special printed enquiry form. (See Fig. 10.2.)

                WOODFIELD COSMETICS

```
                              12 Hall Street
                                   Hull
                             North Humberside
                                HU12 3JT


        Tel:  0482 516783                              3 March 19__



        ENQUIRY FORM

               To:  Natural.Products.Ltd..
                    5.Neath.Avenue........
                    Darlington............
                    DN4.25R...............


        Dear Sir/Madam

        Could you send me details of the following:  Welhair.Shampoo.for.normal/dry/...

        greasy.hair,.bath.salts,.luxury.soap...............................................

        .....................................................................................

        Your reply should include prices, delivery period, carriage and terms.

        Yours faithfully

        Woodfield Cosmetics



        R Ramsden
        Purchasing Officer
```

**Figure 10.2**  Example of an enquiry form

## Quotation, price list and catalogue

The buyer will receive several quotations and information, often presented in leaflets and catalogues. For example, Woodfield Cosmetics may receive a quote from a company called Natural Products, describing the prices and details of various types of:

- shampoo
- bath salts
- soaps
- make-up
- other cosmetics

The quote will also give details of how the goods can be delivered and any terms which are being offered. For example, 5 per cent 30 days, would show that if the bill is paid in 30 days or under there will be a reduction of 5 per cent.

If Woodfield Cosmetics thinks that the best quote comes from Natural Products then an order will be made out for goods. Each order form will be numbered so that it can be traced easily and it is also dated. Upon receipt of the official order, the seller will check the details on it such as prices and delivery.

## Advice note and dispatch note

Before sending the goods, the seller will send an advice note to say that the goods are being sent and that they will arrive shortly. If the goods do not arrive the buyer can then contact the seller so that the delay can be investigated.

## Delivery note

A delivery note is often sent with the goods. It lists the items in the parcels. The buyer can use it to check that all the goods have arrived.

## Invoice

This document (see Fig. 10.3) is needed for any credit transaction. It shows the details of the deal, the amount charged and the terms. The following details could be found on the invoice:

1. *Order number*. This can be used to check the goods delivered against those ordered.
2. *Terms*. This shows how much time buyers have to pay for their goods and the cash discount which is given to buyers if they pay quickly.
3. *Carriage*. This gives details of how transport will be paid for. 'Carriage paid' shows that the seller will pay for transport, 'Carriage forward' shows that the buyer will pay.

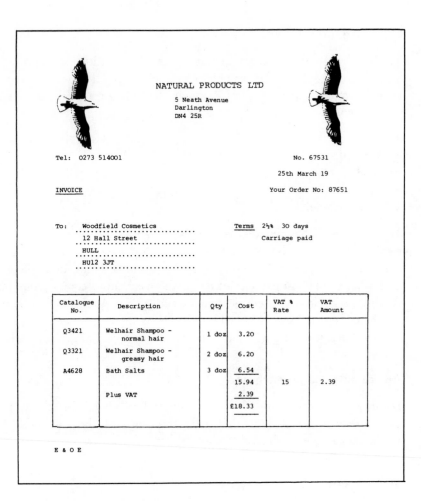

NATURAL PRODUCTS LTD

5 Neath Avenue
Darlington
DN4 25R

Tel:  0273 514001

INVOICE

No. 67531

25th March 19

Your Order No: 87651

To:   Woodfield Cosmetics

12 Hall Street

HULL

HU12 3JT

Terms  2½%  30 days

Carriage paid

| Catalogue No. | Description | Qty | Cost | VAT % Rate | VAT Amount |
|---|---|---|---|---|---|
| Q3421 | Welhair Shampoo - normal hair | 1 doz | 3.20 | | |
| Q3321 | Welhair Shampoo - greasy hair | 2 doz | 6.20 | | |
| A4628 | Bath Salts | 3 doz | 6.54 | | |
| | | | 15.94 | 15 | 2.39 |
| | Plus VAT | | 2.39 | | |
| | | | £18.33 | | |

E & O E

**Figure 10.3**   Example of an invoice

4.  *E and OE.* this stands for 'errors and omissions excepted'. This means that the seller can correct any mistake on the invoice at a later date.
5.  *Trade discount.* This may be given to regular customers in the same line of business and is deducted from the invoice price—e.g., a builders' supply warehouse will give discounts to builders that make regular purchases.
6.  *VAT.* Value added tax is added to the amount appearing on the invoice.
7.  *Invoice numbers.* This makes it possible for the accounts departments of both buyers and sellers to identify the invoice quickly.
8.  *VAT registration number.* Most businesses print their VAT registration number on their invoices, for tax purposes.

There are several copies made of an invoice, on different coloured paper. One copy is normally packed with the goods.

If the seller has not done business with the buyer before, or the buyer has been late with payments in the past, the seller might send the buyer a pro forma invoice. This document is sent to the buyer before the goods are delivered and sets out the charges for goods in advance. Only after the payment is made are the goods delivered.

### Credit notes and debit notes

These are sent by the seller and change the amount that earlier appeared on an invoice.

A credit note reduces the invoice price. This could be for any of the following reasons:

1. A mistake on the invoice.
2. Goods have been returned either because they are faulty or because the wrong goods have been delivered.
3. Fewer goods have been sent than appear on the invoice.

A credit note is often printed in red.

A debit note will increase the invoice price. This could be for the following reasons:

1. A mistake on the invoice.
2. Too many goods have been sent.

### Statement of account

The seller sends all regular customers a statement of account at the end of every month. (See Fig. 10.4.)

This is a copy of the customer's account in the sales ledger and usually contains a record of all transactions with the customer during the month. The debit column shows the sales by the seller to the buyer and includes anything which increases the debt, such as a debit note, while the credit column shows any credit notes or payments and anything which reduces the debt.

## Computerized systems

Computers provide a fast and accurate method for firms to keep a record of transactions; indeed, accounts is an area of business life particularly helped by computers.

When a firm's sales department receives an order, an employee will type the details in on a keyboard and these then appear on a screen. Every customer is given an index number and when the operator types in this number the customer's records and details appear on the screen. The operator can then add the details of the new order—item numbers, prices, terms offered, etc.

The computer then carries out a number of operations:

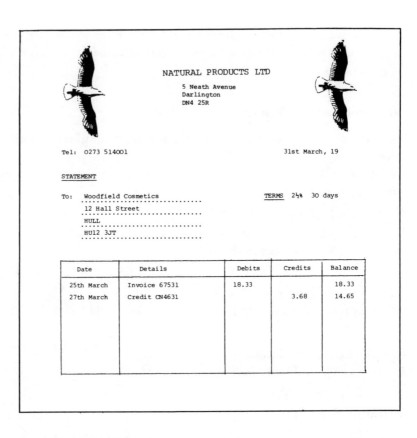

NATURAL PRODUCTS LTD

5 Neath Avenue
Darlington
DN4 25R

Tel:  0273 514001                                      31st March, 19

STATEMENT

To:   Woodfield Cosmetics                TERMS  2½%  30 days
      .............................
      12 Hall Street
      .............................
      HULL
      .............................
      HU12 3JT
      .............................

| Date | Details | Debits | Credits | Balance |
|------|---------|--------|---------|---------|
| 25th March | Invoice 67531 | 18.33 | | 18.33 |
| 27th March | Credit CN4631 | | 3.68 | 14.65 |

**Figure 10.4**  Example of a statement of account

1.  It prepares a packing note for the packaging department to make up the order.
2.  It checks off the items ordered against stock records. If items are running low it prepares a re-order for fresh supplies, or instructs the production department (in the case of a manufacturer) to make more of the items.
3.  It prepares invoices for the customers in relation to goods supplied.
4.  At the end of the month it makes up a statement for that month's transactions.

## Credit control

There are certain dangers in credit transactions. Many customers may take too long to pay their bills and some may not pay their bills at all. This leads to bad debts. Cash discounts are used to encourage customers to pay promptly, but they do not always work.

Large firms employ credit controllers whose job it is to ensure that a regular review is made of all customers, that credit limits are not exceeded and that payments are prompt. Letters and phone calls are used to remind customers about payment and, in some cases, legal action has to be taken.

Businesses can also sell their debts to a factoring company. This simply involves selling off bad debts to a third party for less than they are worth. Many small businesses need cash to keep the business ticking over. It makes sense to sell of debts for less than their face value in order to make more money by producing new goods. Banks in Britain offer a wide range of factoring services for good-quality debts.

During the 1990s many companies have been slow in paying debts. This makes life difficult for other firms that have supplied goods on credit. The government is considering passing a law to limit the amount of time a firm can hold back payment.

Firms can take out bad-debts insurance with an insurance company to cover themselves against non-payment. The disadvantage, of course, is the cost of the insurance premium.

Before granting credit, a firm will usually ask for a trade or bank reference. A trade reference is given by a supplier who has previously given credit to a business, vouching for the reliability of that business.

Before giving credit, the firm could also make enquiries with a credit reference agency, which is a firm specializing in keeping lists of people who have defaulted on payments. It will verify, for a fee, whether a particular firm has ever had problems or whether it has a clean bill of reliability. Study the letter in Fig. 10.5 on page 198.

1.  Who are the two parties involved in the letter shown and what is the nature of their business?
2.  What is the letter being sent in response to?
3.  Find out the meaning of the following terms: (i) nouveau produit (ii) avant de passer commande (iii) les conditions de vente (iv) le délai exact de livraison (v) Responsable des Achats.
4.  What details does Jeanne Schmidt require before placing an order?
5.  Explain the purpose of the letter in about 40 words.
6.  Draft out a letter in English which Société Hi-Tek might send out in response to this letter. Perhaps you could do this in the form of a pro forma invoice setting out details and terms. Invent the details of this invoice.

## Questions

1.  Complete the following sentences using the terms listed below:

| | |
|---|---|
| E and OE | Invoice |
| Proforma invoice | VAT registration number |
| Advice note | Statement |
| Quotation | Payment |
| Order form | Enquiry |

SOCIETE HI-TEK
15, bd de Grenelle
69001 LYON

Computechnix
John Adam Street
London WC2N 8PL
ANGLETERRE

N/Réf: ZS/2401/B                                      Lyon, le 30 mai 1989
Objet:   Renseignements pour un
              nouveau produit

Messieurs,

    Nous avons bien reçu votre brochure dans laquelle vous nous présentez votre tout dernier circuit imprimé.

    Nous tenons un commerce de détail à Lyon et nous sommes très intéressés par ce nouveau produit. Cependant, avant de passer commande, nous voudrions obtenir de plus amples renseignements.

    En effet, vous serait-il possible de nous indiquer les conditions de vente que vous pratiquez?

    Pourriez-vous également nous préciser les quantités minima à l'achat que vous acceptez ainsi que vos conditions de paiement et vos tarifs? Nous voudrions aussi savoir si vous accordez des remises pour des commandes importantes.

    De plus, nous tenons à connaître le délai exact de livraison.

    Dans l'attente de votre réponse, nous vous prions d'agréer, Messieurs, nos salutations distinguées.

Jeanne Schmidt
Responsable des Achats.

**Figure 10.5**   Letter to
Computechnix

(a)   A buyer wishing to find out details from a seller will start off by
       sending a letter of . . . . . . . .
(b)   When the seller has made up the order he or she will send the buyer
       an . . . . . . . . to give details of when and how delivery will be made.
(c)   For tax purposes a . . . . . . . . will be printed on an invoice.
(d)   A seller will send a buyer a . . . . . . . . indicating the types of goods and
       the prices and terms under which he or she would be prepared to
       supply.

(e)    A . . . . . . . would be sent by a seller dealing with a buyer for the first
       time.
(f)    The letters . . . . . . . printed on an invoice give the seller the right to
       put right mistakes on that invoice.
(g)    . . . . . . . . can be made by cheque.
(h)    There are several copies made of an . . . . . . . . , one of which is packed
       with the goods.
(i)    An . . . . . . . will be used when placing an order for goods.
(j)    A . . . . . . . gives a record of all transactions made within a certain
       time period.
2.   Maureen Coombs, a retail grocer, deals regularly with a wholesale firm,
     Suppliers Ltd, and one transaction took place as follows:
(a)    Coombs ordered food worth £300 from Suppliers Ltd on 14 April 1992
       and the goods were delivered by Supplies Ltd's own van on 20 April.
       The foods consisted of 100 kilograms of butter at 40p a kilo; assorted
       cereals with a total cost of £60; 100 tins of fruit salad at 30p a tin and
       tinned meat totalling £170.
(b)    On 21 April, Coombs found out that the butter delivered in one of the
       boxes had turned rancid. She informed Suppliers Ltd, who arranged
       for her to send back the goods which were valued at £10.
          Make out the documents you would expect to be used in the
       transaction above, explaining how each document is used.
3.   Explain the following terms which might appear on an invoice:
(a)    Four per cent cash within one month.
(b)    Less trade discount 10 per cent.
(c)    Pro forma invoice.
(d)    VAT.
4.   The statement in Fig. 10.6 is the one currently used by a stationery
     supplier called 'Pens and Paper'. The owner of the shop is unhappy
     because:
(a)    it looks dull.
(b)    it is difficult to write neatly on it.
(c)    debtors are slow in paying up.
(d)    suggest ways in which the statement design could be improved.
(e)    how could debtors be encouraged to pay more promptly?
5.   What do the following mean? (Look them up in a dictionary of business
     terms.)
(a)  COD        (b)  CWO        (c)  Net
6.   List the details normally shown on an invoice.
7.   In many firms, several carbon copies of invoices are made. Why is this
     done and how are the carbon copies used?
8.   List ten benefits of using computers to produce and keep details of
     business documents.

```
┌─────────────────────────────────────────────────┐
│                                                   │
│   Pens and Paper                                  │
│   8 Castle Street                                 │
│   Lincoln                                         │
│   LN8 4RD                                         │
│                                                   │
│                                                   │
│   Statement To:                        Date:      │
│                                                   │
│     Date    │   Details   │   Balance Owing       │
│─────────────┼─────────────┼───────────────────    │
│             │             │                       │
│             │             │                       │
│             │             │                       │
│             │             │                       │
│             │             │                       │
│             │             │                       │
└─────────────────────────────────────────────────┘
```

**Figure 10.6**   Stationery statement

9.  What is the current rate of VAT?
10. Outline the various stages of a credit business transaction, mentioning each of the documents likely to be used.
11. What are the main differences between the following:
    (a) a quotation and a catalogue
    (b) an advice note and a delivery note
    (c) an invoice and a statement
    (d) trade discount and cash discount
    (e) a credit note and a debit note.
12. What is a statement of account? What do each of the following record?
    (a) The debit column.
    (b) The credit column.
    (c) The balance.

## Coursework

1. Students could organize themselves into pairs and run through a set of business documents acting as buyer and seller.

2.  Collect invoices from business concerns. What are the strengths and weaknesses of each one's layout. Pick one that you feel can be improved. Explain why you think that you have improved the invoice. Write up the piece of work under the heading: 'How can I improve a real business invoice?'
3.  How do firms computerize their business documentation? This could be a useful study during a period of work experience.
4.  Using a desk-top publishing program, create an invoice which could be used by your school or college for casual room lettings.
    Create the document.
    Enter a heading.
    Enter text.
    Enter a drawing or create a box for your own artwork.
    Save the page or pages created.
    Edit the page.
    Print out the page.
    Present your document to the school or college officer responsible for room hire.

# 11

# Finance and financial control

## Cash budgets—'bringing order to disorder'

When it comes to looking after our own finances we all know that we have to exert some form of responsibility. If we spend too much, too quickly we will soon run out of money and not be able to have many of the things that we might need or, we might have to borrow to get them. But, if you borrow, can you pay back the person who has lent you the money?

Organizing our personal cash income and expenditure, in the form of a cash-flow forecast or cash budget, will help us to predict if we are able to meet our financial commitments as and when they arise. Cash-flow forecasts are statements which enable users to analyse their expenditure and income over a period of time.

### Case Study—Cash-flow exercise

Imagine that you have left school and started work. You earn £80 a week and out of this you have certain fixed weekly expenses.

|                         | £  |
|-------------------------|----|
| Rent to parents         | 20 |
| Daily fares             | 5  |
| Lunches                 | 10 |
| Weekends                | 12 |
| Records, magazines, etc.| 10 |
| Total                   | 57 |

On 2 January you receive your wages of £80. You owe your father £40 from December. There are some clothes that you want to buy costing £15 in a sale that ends on 6 January. A deposit of £30 for a holiday must be paid during the second week. This week you are taking three

friends to the cinema which will cost you £9 and you have to pay a dry-cleaning bill of £2. There are four weeks in January and in the third week you will economize and not buy any records and magazines.

A cash-flow forecast will enable you to see if you can afford to do all of these things and predict how soon you can pay back the loan from your father. Look carefully at the cash-flow forecast drawn up below and analyse all of the different expenditures.

|                          | 1     | 2     | 3      | 4      |
|--------------------------|-------|-------|--------|--------|
| INCOME                   | 80    | 80    | 80     | 80     |
| EXPENSES                 |       |       |        |        |
| Rent                     | 20    | 20    | 20     | 20     |
| Fares                    | 5     | 5     | 5      | 5      |
| Lunch                    | 10    | 10    | 10     | 10     |
| Weekends                 | 12    | 12    | 12     | 12     |
| Records, magazines, etc. | 10    | 10    | –      | 10     |
| Clothes                  | 15    | –     | –      | –      |
| Cinema                   | 9     | –     | –      | –      |
| Dry cleaning             | 2     | –     | –      | –      |
| Holiday                  | –     | 30    | –      | –      |
| TOTAL                    | 83    | 87    | 47     | 57     |
| NET                      | (3)   | (7)   | 33     | 23     |
| Loan—mother              | (3)B  | (7)B  | (10)R  | –      |
| Loan—father              | –     | –     | –      | (40)R  |
|                          | –     | –     | 23     | 6      |

(B) = Borrowing
(R) = Repayment

The cash-flow forecast has indicated that you need to borrow from your mother in weeks 1 and 2, but can pay her back in week 3, and that you can pay your father back in the last week of the month.

Cash flow has, therefore, provided the planning necessary to cope with the timing of various financial commitments.

*Questions*

1. Using a similar format, produce a cash-flow forecast of your income and expenditure for the next month.
2. What sort of benefits would you gain if you regularly used this sort of technique for monitoring your finances?

## Sources of finance

In the case study when money was needed for a cash shortfall, it was borrowed from both a mother and a father. Unless someone in business is very lucky such an instant and convenient source of finance is rarely available. Operating any form of business can involve considerable expenditure. *Capital expenditure* is associated with the purchase of assets which are expected to have some permanency in their use and will last for many years. *Revenue expenditure* is spending concerned with all of the running expenses of the firm which are used up over a year. Whatever an organization's requirements are, a decision has to be made about where to obtain the necessary finance.

Much of the finance for starting a business or running a business must come from a business person's own resources, e.g. savings, redundancy money or the releasing of equity in the home. However, more often than not, further finance is required to support the venture and, in order to convince potential backers of the viability of the idea, a business person will draw up a *business plan* to show that the proposals will work.

A business plan will work out the financial needs of the business. It will be a practical working document designed to become a blueprint for its activities. It will involve detailed analysis of:

(a)   the strengths of the business idea.
(b)   the qualities of the people in the business.
(c)   the potential market.
(d)   premises, equipment and start-up costs.
(e)   forecast sales, prices, cash requirements and profits.

Solutions to a business's cash requirements may include:

1.   *Bank loan.* This is a fixed sum lent for a specific purpose, over a time period for which interest is paid.
2.   *Bank overdraft.* An overdraft limit is agreed with the bank and can provide a flexible form of short-term finance.
3.   *Shares.* Private and public limited companies can issue shares in order to raise finance. This creates a larger number of part-owners and profits have to be divided between more people. Similarly, a sole trader might wish to obtain a partner and a partnership might wish to take in further partners.
4.   *Trade credit.* Delaying the payment of bills can provide short-term funds and ease cash-flow problems but, this could ultimately lead to difficulties in obtaining raw materials and to the running down of stocks.
5.   *Hire purchase.* Goods can be obtained and paid for in instalments but they remain the property of the lender until the last payment is made.
6.   *Credit sales agreement.* Goods bought become the property of the purchaser after the deposit or first instalment.

7. *Leasing*. The goods can be obtained immediately but ownership is never obtained. This enables capital goods to be paid for from revenue expenditure and makes it easier to predict costs.
8. *Venture capital firms*. These are firms which specialize, either by area or by industry, in providing capital for investment.
9. *Government grants*. Schemes such as the Enterprise Allowance Scheme and the Small Firms Loan Guarantee Scheme may help businesses to develop.

### Case Study—What is the bank manager looking for?

Your Barclays Bank manager sees your business plan as fundamental to your relationship with Barclays. He or she needs to understand how you see your business developing and how you are going to prepare for its growth. But what exactly does Barclays expect from you? Certainly nothing that you should not expect from yourself.

Broadly speaking, before meeting you your Barclays manager will ask some key questions:

- Do you need Barclays to lend you money?
- If so, how much will you need?
- And when?
- How are you going to pay it back?
- Do you have any security you could offer Barclays?

Figure 11.1  Barclays logo

Your Barclays manager will expect you to know the answers to these questions at the very outset, as they will frame the manager's view of your prospects.

The picture is filled in by assessing your ability and reliability, for instance, your capacity to stay in business and fulfil the promise of your business plan, as well as your current relationship with Barclays.

You need to think carefully about these important questions, as your ability to answer them will determine the manager's response to your approach.

(*Source*: Barclays Bank plc)

*Questions*

1.  Why is it important for a business to foster a good relationship with its bank and how might a business plan help?
2.  Look at the key questions the Barclays manager will ask. Why do you think they will scrutinize the answers to such questions?

## Why do we need accountants?

Different businesses will have different objectives but, whatever these are, they will always need to keep one eye on their financial position. Accountants will help businesses to gain insight into the world of business, finance and administration. Such financial expertise will help managers to answer crucial questions which might concern substantial investments, such as:

*   How are we doing?
*   What sort of return are we going to get?
*   Can we meet our debts?
*   Should we expand?
*   What about taxation?
*   Where does our future lie?

As well as helping *managers* to manage the business more efficiently, information supplied by accountants might help:

*   *shareholders* to assess the value of their investment.
*   *suppliers* to assess whether a company can pay its debts.
*   *providers of finance* to know whether repayments are possible.
*   *employees* to know how a company is performing.
*   *Inland Revenue* to make an accurate tax assessment.

Accounting data prepared by accountants therefore provides *information* which can be used by a variety of different people for decision-making purposes.

## What is accounting?

Accounting involves the recording and interpretation of business activity. Records are kept of business transactions and full sets of accounts are produced at regular intervals, using these records. From a set of accounts it is possible to use ratios and percentages to analyse the behaviour of the firm, detect difficulties and to take action to improve efficiency.

Accountancy falls into two broad areas. *Financial accounting* involves fulfilling the legal requirement to keep books of account and prepare annual accounts for shareholders and the Inland Revenue. Limited companies have a requirement to have their books audited by a qualified chartered or certified accountant to vouch that the accounts are a 'true and fair' view of that company's financial affairs. *Management accounting* provides detailed information about many aspects of a business and helps managers with decisions they have to make.

Accountants work in three main fields:

- In *private practice* accountants work for firms which provide a wide range of services to fee paying clients. Such firms range from large international organizations to small practices of just one accountant.
- In industry and commerce accountants work in almost every organization.
- In public service, such as central and local government and the National Health Service, the work of accountants is fundamental to allocating resources efficiently.

**Figure 11.2** The accountant has a major role in looking after the company's finances (Source: Kim Hooper, Reading)

Accountancy bodies include:

- ICAEW—The Institute of Chartered Accountants in England and Wales.
- CIMA—The Chartered Institute of Management Accountants.
- CIPFA—The Chartered Institute of Public Finance Accountancy.
- ACCA—The Chartered Association of Certified Accountants.

### Recording transactions

The recording of business transactions provides accounting information. Records of transactions are taken by bookkeepers, who initially record transactions in day books, the journal or a cash book before transferring them to a series of ledgers. (See Fig. 11.3.)

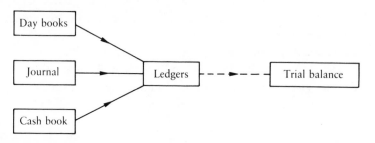

**Figure 11.3**  Recording transactions

In ledgers, transactions are recorded using the double-entry system whereby, with each transaction, one account is debited and another account is credited. This means that for every debit entry in one account, there is always a corresponding credit entry into another account. Such a system assumes that all entries into an accounting system reflect a process of exchange. It takes into consideration the fact that every transaction involves two parts and both of these are recorded in the books of account. For example, if we buy equipment for cash, we lose cash but gain equipment. We must therefore record both the loss in cash in a cash account and the gain of equipment in an equipment account. This dual element is carried through to the trial balance and then on to the final accounts. The use of information technology has meant that today integrated software packages contain the books of first entry and these are linked to a system which updates all records whenever a transaction takes place.

The *trial balance* is a list of all the accounts from all of the ledgers. It should balance because for every debit entry into one account there should have been a corresponding credit entry into another. This list of balances provides the raw material for accountants to draw up the final accounts.

### Final accounts

Earlier in this chapter we looked at the need for accountants and we said that they helped to provide valuable information to answer crucial questions. Much of the information they provide appears in the form of final accounts. These are drawn up regularly by each organization's auditors and are used to assess performance.

Final accounts are made up of the following three elements:

1. A trading account
2. A profit and loss account
3. A balance sheet

The *trading account* shows the *gross profit* made over an accounting period. Gross profit is the difference between the value of sales/turnover and the cost of obtaining the goods (purchases) or the production cost of manufactured goods.

*Note* Getting the goods ready to sell either through purchase or manufacture is known as the cost of sales.

### SALES – COST OF SALES = GROSS PROFIT

Cost of sales is found by applying the following:

### OPENING STOCK + PURCHASES/
### COST OF MANUFACTURE – CLOSING STOCK

Stock appears in this equation as the *opening stock*. It is effectively a purchase because it will be sold in the current trading period and the *closing stock* must be deducted from purchases because it will be sold next year.

Let us imagine that the business of B Cross *sells* or has a *turnover* of £15,000 of widgets, from the beginning of January to the end of December during 1992. At the beginning of January her *opening stock* was £4,500. During the year her *purchases* were £9,000 and at the end of the year her *closing stock* was £6,400. From this basic information we can draw up her trading account which is shown below:

*The Trading account of B Cross for the year ended 31/12/92*

|  | £ | £ |
|---|---|---|
| SALES | | 15,000 |
| *LESS COST OF SALES* | | |
| Opening stock | 4,500 | |
| Add purchases | 9,000 | |
| | 13,500 | |
| Less closing stock | 6,400 | 7,100 |
| GROSS PROFIT | | £7,900 |

*Tasks*

Complete the following examples from the information provided:

(a) At the end of 1992, A Tree had a sales figure of £23,200. His opening stock had been £3,760 and his closing stock figure was £8,564. During the year he has purchased £14,530 of goods. Draw up his trading account and calculate his gross profit.

(b) R Terry runs a manufacturing concern. At the end of 1992 his turnover for the year was £34,532. His opening stock of finished goods at the beginning of the year had been £3,456 and at the end of the year a stock check of finished goods revealed a cost value of £4,553. The production cost of manufacture was £18,767.

   *Note*   Remember the cost of manufacture will appear in the same place as purchases.

   Draw up the trading account and calculate the gross profit.

The *profit and loss account* appears immediately below the trading account where it deducts all of the organization's expenses from the gross profit, in order to achieve the final profit known as *net profit*.

### NET PROFIT = GROSS PROFIT − EXPENSES

   In the example of B Cross on page 209 we calculated her gross profit at £7,900. To find her net profit we have to take into consideration all of her expenses. These are: administrative expenses £423, rent £325, insurance £227, salaries £2,141, advertising £625 and interest paid £152.

*The Profit and Loss account of B Cross for the year ended 31/12/92*

|  | £ | £ |
|---|---|---|
| GROSS PROFIT |  | 7,900 |
| *LESS EXPENSES* |  |  |
| Administrative expenses | 423 |  |
| Rent | 325 |  |
| Insurance | 227 |  |
| Salaries | 2,141 |  |
| Advertising | 625 |  |
| Interest paid | 152 | 3,893 |
| NET PROFIT |  | £4,007 |

*Tasks*

Complete the following examples from the information provided:

(a)   At the end of 1992, A Daley has a gross profit of £12,110. During the year he incurred the following expenses: rates £1,140, rent £861, advertising £432, salaries £4,953, light and heat £639, bad debts £45 and sundry expenses £55. Draw up his profit and loss account and calculate his net profit.

(b)   Copy out the following trading and profit and loss account and insert the missing figures:

*The Trading and Profit and Loss account of D Boy for the year ended 31/12/92*

|  | £ | £ |
|---|---|---|
| Sales |  | xxxxx |
| LESS COST OF SALES |  |  |
| Opening stock | 3,100 |  |
| Add purchases | 4,215 |  |
|  | xxxx |  |
| Less closing stock | 1,218 | 6,097 |
| GROSS PROFIT |  | 1,2058 |
| LESS EXPENSES |  |  |
| Rent | 132 |  |
| Rates | 85 |  |
| Salaries | xxxx |  |
| Advertising | 327 |  |
| Interest paid | 95 |  |
| Light and heat | 41 | 2,136 |
| NET PROFIT |  | £xxxx |

A *balance sheet* is a picture of what a firm owns and owes on a particular date. It is a statement of the assets, liabilities and capital of a business at a particular moment in time (usually the end of an accounting period). We will look at each part of the balance sheet in detail.

A business owns assets and these are divided into *fixed assets* and *current assets*. Fixed assets are tangible assets which have a lifespan of more than a year and tend to be used in the business over a long period, e.g. land and buildings and motor vehicles. Current assets constantly change because they are involved in continuous business activity and, for this reason, they are sometimes called circulating assets. For example, a business will hold stocks so that it can respond to the needs of its customers. When a sale takes place, if it is on credit, it will create debtors who owe the business money. After a reasonable credit period, payment will be expected. Thus the firm has a cash cycle. (See Fig. 11.4.)

Liabilities are owed by a business. They are divided into *current liabilities* and *long-term liabilities*. Current liabilities are debts of the business which need to be paid in a fairly short period of time (normally within the year). For example, when you buy supplies of goods on credit the people you owe money to are known as creditors and they need to be paid after a reasonable period. Other current liabilities might include a bank overdraft or any bills that might

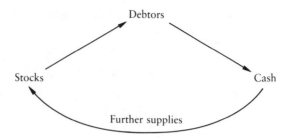

**Figure 11.4**  The cash cycle

be outstanding at the time the balance sheet is drawn up. A long-term liability is not due to be paid until quite a long time in the future. These would include any long-term loans to the business such as a bank loan or a mortgage.

In business accounts, we always treat the business owner (or owners/ shareholders in the case of partnerships or companies) as a separate legal entity from the business itself. The *capital* provided by the owner(s) is therefore deemed to be owed to the owner by the business and is updated annually.

A frequently drawn analogy is that the balance sheet is a snapshot of a business at a particular point in time, while the trading and profit and loss account is like a video running until the next snapshot. All of the figures for the balance sheet will come from the trial balance, except for the net profit which will link the trading and profit and loss account to the balance sheet.

The balance sheet opposite is presented in a *vertical style*. Assets are traditionally arranged in an inverse order of liquidity. This simply means that the items which would take longest to turn into money are put at the top and the items which can quickly be turned into money are at the bottom. Current liabilities are deducted from current assets in order to achieve the *working capital*. This helps a business to quickly assess how easily short-term debts can be turned into cash and how easily bills can be paid. Long-term liabilities are deducted from the total of working capital and fixed assets to achieve net assets.

The capital section of the balance sheet is adjusted with each statement by adding the net profit taken from the profit and loss account and then deducting *drawings* which are the amounts taken from the business for the owner's use.

*Tasks*

Complete the following examples from the information provided:

(a)    At the end of 1992, the following figures were extracted from the trial balance and profit and loss account of K O'Leary: land and buildings £23,200, motor vehicles £6,700, closing stock £840, debtors £600, bank £305, creditors £803, mortgage £5,000, capital £20,000, net profit £7,321 and drawings £1,479. Organize the figures into a balance sheet as at 31/12/92.

*The balance sheet of B Cross as at 31/12/92*

|  | £ | £ |
|---|---|---|
| **FIXED ASSETS** | | |
| Land and buildings | 25,000 | |
| Motor vehicles | 3,000 | 28,000 |
| **CURRENT ASSETS** | | |
| Closing stock | 1,500 | |
| Debtors | 1,017 | |
| Bank | 325 | |
| | 2,842 | |
| **LESS CURRENT LIABILITIES** | | |
| Creditors | 1,500 | |
| Working capital | | 1,342 |
| | | 29,342 |
| **LESS LONG-TERM LIABILITIES** | | |
| Mortgage | | 10,000 |
| Net assets | | £19,342 |
| Financed by: | | |
| CAPITAL | | 15,935 |
| Add net profit | | 4,007 |
| | | 19,942 |
| Less drawings | | 600 |
| | | £19,342 |

(b) P Brown is in a dilemma and has approached you for help. He understands how to work out his profit and has calculated that he has made £2000 net profit during 1992, but he needs to draw up a balance sheet and has sought your advice.

(i) Briefly explain to Philip the importance of drawing up a balance sheet and how a balance sheet is organized.

(ii) Draw up his balance sheet as at 31/12/92 from the following information he provides: land and buildings £8,150, motor vehicles £2,000, machinery £6,000, closing stock £850, debtors £400, bank £20, creditors £1,200, bank loan £6,000, capital £10,000 and drawings £1,780.

(iii)   Philip has only got £20 in the bank and his working capital is very small. Outline to him how this might affect his ability to run his business. Might it mean that his business could go the way of all dinosaurs?

## Making use of the final accounts

We know that final accounts show what a business owns and owes, as well as profitability, but they can also be a very useful source of other information for a business. Obtaining this information by interpreting the final accounts, using ratios and percentages, enables comparisons to be made between one year and another, or one organization and another, to improve efficiency.

The following figures can be extracted from the trading and profit and loss account:

(a)   **Gross profit percentage on turnover**

$$\frac{\text{Gross profit}}{\text{Sales}} \times 100$$

This indicates the percentage gross profit made upon sales. It is an important figure because if it falls it could indicate theft of stock or losses from the till. It would also indicate changes in the prices of raw materials and changes in pricing policy.

(b)   **Net profit percentage on turnover**

$$\frac{\text{Net profit}}{\text{Sales}} \times 100$$

This indicates how much final profit is made as a percentage of sales. If the gross profit percentage is consistent, any change in net profit percentage might indicate an increase in overheads and a need to make economies.

(c)   **Stock turnover**

$$\frac{\text{Cost of sales}}{\text{Average stock}}$$

*Note*   Average stock = $\dfrac{\text{Opening stock} + \text{Closing stock}}{2}$

Stock turnover is the average length of time an item of stock is held in store before it is used or sold. This will vary according to the nature of the

the business. An increasing stock turnover will mean increasing profits and comparisons can be made with previous years.

The following figures can be extracted from the balance sheet:

(a)  **Working capital ratio**
This is the ratio of current assets to current liabilities. A prudent ratio is sometimes said to be 2:1. Organizations must pay close attention to this ratio to ensure that they can meet all of their short-term debts.

(b)  **Asset utilization**

This is calculated by the formula $\dfrac{\text{Sales}}{\text{Fixed assets}}$

This ratio indicates how effectively fixed assets are being used to generate sales.

(c)  **Return on capital**

$$\dfrac{\text{Net profit}}{\text{Capital invested}} \times 100$$

This will show whether the business is justified in continuing or whether the business ought to cease operations. If the return on capital is low the entrepreneur would have to consider the alternatives.

## Break-even analysis

By understanding their organization's final accounts, managers are provided with valuable information which enables them to improve the quality of their decisions. However, within the organization management accounting takes this aspect further and works in close unison with all departments in order to maximize efficiency through the supply of the right information to the right person at the right time. One technique of doing this is break-even analysis.

Breaking even is the unique point at which a business makes no profit and no loss. If sales are beyond the break-even point profits are made and, if they are below the break-even point, losses are made. A basic understanding of costs is fundamental to its calculation. *Fixed costs* are costs which do not increase as total output increases and are often referred to as overheads. These might include the salaries of office staff, factory rent and rates, etc. *Variable costs* are costs which increase as output increases and would include, for example, raw materials or the wages of machine operatives.

To calculate the break-even point:

1.  Calculate the *unit contribution* (selling price less variable costs).

2. Divide the fixed overhead costs by the unit contribution. This will provide the number of units it is necessary to produce in order to break-even. *Note* The sales value of this break-even point (BEP) can be calculated by multiplying the number of units at BEP by the selling price.

### Case Study—Trio Toys

Ron Todd, the dynamic entrepreneurial Chairman of Trio Toys, has been carefully monitoring the baby buggy division of his company. Each baby buggy sells for £12 and the variable costs encountered in manufacture include:

- £4 direct labour per unit
- £3 direct materials per unit
- £1 other variable overheads per unit

The fixed costs of the baby buggy division are £80,000.

*Working out the BEP*

The unit contribution for each buggy produced will be:
£12 (selling price) − £8(£4 + £3 + £1 variable costs) = £4

$$BEP = \frac{\text{fixed costs}}{\text{unit contribution}}$$

$$= \frac{£80,000}{4} = 20\,000 \text{ units to break-even}$$

Sales value to break-even = 20 000 units × £12 selling price
= £240,000

*Aiming for a profit target*

Ron hopes to make a profit of £30,000 on his buggies. To find out how many units he has to sell to achieve this, he must add his profit target to his fixed costs and divide this by the contribution.

$$\frac{£80,000 \text{ (fixed costs)} + £30,000 \text{ (profit target)}}{4} = \frac{110\,000}{4}$$

= 27 500 units to achieve this target

The sales value required to make this profit =

27 500 units × £12 selling price = £330,000

## The break-even chart

Ron Todd could have discovered the above information from a break-even chart. A break-even chart will show the position at which a business breaks even and the profits and losses it will make at various levels of activity. It is constructed by:

1. Labelling the horizontal axis for units of production and sales.
2. Labelling the vertical axis to represent the value of sales and costs.
3. Plotting fixed costs.
   *Note* These will remain at the same level over all levels of production.
4. Plotting variable costs. These are shown rising from where the fixed cost line touches the vertical axis and will also represent total costs. It is plotted by calculating total costs at two or three random levels of production. (See Table 11.1.)
5. Sales are plotted by taking two or three random levels of turnover and will rise from the intersection of the two axes. (See Fig. 11.5 on page 218.)

For example, for Trio Toys:

| | 10 000 units £ | 20 000 units £ | 30 000 units £ |
|---|---|---|---|
| Variable costs = £8 per unit | 80 000 | 160 000 | 240 000 |
| Fixed costs | 80 000 | 80 000 | 80 000 |
| Total cost | 160 000 | 240 000 | 320 000 |
| Sales £12 per unit | 120 000 | 240 000 | 360 000 |

Table 11.1 Calculating total costs and sales at three random levels.

## Case Study—Cash flow

You are the accountant for a small firm. The firm is expected to take cash receipts of £50,000 per month for the first six months of the year. Its raw material and labour costs are also expected to be constant at £40,000 per month.

The firm wants to buy a new machine in March for £30,000. Fill in the firm's projected-cash-flow table (Table 11.2) from January to June starting with a balance of zero.

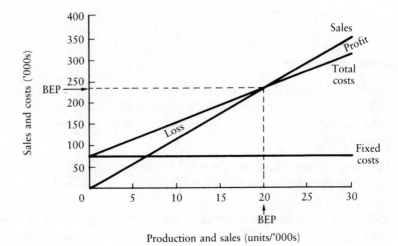

**Figure 11.5**  Breakeven chart of Trio Toys

**Table 11.2**  Table for the firm's projected cash flow from January to June

|  | Jan. | Feb. | Mar. | Apr. | May | June |
|---|---|---|---|---|---|---|
| Balance b/f from last month |  |  |  |  |  |  |
| Receipts |  |  |  |  |  |  |
| Raw materials and wages |  |  |  |  |  |  |
| New machinery |  |  |  |  |  |  |
| Balance c/f to next month |  |  |  |  |  |  |

## Questions

1.  What would be the balance carried forward to July?
2.  What is the purpose of doing a projected-cash-flow analysis?
3.  What could make the projected cash flow turn out to be wrong?

## Case Study—JR Ewett

JR Ewett constantly searches every avenue to achieve financial success. His previous projects have nearly always provided him with substantial rewards. You have just approached JR with a proposition concerning the production of computer software. You have worked hard developing this software and know that you could sell each unit for £30. Having researched the project you have calculated that variable costs would include:

- £4 direct labour per unit
- £6 direct materials per unit
- £3 other variable overheads

Fixed costs are estimated to be £140,000.

(a)   Work out the break-even point for JR in both units and sales value.
(b)   JR is looking for a profit target of £40,000. Indicate to him how many units of sales you would need to clear to achieve this.
(c)   How would increasing the prices by 20 per cent affect the figures above?


## Case Study—Accountants hooked on computers

A recent survey revealed that accountants are daily becoming more dependent on computers. Nearly 80 per cent of those questioned reckoned that they now use a computer for between one and six hours a day, with over half of them using one for at least three hours a day. Seven per cent of accountants questioned said they used a computer for more than six hours a day! The survey was conducted by *Career Accountant* among more than 700 accountants throughout the UK.

It also revealed that:

*   90 per cent of accountants used spreadsheets
*   two-thirds used financial business systems software
*   65 per cent used word processing packages.


*Questions*

1.   Describe how important you feel a computer is for an accountant.
2.   Why might an accountant use spreadsheets, financial software and word processing packages?


## Case Study—Valeo

Valeo is a French motor component company and the leading maker of security and air-conditioning systems for the European automotive industry. Current conditions are not favourable for Valeo. Throughout 1990, Peugeot and Renault ran down stocks. Car manufacturers in both the US and Brazil have also been cutting production. Redundancies of 2500 have just been announced.

During 1991 margin pressure has remained and turnover for 1991 has been down by seven per cent. Though profits are down, the company point to their potential for recovery.

*Questions*

1.  Explain what is meant by:
    (a)  turnover
    (b)  margin pressure
2.  Why might many car manufacturers run down stocks?
3.  How would you feel as a shareholder if the company you had invested in announced 2500 redundancies?
4.  Why might a company which has gone through a recession point to their potential for recovery?

## Questions

1.  Compete the following sentences using the terms below:

| | |
|---|---|
| Balance sheet | Credit |
| Asset | Trading account |
| Liability | Profit and loss account |
| Net profit | Expenses |
| Gross profit | Capital |
| Debit | |

(a)  The sum of money contributed to a business by its owners is known as . . . . . . . .
(b)  A snapshot of a company's position at a particular moment is known as a . . . . . . . .
(c)  An account that is owed money is said to be in . . . . . . . .
(d)  An account that owes money is said to be in . . . . . . . .
(e)  Lighting and heating are examples of . . . . . . . .
(f)  An . . . . . . . . is something owned by a business or owed to a business.
(g)  Expenses are deducted from gross profit to arrive at net profit in the . . . . . . . .
(h)  . . . . . . . . will be greater than . . . . . . . .
(i)  The . . . . . . . . is calculated to show gross profit.
(j)  A . . . . . . . . is something owed by the business.

2.  Your friend intends to start a small business. Explain to him the need for:
    (a)  A business plan.
    (b)  A cash flow forecast.
    (c)  A bookkeeping system.

3.  Find out the difference between the following:
    (a)  Capital and revenue expenditure.
    (b)  Fixed assets and current assets.
    (c)  Fixed costs and variable costs.
    (d)  Financial accounting and management accounting.

4.    Lucy prepared the following estimates for a new line of hats.

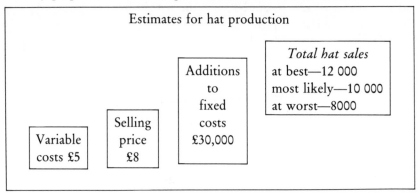

(a)    What might be the 'additions to fixed costs'?
(b)    Where might the firm raise the additional finance for the 'additions to fixed costs'?
(c)    From the estimates, advise Lucy whether the new line of hats should be introduced.
       (*Source*: Extract from Northern Examining Association.)
5.    Dymark is a small business partnership specializing in the manufacture of doors. Study the figures in the following profit and loss account of Dymark for the years 1988/89 and 1989/90 and answer the questions which follow.

DYMARK DOORS
PROFIT AND LOSS ACCOUNT
for the year ended 5 April 1990

| 1988/89 | | | 1989/90 |
|---|---|---|---|
| 24 000 | GROSS PROFIT | | 24 300 |
| 4300 | Wages | 5180 | |
| 1000 | Insurance | 1050 | |
| 2000 | Rent | 2100 | |
| 1000 | Rates | 1020 | |
| 800 | Lighting and heating | 850 | |
| 900 | Advertising | 1100 | |
| 10 000 | TOTAL EXPENSES | | 11 300 |
| 14 000 | NET PROFIT | | |
| 24 000 | | | 24 000 |

(a)   Explain what is meant by the term 'gross profit'.
(b)   Explain what is meant by the term 'net profit'.
(c)   Calculate the net profit for 1989/90.

(d)       The following were the net sales for both years

| 1988/89 | 1989/90 |
|---------|---------|
| £80,000 | £81,000 |

Using the information available, identify the better trading year, giving a reasoned explanation for your answer.
(e)   How might this firm use its net profit?
(f)    Why is it important for Dymark to produce a set of accounts?
       (*Source*: Northern Ireland Schools Examination and Assessment Council)
6.    Mark Marsh and Geoff Taylor run a successful partnership producing garden equipment. A new product they have just introduced (a lightweight garden fork) is expected to sell well and to become one of the market leaders. Geoff Taylor has calculated the following figures showing the costs involved in manufacturing the forks.

| Forks produced (thousands) | Total costs (£'000s) |
|---------|---------|
| 0 | 16 |
| 2 | 26 |
| 5 | 41 |
| 8 | 56 |
| 12 | 76 |
| 15 | 91 |

(a)   What action could the partners take to prevent rival firms from copying their design for the lightweight fork?
(b)   The partners have to pay fixed costs whatever their level of output.
      (i)   Give an example of a fixed cost.
      (ii)  What amount of fixed costs do the partners have to pay when producing the fork?
(c)   The partners have decided that the selling price of the new forks will be £7 each, assuming all the forks they produce will be sold.
      **Showing all your calculations**:
      (i)   How many forks will they have to produce next year in order to break even?
      (ii)  If they actually produce 12 000 forks next year, how much profit would they earn?

    (iii)   If the partners decide to increase their selling price to £7.50, what would be the new profit level if sales were maintained at 12 000 forks?

(*Source*: Southern Examining Group)

7.  Give a list of fixed assets you might include in the following types of business:
  (a)   A disco
  (b)   A driving school
  (c)   A corner shop
  (d)   A manufacturing firm
  (e)   A cinema

8.  Draw up what you consider to be:
  (a)   A healthy balance sheet
  (b)   An unhealthy balance sheet

9.  Bulco Ltd plans to expand production and next year it hopes to produce 30 000 units and sell them for £8 each. Variable costs are £4 per unit and fixed costs are £50,000. Draw a graph to find the break-even point for Bulco Ltd. Calculate total costs.

## Coursework

1.  If you run a mini-company or enterprise, do an analysis of the balance sheet. Alternatively, see if you can get the figures from a small local business. What scope is there for improvement?

2.  How do we set out a trading account and profit and loss account?
    See if you can obtain the relevant figures from a firm and then set them out as a trading and profit and loss account.

3.  How do we rank assets in order of liquidity?
    Visit the premises of a local business and by observation try to rank its assets in order of liquidity. This could be done as a class exercise so that a lot of information is brought together. You can then analyse the information to find out which sorts of business have a high ratio of fixed to variable capital. You can then take this further and look at causes, problems, advantages and disadvantages, etc.

# 12

# The personnel department

## Human needs at work

People spend a considerable part of their lives at work. It is not surprising, therefore, that we come to expect a certain amount of satisfaction from the jobs that we do. To some people work is a great pleasure, giving them a great sense of personal fulfilment, but for others it is just a necessary way to make a living.

### Case Study—Finding the motivation

A senior director of a large company was recently surprised with the performance of an employee who had only been in post for three years. The person in question had the right qualities for the job and the relevant technical skills but was not doing as well as expected. The appointee had been running a technical department with 30 highly-qualified specialists. His role was to lead and motivate the team in order to meet the company's objectives. Despite a generous salary, relocation package, health insurance, company car and pension scheme, his heart did not seem to be in the job and, instead of taking pride in running his department, he busied himself in technical work where he could see the fruits of his labours.

After talking with this employee it was found that he felt that he had sorted out his job and that the role was no longer challenging. He had been recruited on the basis of his technical competence and management potential but, they had not realized that he needed to be constantly involved in challenging projects that were actually using his skills.

Often attitudes to work are dependent upon how much opportunity individuals are given to express their talents and skills. Though the individual in this case study was being well rewarded, the post in question was not providing the vital *motivation*. As a result of research by the senior director it was found that this individual was frustrated and he was put in charge of a small team of project design experts where he could see the direct results of his efforts.

*Questions*

1. Explain why material rewards are not the only things that people look for in a job.
2. What would you look for in a job?
3. What is meant by motivation?

Job satisfaction is often a very personal thing. Some people enjoy having no responsibility and getting on with repetitive work. Some enjoy being told what to do, while others look for the freedom to make their own decisions and the flexibility to work in the way they want. The following is a list of some of the factors different people might look for in a job:

1. A good rate of pay.
2. Good opportunities for promotion.
3. Long breaks and holidays.
4. Prestige.
5. The opportunity to combine work and family life.
6. Job security.
7. Friendship with workmates.
8. Opportunities to be creative.
9. A degree of independence.
10. Responsibility.

*Task*

Interview a cross-section of people to find out what gives them job satisfaction.

Generally, satisfaction will be greatest for individuals who have the greatest freedom to choose a job and this will be those who have had the opportunity to acquire the most widely accepted range of qualifications and skills. Most jobs have some disadvantages but workers will enjoy work more if these disadvantages can be minimized.

# The role of personnel

Everyone who manages people has a personnel function because they are responsible for the actions of others. Personnel management is, however, a specialist function of management which is concerned with all matters relating to *interpersonal* relationships within a firm. This includes hiring, dismissal, training, discipline, pensions, wage negotiations and other matters.

Personnel work includes:

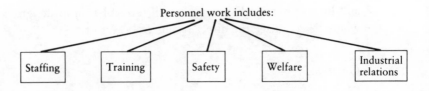

**Figure 12.1**  The functions of the Personnel Department

| Staffing | Training | Safety | Welfare | Industrial relations |

In addition to these functions, modern personnel departments are also expected to be involved in assessing the implications of change for the employees of the organization.

## Recruitment

From the personnel viewpoint the purpose of recruitment is to buy in the best available human resources to meet a company's needs. For the individual, however, finding paid employment is not always easy. In the UK, the most common way of finding a job is by directly contacting a firm or place of employment. Sometimes people apply for a job as a result of a personal contact such as, a relative already working for a firm.

### Recruiting through newspaper advertisements

Newspaper advertisements are an obvious place to scout for jobs. A good newspaper advertisement gives a substantial amount of information. Personnel managers place adverts in the most suitable medium. Jobs demanding limited skills can often be advertised locally, whereas jobs requiring specialist skills need to be advertised in specialist media. Adverts for teachers, for example, will appear in *The Times Educational Supplement* and adverts for doctors' posts will be advertised in *The Lancet*. (See Fig. 12.2.)

**Figure 12.2**  Advertisement placed by Leigh Rugby League Club in a Welsh newspaper – the aim was to attract quality players in an area where such players abound (Source: Western Mail)

When recruiting labour the personnel manager will therefore do the following:

1.  Target the recruiting campaign at the most suitable audience.

2.  Advertise in the most cost-effective way (i.e., use the cheapest method possible to get the right sort of people).

To ensure that a newspaper gets the right response it will be necessary to make at least some of the following points clear (see Fig. 12.3):

**BOOKKEEPER**
*REQUIRED CENTRAL LEEDS* (1)

Janet Davis Advertising Agency,
starting salary £6000 per annum. (2)

We are looking for a bookkeeper who has had experience of (3) (4)
handling the purchase ledger and other account books and
is familiar with operations leading to a trial balance.
The successful applicant will be entitled to luncheon (5)
vouchers and transport expenses to work.

Please apply in writing to Mrs. S. Grose (6)
Personnel Manager, The J. Davis Advertising Agency,
Prince Street, Leeds, LSU 9BJ.
*(Please state names and addresses of two referees.)*

**Figure 12.3** Advertisement appearing in a West Yorkshire evening paper. (The numbers in brackets refer to the list of points a job advertisement should include)

1.  Where the job is located.
2.  How much the job pays.
3.  What qualifications are required to do the job.
4.  What the job involves.
5.  What fringe benefits are available.
6.  How to go about applying for the job.

*Jobcentres*

The Department of Employment is responsible for the running of jobcentres, which can be found in a prominent position in major towns. The jobcentres run window displays of jobs and people seeking work are encouraged to come in and look at the cards with details of job vacancies which are on open display (see Fig. 12.4).

**JOBCENTRE**

| | |
|---|---|
| **JOB** | FULL-TIME SALES ASSISTANT |
| **DISTRICT** | CENTRAL NORTHAMPTON |
| **SALARY** | £3.00 per hour. Annual staff bonus. Fringe benefits. |
| **HOURS** | 40 hour week, 6 day flexible work pattern. |
| **DETAILS** | Ladies' fashion department. Age 25 – 45. Experience essential. |
| **JOB NO.** | 15 |

**Figure 12.4** Jobcentre advertisement for a sales assistant

Some firms regularly use jobcentres as a method of recruiting labour because it is a cheap and quick way of reaching an interested audience.

### Private employment agencies

There are a wide range of private employment agencies which help businesses to recruit staff. Fields in which these agencies are particularly common are secretarial work, high-technology areas, nursing and casual work.

*Note*   Recently some agencies have responded to shortages of teachers and set up to provide supply teachers for schools.

The agency will take a commission on the salary of the worker. In the case of secretarial staff, wages will often be paid by the employing firm to the agency who will then pay the worker.

### Other forms of recruitment

One function of the Department of Employment is to constantly revise its strategy to respond to changes in the employment marketplace. On two occasions since 1980, through two recessions, we have seen massive rises in numbers unemployed and the general nature of those unemployed differed in both instances. We have seen initiatives such as Employment Training, Job Clubs and The Enterprise Allowance Scheme, all designed to create opportunities for those without work.

In the Midlands a scheme has been introduced allowing unemployed people to find a job from the comfort of their armchairs. Under the scheme, launched by Central Television and the Department of Employment, after the end of normal programmes, up-to-date job vacancies are shown in teletext form. Job-seekers can then enquire by telephone about the jobs that interest them, without having to go to a jobcentre. An advantage of this scheme is that it reduces wasted travel expenses and it is a particularly useful scheme for the disabled.

## Methods of selection

These will tend to vary according to how the job has been advertised and the experience, skills and expertise required of the successful applicant. The aim will be to seek the best possible candidate on the basis of their ability to perform the job required.

Sometimes employers will ask candidates to apply by letter. A good letter of application will tell the organization whether the candidate is worthy of an interview. (See Fig. 12.5.)

```
                                         158 Franklin Road,
                                         Harrogate,
                                         Yorkshire,
                                         HG1 SEN


                              (Telephone:   0423 886412)

Mrs S. Grose,
J.Davis Advertising Agency,
Prince Street,
Leeds, LSU 9BJ                            10 August 19__


Dear Mrs Grose,

      With reference to your advertisement in the 'Evening Post' of the 8th August
for a Bookkeeper to Trial Balance, I would like to apply for the vacancy.

      I am 34 years old and have worked for several years in the Accounts Department
of Heels Department Store in Central Leeds.  I have been in charge of the purchases
section there and have regularly prepared the trial balance.  The firm is currently
re-locating in Glasgow and it is impossible for me to move with them because of
family ties.

      I have been an active member of the social club at Heels and am currently
acting treasurer of this body.

      I was very interested in your job advertisement and would be pleased to attend
an interview at your convenience.

      My referees are Mr S. Heel, Managing Director, Heels, and Mr S. Bartholomew,
Accounts Manager, Heels.

                        Yours sincerely,

                          Elizabeth Howard

                        (Elizabeth Howard)
```

**Figure 12.5**  A personnel manager will be attracted to a letter that is well written and well presented, as this one is

Sometimes organizations ask candidates to fill in a printed application form. An application form enables applicants to set out information about themselves in a standardized way and this helps with analysis. (See Fig. 12.6.)

The interview is the most common technique used for selection purposes. Often before an interview an organization will send for references.

Questioning plays a vital role in a selection interview. It is the means by which information is obtained about the suitability of the candidate and an

HUNTLEY, BOORNE & STEVENS LTD.

APPLICATION FOR EMPLOYMENT — HOURLY PAID EMPLOYEE

*(Please complete this Form in your own handwriting)*

| | |
|---|---|
| Surname: | Christian Names: |
| Address: | Position required: |

| Age: | Date of Birth: | Married Single Divorced Widowed | Dependants: |
|---|---|---|---|

Name and Address and Telephone No. of person to be informed in case of emergency.

| Relatives with Company: | Place of Birth and Nationality: |
|---|---|
| Education Details: | Details of any apprenticeship served: |

Previous employment with the Company (if any):

Have you ever suffered from –

(a) Accident of serious illness?  ...........................................................
(b) Dermatitis or skin condition?  ...........................................................
(c) Hay fever or asthma?  ...........................................................
(d) Fainting or giddy fits?  ...........................................................
(e) Epilepsy?  ...........................................................
(f) Heart or chest conditions?  ...........................................................

Are you a Registered Disabled Person? If so, Registered No. ................................
Date of Expiry: .........................................................

Are you prepared to work shifts?

PRESENT OR PREVIOUS EMPLOYMENT
Last or present employer: ........................................ Clock no. ............................
.......................................................................... Foreman: ............................
Occupation: ..................................................... Rate: ............................
Length of Service: .............................................. Date left: ............................
Reason for leaving: ...........................................................

| Date: | Signature of Applicant: |
|---|---|

Remarks: .......................................................................................................
...........................................................................................................................

| Engaged as: | Clock No.: | Department: |
|---|---|---|
| By: | Wage Rate, etc. | |
| Starting Date: | | |

| Date | Signature of Interviewing Officer: |
|---|---|

**Figure 12.6** Huntley, Boorne and Stevens regularly takes on new employees and so issues a standard application form

**Figure 12.7** Personnel director Mary Macdonald interviews an applicant for a job (Source: Kim Hooper, Reading)

opportunity to assess the candidate as a person. Questions help to find out if the candidate is the person for the job and also the sort of person who will fit into that particular work environment. Interviews are not always the best means of assessing technical ability and they are often supported with some means of test which is specially designed to find out the skills and capabilities of the candidates.

*Task*

Work in groups of four.

1. The first pair should prepare an advertisment for a job as an accounts clerk in a firm called Merryweather Ltd. The second pair should prepare an advertisement for a job as an office junior for a firm called ABCDE Ltd. Make up details where necessary.
2. Each pair should now send a letter of application for the job advertised by the other pair.
3. Each pair should now write to the other pair inviting them for interview.
4. Hold the interviews so that all four candidates are interviewed. If it is practical to do so, make a video.
5. Analyse the performance of both interviewers and candidates and then make a list of interviewing techniques which ought to be used by an interviewer, as well as a list of interviewing techniques which ought to be used by an applicant.

## Staffing

Human resources are one of the most valuable of an organization's resources. As with any other resource they need to be looked after if they are to achieve their full potential. Motivation, communication, leadership, the structuring of work and disputes will all involve issues which constantly have to be handled by the personnel department.

When someone starts work, a host of factors will determine their pay or *monetary rewards*. These might include:

1.  Qualifications and skills
2.  Experience
3.  Payment for results
4.  The demand and supply of labour
5.  Location
6.  Whether the job is dangerous or unhealthy
7.  Responsibility

Other *non-monetary* rewards might also be available such as:

1.  A pension scheme
2.  A company car
3.  Private medical insurance
4.  Generous holidays

New employees will usually be asked to attend an *induction scheme* which will initiate their training needs. They must also be given a written *contract of employment* within 13 weeks of starting the job.

Under the Contract of Employment Act 1972, the written contract must include the following:

1.  Title of the job.
2.  Date the job starts.
3.  Hours of work.
4.  Rate and method of pay.
5.  Holiday arrangements.
6.  Period of notice that must be given.
7.  Pension scheme arrangements.
8.  Rights concerning trade unions.
9.  The organization's discipline rules.

## Training

This is another major area of the personnel function. Many large firms will have a detailed training scheme which is executed on an 'in-house' basis. This is particularly true of larger public companies such as banks and insurance companies. In conjunction with this, staff may be encouraged to attend college courses to learn new skills and get new qualifications. Training thus takes place in the following ways:

1. On the job—learning skills through experience at work.
2. Off the job—learning through attending courses.

### Case Study—Making use of your employees

Sir John Harvey-Jones recently gave the closing address at the Conference of the Institute of Personnel Managers (IPM). In his speech he indicated that even the best companies were only using about 40 per cent of the potential of their people.

Sir John pointed out that 'People have been looked upon as buyable and sellable like machines or widgets' yet companies keep declaring that 'our people' are 'our greatest asset'. The fault was that selecting, training, developing, motivating, organizing and rewarding or punishing seem to occupy very little time in the average board agenda.

He finished by pointing out that in the future personnel will occupy a pole position and competition will involve mobilizing and motivating peoples' minds.

### Questions

1. Briefly describe why personnel has involved so little time in an average board agenda.
2. Explain why you think personnel might become a more important function in the future.

Promotion within a firm often depends on acquiring qualifications to do a more advanced job. In banking, for instance, staff will be expected to pass banking examinations. At the same time, a candidate for promotion must show a flair for the job. It is the responsibility of the training department within a business to make sure that staff with the right skills are coming up through the firm or being recruited from outside.

Training and Enterprise Councils (TECs) have been promoting the importance of training as an economic issue. They have been encouraging employers to take the lead in training and to enable individuals to take responsibility for their own development. One way they have done this is by allowing companies meeting a new national standard in training and staff development to display the quality training 'kitemark'. (See Fig. 12.8.)

**Figure 12.8**   Training kitemark

**Case Study—Where training has the pride of place**

In Germany, the amount of money spent on vocational training continues to rise. Every German firm of repute regards it as its duty to take on apprentices and offer vocational training.

German strength in training has always been attributed as one of the key reasons for its economic success. Geerd Woortmann from the Chamber of Commerce explains that 'If you are in a country with high costs you know that you stand little chance on price competition. Your best option, therefore, is quality, but you only maintain that with quality labour. Then price becomes a secondary factor.'

Germany industry believes that by investing in training it keeps the workforce constantly moving ahead towards improving quality and economic success.

*Questions*

1.  Why do German firms regard it as their duty to provide training?
2.  Explain how training will·help to improve quality.

## Safety

The personnel department will also normally be concerned with safety at work. This might involve the employment of a specialist safety officer. There are many hazards in the workplace and the safety officer has a particularly difficult job in making sure that the firm complies with the law on health and safety. Unions are also particularly concerned with this issue.

The three main laws concerned with health and safety are:

### The Factories Act 1961

This act covers most businesses that use mechanical machinery and therefore includes a wide range of premises such as garages, printing works, building sites and engineering establishments. Provisions of this act cover toilet and washing facilities, ventilation and heating, fenced screens and guards and fire escapes.

### The Offices, Shops and Railways Premises Act 1963

This is particularly important in relation to office and shop conditions and covers areas such as temperatures, the supply of air, toilet and washing facilities, lighting and floor space.

### The Health and Safety at Work Act 1974

This act establishes a responsibility of both employers and employees to provide safe conditions at work. The *employer's duty* is to ensure, as far as is reasonably practical, the 'health, safety and welfare at work of all employees'. The *employee's duty* is to take reasonable care to ensure both his or her own safety and the safety of others who may be affected by what he or she does or does not do. Employers or employees who do not abide by these rules can be punished in a court of law. This is backed up by a Health and Safety Executive which includes representatives of employers, employees and local authorities.

Not only must the safety officer be aware of general laws but there are also codes relating to specific industries. For example, there are laws relating to workers in mines, the explosives industry and textiles. On top of this, many industries establish their own safety regulations, often in conjunction with trade unions.

## Welfare

The final major responsibility of a personnel department looked at in this chapter is the physical and general well-being of the workforce. This will involve social facilities, Christmas activities, complaints at work and many other related areas.

Members of the personnel department should know quite a lot about the employees of the firm. Not only will they meet them through recruitment and training, but they will also make it their business to keep records relating to employees' families, absences from work, qualifications, problems at work and to generally respond to the needs of their employees.

Staff appraisal is an important feature in many companies and enables personnel to assess the performance of employees and to utilize their strengths in order to achieve their full potential. It also helps them to set targets for staff to achieve and helps to prepare staff for promotion.

### Case Study—Nissan Motor Manufacturing (UK) Limited

On 1 February 1984, Nissan and HM Government signed an agreement to build a car plant in the north-east of England, near Sunderland. Within months they had appointed their first British employee, the director of personnel. Since then their short British tenure has been a success story with forecast production of 220 000 cars by 1993, half of which will be exported.

The Nissan philosophy is to build profitably the highest quality car sold in Europe. They also want to achieve the maximum possible customer satisfaction and ensure the prosperity of the company and its staff. To assist in this, Nissan aim to achieve mutual trust and cooperation between all people in the company and to make Nissan a place where long-term job satisfaction can be achieved. 'Kaizan' is a word much used at Sunderland. It is a Japanese word, the literal translation being simply—*continuous improvement*. It is improvement gained by slow steady change, that, once achieved, is maintained at that level until such time as the next step of improvement takes place. As people are their most valuable resource they feel that:

- all staff have a valuable contribution to make as individuals and that this can be more effective in a team working environment.
- Nissan Motor (UK) Limited will not be restricted by tradition and in all actions will have a flexible approach.
- Kaizan team activity will help to develop leadership and presentation skills, as well as enable people to learn from others.
- Kaizan enables all staff to consider issues which affect their place of work.

**Figure 12.9** Nissan Motor Manufacturing (UK) Ltd – Sunderland (Source: Nissan Motor Manufacturing (UK) Ltd)

**Figure 12.10** Nissan Final Assembly – Nissan Sunderland (Source: Nissan Motor Manufacturing (UK) Ltd)

Kaizan assumes the total involvement of all employees but recognizes that the success of participation depends on individuals feeling that they are part of the 'Nissan team'.

At Sunderland, all of the office accommodation is open plan. Communications meetings are held every day with staff and everyone works under the same terms and conditions of employment. There are single status subsidized canteens and no privileged parking.

*Questions*

1. Explain why a company has a 'philosophy'.
2. What are the benefits for Nissan of producing a workplace where job satisfaction can be achieved?

**Figure 12.11** Nissan Final Assembly Area – Nissan Sunderland (Source: Nissan Motor Manufacturing (UK) Ltd)

3. Explain why improvement is a suitable belief to have.
4. How will open and frequent communications help employees to feel more valued?

One area of particular importance for the personnel officer is to make sure that there is no discrimination in the workplace. Discrimination against anyone on the grounds of their sex, race, colour or national origin is illegal, whether it be in recruitment, conditions of work, promotion, training or dismissal. Job advertisements must not discriminate. (See Fig. 12.12.) It is also necesssary to make sure that interviews are fair, pay is equal for similar work, there is no sexual or racial harrassment; that, in fact, there is no discrimination of any sort. If there is a case of discrimination it can be taken to an industrial tribunal.

**Figure 12.12** Job advertisements must not suggest that someone of a particular sex (except for certain jobs) race, colour or nation origin will be preferred

- An **industrial tribunal** is set up to investigate grievances at work. Its decision is binding on parties. It is made up of a legally qualified chairperson, an employers' representative and a trade union representative. Industrial tribunals sit regularly in all areas of the country.

## Personnel issues

### Redundancy

This occurs when a business or firm closes down, when part of a business closes down, or when particular types of workers are no longer required. On being made redundant, a worker has certain legal rights for compensation. To receive redundancy pay, a worker must have been with a firm for at least two years.

### Dismissal of staff

Over the years an elaborate system for the dismissal of staff has developed, as a result of the large number of cases which have been brought before industrial tribunals and other courts. The heart of the matter lies in the difference between what is termed *fair dismissal* and what the court regards to be *unfair dismissal*.

## Fair dismissal

It is up to an industrial tribunal to decide on the 'fairness' of a dismissal. A worker can be 'fairly' dismissed without notice. This would involve proving a case against the worker on grounds such as:

1. Wilful destruction of company property.
2. Sexual or racial harrassment.
3. Continuous bad timekeeping.
4. A negligent attitude to work.
5. Inability to do the job which the employee was appointed to do.
6. Sleeping on the job.

Some of these may lead to instant dismissal where there has been gross misconduct, e.g. theft from a factory. Sometimes an employee may receive a written warning before dismissal.

## Unfair dismissal

Dismissal for the following reasons would be 'unfair':

1. *Pregnancy*. You can only be sacked if you are unable to do your job properly, e.g. a shelf stacker.
2. *Race*. A worker cannot be sacked on the grounds of race.
3. *Homosexuality*. If a worker is homosexual there is no reason why he or she should be sacked, unless it can be proved that it affects his or her standard of work.
4. *Union membership*. An employer cannot sack a worker for belonging to a trade union.
5. *Criminal record*. If an employer does not find out about an employee's criminal record until some time after employing him or her, the employer cannot sack the worker on these grounds unless it was a relevant crime.
6. *Religion*. An employee cannot be sacked on grounds of their religious beliefs.

## Women at work

The Equal Pay Act 1970, aimed to eliminate discrimination on grounds of sex in relation to pay, overtime, piecework rates and holiday entitlements. It gave all employees the right to equal treatment as that given to an employee of the opposite sex in the same employment who is doing the same or 'broadly similar' work.

The Sex Discrimination Act 1975, made sex discrimination unlawful in employment training and related matters.

The main problems for women as a group have been low pay and a concentration in low-paid occupations. Economic expansion in the UK from the 1950s onwards created more and more jobs for women. There has been a growth particularly in the proportion of married women at work, so that over half now work.

### Case Study—Mission impossible

Are women making real progress in the world of employment? Women represent 43 per cent of the British workforce, hold only 11 per cent of managerial positions, make up just 9 per cent of senior management, 5 per cent of directors and less than 1 per cent of chief executives! As the Hansard Society Commission's report 'Women at the top' boldly states, 'If boardrooms are where power and influence reside, then women are clearly excluded'.

Though there is no doubt that many of Britain's most influential chairmen recognize that more needs to be done to attract women to business and are actively promoting women to senior positions, this revolution might still be a struggle for some men who still think of the 'male as the breadwinner'.

*Questions*

1. Why do you think so few women are in senior positions in companies?
2. What provisions, encouragement, facilities and opportunities could organizations provide to encourage women to develop their careers?

The major problem for women is that they tend to work in industries where unions are weak, they are often unable to do overtime because of family commitments and their jobs are often part-time. Women are concentrated in a very narrow range of occupations. Catering, cleaning, hairdressing, bar work and other services occupy over half of women manual workers and office work employs a large proportion of non-manual workers.

A feature of the UK in recent years is that women now have more qualifications, which should lead to advancement in earnings. Women with better qualifications are choosing from a wider range of careers.

Today it is the fastest-growing industries which are taking most women into their senior ranks, e.g. the information industry (including public relations, computer services and the press), financial services, tourism and design. The

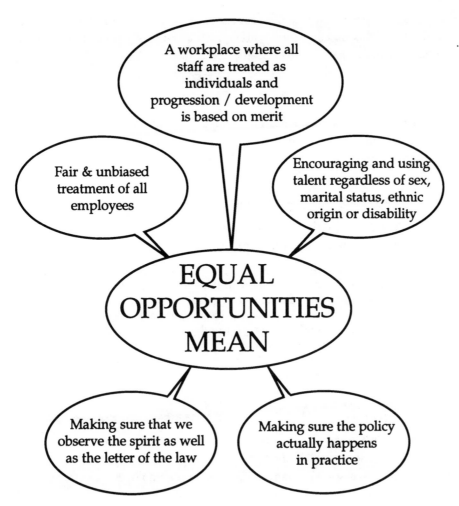

**Figure 12.13** Equal opportunities
(Source: Shell UK Ltd)

parts of the economy where women are rarest—upper and middle management in medium-sized and larger companies, especially in manufacturing—are generally those now entering into relative decline.

### Job splitting and job sharing

The practice of job splitting is most common in large offices where the employer finds it impossible to recruit full-time staff. A common arrangement is for the employer to employ staff who work alternate weeks. Another arrangement is for staff to use the same desk and equipment for different hours of the day.

Job sharing occurs when two employees agree to share a job. An example of this would be if 20 posts were offered, to be taken on by 40 workers who would share out the responsibility for each job as a pair. Job sharers are entitled to the full rights of a full-time worker such as rates of pay, maternity leave, holidays and sick pay.

## The Race Relations Act 1976

This act sought to eliminate discrimination of all kinds on the grounds of racial origin. It is illegal to discriminate in training, recruitment, employment and promotion.

### Case Study—Job satisfaction (1)

The following is an extract from an interview with a worker on the production line at a car factory:

> 'I find work here really boring. The pay is good but it has to be because the work is so tedious. I just try to think about what I'm going to do at the weekend or how I am going to spend my money. I feel that I am stuck with this job because there is nothing else going and all the time I am counting up the money against the hours. The problem is that we have to repeat the same task time after time and we don't get the chance to put something of our own personality into the work. I would like to be a footballer but I would never make the grade.'

*Questions*

1. Why do you think that job satisfaction might be low in a production line job?
2. What sort of compensation might an employer have to offer for low job satisfaction?
3. How might it be possible to increase job satisfaction for production line workers?

### Case Study—Job satisfaction (2)

The following is an extract from an interview with a textile worker who had been made redundant (from *Redundant Women* by Angela Coyle, The Women's Press, 1984):

> Roger Firth rarely had to recruit labour on the open market. Once employed, their people tended to draw in members of their own family. When people said that the factory was like 'family', there was some measure of truth in that, as well as indicating their attachment to the factory.
>
> I enjoyed every minute, because all my friends were on that section. We used to have a right laugh and joke and I miss them all now. We could chat when we were working, that's what I liked.

*Questions*

1.  What elements of job satisfaction are expressed in the above extracts?
2.  Why did the firm find it easy to recruit labour?
3.  Would you expect wages to be high or low in the above firm?

### Case Study—Contract of employment

The document in Fig. 12.14 is the first part of a copy of a contract of employment produced by Huntley, Boorne and Stevens.

What other details would you expect to be included in the contract under the Contract of Employment Act?

---

**HUNTLEY BOORNE & STEVENS LIMITED**
**PARTICULARS OF TERMS OF EMPLOYMENT**
**HOURLY PAID EMPLOYEES**

This document defines the terms and conditions for hourly paid employees of Huntley Boorne & Stevens Limited and is compiled in accordance with the requirements of the Contracts of Employment Act 1972 and the Amendments thereto under the Employment Protection Act 1975.

To: (Name) ...............................................................................

of (Address) .............................................................................

.............................................................................................

Job title: ...............................................................................

This Contract to take effect as at .................................................

your employment with Huntley Boorne & Stevens Limited having commenced

on .......................................................................................

1.  REMUNERATION

Your rate of pay and overtime rate is as established by the Domestic Agreement between the General and Municipal Workers' Union and the Company.

A copy of this Agreement is available for reference in the Personnel Department.

Your current rate of pay is £_____ per week of 40 hours, made up as follows:

.............................................................................................

and is paid weekly in arrears, normally on the Thursday.

Each payment will be accompanied by an itemised pay statement.

The pay week commences on Monday morning and ends on Sunday midnight.

In addition to the above rate of pay, the Company operates an Incentive Bonus Scheme for direct operatives. A copy is available in the Personnel Department for reference.

**Figure 12.14** The first part of a contract of employment produced by Huntley, Boorne and Stevens

### Case Study—The Sex Discrimination Act

The advertisement in Fig. 12.15 is commonly displayed in the job advertisement columns in newspapers.

*Questions*

1.  What is the purpose of the advertisement in Fig. 12.15?
2.  Collect adverts from the press which you think comply with the rules.
3.  Collect advertisements from the press which you think are trying to stretch the rules.

**Figure 12.15** An advertisement commonly displayed in the job advertisement columns of newspapers (Crown Copyright)

> # SEX
> ## DISCRIMINATION ACT, 1975
>
> No job advertisement which indicates or can reasonably be understood as indicating an intention to discriminate on ground of sex (eg by inviting applications only from males or only from females) may be accepted, unless
>
> 1. The job is for the purpose of a private householder or
> 2. It is a business employing fewer than six persons or
> 3. It is otherwise excepted from the requirements of the Sex Discrimination Act.
>
> A statement must be made at the time the advertisement is placed saying which of the exceptions in the Act is considered to apply.
>
> In addition to employment, the principal areas covered by the section of the Act which deals with advertisements are education, the supply of goods and services and the sale or letting of property.
>
> It is the responsibility of advertisers to ensure that advertisement content does not discriminate under the terms of the Sex Discrimination Act.

### Case Study—Industrial tribunals

Three members of the class will represent an industrial tribunal in the following exercise. Another two members of the class will represent the spokesperson for a firm which has sacked workers for various reasons. Another three members of the class should represent workers who claim to have been unfairly dismissed. It is the responsibility of the industrial tribunal to decide whether the cases represent fair or unfair dismissal in the light of the evidence.

For each case the class must write down the name of the person whose case is being heard, his or her age and job description, the reason for dismissal and the verdict of the panel with the reason given. The normal procedure will be for the panel to ask the employer's spokesperson to present the employer's side first and then for the employee to present his or her case.

*Information for the employer's spokesperson*

*Case 1*
Name: Bill Davis
Age: 22
Position: Accounts clerk

Bill has been working at the firm for two years. He is good at his job. He has been dismissed without notice for continually being late for work. Last year he was late for work on 103 occasions. He has repeatedly been warned about the offence. This year he has been late for work on 17 occasions (by the end of March). Last week you warned him not to be late again but on Friday he was seen leaving a chemist's shop 20 minutes after he should have reported for work. He was dismissed when he then turned up for work an hour late.

*Case 2*
Name: Sharron Foxwell
Age: 23
Position: Gardener in a garden centre

Sharron has been working for you for two years but has never been a very effective worker. She tends to take breaks that are too long and has a fairly casual attitude. She is now pregnant (two months) and so you have informed her that you no longer require her services—she has been dismissed immediately.

*Case 3*
Name: Sarah Groves
Age: 24
Position: Printer

Sarah has been working for the company for six years but is known to have a grudge against the supervisor. They have not been on speaking terms for several years. Last week somebody sprayed an abusive message with an aerosol on the canteen wall. Sarah was suspected and sacked immediately.

*Information for the employees' spokesperson*

*Case 1*
Name: Bill Davis
Age: 22
Position: Accounts clerk

You have been working at the firm for two years. You have been dismissed without notice. You are a single parent and have to take your child to a nursery every morning. Unfortunately the nursery is rarely open on time and this frequently makes you late for work. You cannot afford to pay someone to take your child to the nursery. You have been warned about your lateness but you feel that the personnel manager is picking on you, because other workers are also late and they are rarely told off.

Last Friday your child was sick. You left the child at your mother's and picked up some medicine, but by the time you got to work the personnel manager was standing there waiting for you to tell you that you were fired. You were so angry that you just walked off.

*Case 2*
Name: Sharron Foxwell
Age: 23
Position: Gardener in gardening centre

You have been working for two years. You enjoy the work very much and get on well with your fellow workers. You have just become pregnant and have been joking about it at work. You wanted to work for another four months, to have a few months off and then come back to work. It came as a bombshell to hear that you were being laid off because pregnant women were not allowed to work in the centre.

*Case 3*
Name: Sarah Groves
Age: 24
Job: Printer

You have been working for the company for six years. You enjoy work but there is one supervisor who really has it in for you and you don't get on at all. Last week you were present when a friend sprayed some graffiti about the supervisor on the canteen wall. You were blamed and as you would not split on a friend you have been given the sack.

## Case Study—French job advertisement

*Questions*

1. What type of post is being advertised in the advertisement in Fig. 12.16?
2. What sort of person are they looking for?
3. How would you go about applying for this job?

Le Groupe CGG (près de 3 milliards de C.A., 3500 personnes), leader mondial de la prospection pétrolière, opère sur les cinq continents. Nous recherchons pour notre siège basé à Massy, banlieue parisienne, un

# **t**raducteur - **r**édacteur

## DE LANGUE MATERNELLE ANGLAISE

Vous avez entre 25 et 35 ans et bénéficiez d'une formation supérieure (B.A., M.A., éventuellement post-graduate diploma in translation). Doté d'une première expérience, vous pratiquez le traitement de texte.

Au sein de notre département Communication/Promotion, vous traduirez nos textes publicitaires et rédigerez en anglais certains de nos documents.

Nous vous assurerons une formation technique spécifique à nos produits.

Ce poste vous intéresse, adressez-nous lettre, C.V. et photo - CGG Service du Personnel - 1, rue Léon Migaux - 91341 MASSY CEDEX.

MEDIAPA

## Compagnie Générale de Géophysique

**Figure 12.16** French job advertisement

## Questions

1. Complete the following sentences using the terms below:

Personnel        Sex Discrimination Act
Jobcentres        The Factories Act
Contract of employment        Health and safety inspectors
In-house training        Employment Protection Act
The Health and Safety at Work Act        Equal Pay Act
Industrial tribunal

(a) One effect of the . . . . . . . is that jobs must be advertised in such a way as to show equal favour to both men and women.
(b) . . . . . . . . applies to all premises using mechanical machinery.
(c) When workers learn skills at the workplace, this is known as . . . . . . . .

(d)  The . . . . . . . . department of a firm has responsibility for the safety, training, recruitment and welfare of employees.

(e)  The Department of Employment supervises high-street . . . . . . . .

(f)  The . . . . . . . states that both sexes should get the same wage for doing the same jobs or jobs involving broadly similar work.

(g)  An . . . . . . . . consists of representatives of the trade unions and employers and an independent chairperson.

(h)  Employment starts when an employee enters into a . . . . . . . .

(i)  The . . . . . . . lays down the employer's duty to ensure safety at work.

(j)  This Act is supervised by . . . . . . . .

(k)  The . . . . . . . lays down minimum periods of notice that must be given when workers are made redundant.

2.

(a)  You work in the personnel department of a large department store. You are preparing a job application form to send to applicants. You must design this form in order to find out as much information as possible relevant to their employment with you. Set out the form in a neat and clear way.

(b)  Explain why you would require eight of the items of information you have asked for.

3.  Figure 12.17 below is a job outline produced by the personnel manager of Huntley, Boorne and Stevens. Write a letter of application for the job.

4.  Alana owns a small clothes shop in a high street. She works in the shop and employs two sales assistants. Alana has to obey the Health and Safety at

HUNTLEY, BOORNE & STEVENS

JOB TITLE:              Machine Operator

FUNCTION:               Aerosol Department.

RESPONSIBLE TO:         Aerosol Operators Manager

AGE INDICATOR:          18 or over.

HOURS OF WORK:          Monday to Wednesday   2.00 p.m. - 12.00 midnight
                        Thursday              2.00 p.m. - 11.00 p.m.

DATE OF APPOINTMENT:    As soon as possible.

CLOSING DATE:           12th November, 1986.

APPLICATION TO          Applications in writing to :

                        Mr A. Robinson,
                        Personnel Manager.
                        Huntley, Boorne & Stevens,
                        Headley Road East,
                        Woodley.

A. Robinson,
Personnel Manager.

**Figure 12.17**  Job description          AR/BRB.  5.11.86

Work Act 1974. How will this Act affect her as an employer?
(*Source*: London East Anglian Group)

5. You are the personnel manager of a local high street bank. You must design a job advertisement to be placed in the local paper. The job is for a school-leaver to start off a career in banking. Make sure you state the qualifications you would expect and a sensible starting salary.

6. Haylake Waste Disposal Services Ltd of Faversham-on-Sea specialize in the treatment and disposal of industrial waste. The directors have decided to apply to the Department of Trade and Industry for a licence to process toxic waste. This would mean that the company would dispose of materials which are more dangerous. If the company is successful in obtaining the licence it will mean a major expansion of the company's activities. Imagine that you are Haylake's personnel manager and so responsible for looking after its workforce.

   (a) State the main functions that make up the job of personnel manager.

   (b) What difficulties might you experience in your job if the company is successful in its application for the licence to process the more dangerous toxic waste?

   (*Source*: Southern Examining Group)

7. Rank the following in order of importance to you when apply for a job:

   (a) Good rate of pay            (g) Good working environment
   (b) Opportunity for promotion   (h) Opportunity to be creative
   (c) Good holidays               (i) Independence
   (d) Prestige                    (j) Responsibility
   (e) Good fringe benefits        (k) Short distance to travel to work
   (f) Job security

8. Which of the following cases probably involve 'fair' and which 'unfair' dismissal?

   (a) John Jones is sacked for wearing a 'gay pride' badge.
   (b) The accountant is sacked for taking money out of the wages account.
   (c) A young apprentice is sacked for deliberately sabotaging a machine.
   (d) Melissa O'Rourke, a company wages officer, is sacked when she becomes pregnant.
   (e) The works manager is sacked for regularly pinching women's bottoms at work.
   (f) Two members of the night shift are sacked for sleeping at work.

9. Explain the main laws relating to a worker's rights at work.

## Coursework

1. How do local firms check the time worked by employees? Do a study of the different methods used to check different workers.

2. How do local firms motivate workers? Do a study of the monetary and non-monetary incentives used by firms to encourage work.

3. What does a personnel manager/union official do? Find out the typical working pattern of these employees.

4. How do local firms train workers? Do a study of the in-house and outside training of workers done by a local firm.

5. How do people find work?

    Interview people to find out what methods they used to find work. Interview a personnel manager to find the most effective methods of recruiting labour.

6. What is the purpose of an industrial tribunal?

    Study articles in newspapers to monitor cases which have been before industrial tribunals. Study the work of a local industrial tribunal.

7. What happens when workers become redundant?

    Study the local newspaper for an example of a firm laying off workers. Interview the firm to find out the causes of the cutbacks and how the workers were laid off. What scope is there for the redundant workers to find alternative employment in the area?

8. What is the purpose of a jobcentre? Interview the local jobcentre manager to find out how it functions and what it does.

# 13

# Industrial relations in the workplace

In this chapter we will be looking at the way in which the personnel department and the trade unions communicate with each other to handle industrial relations.

Industrial relations are concerned with communication between the representatives of employers and the representatives of employees. Much of industrial relations will be based on employees and employers working together. Indeed, part of European Community policy today is to create a system of shared responsibility of employers and employees for working practices, conditions and other areas of working life. Employers and employees, however, do not always agree and this can lead to argument and disputes.

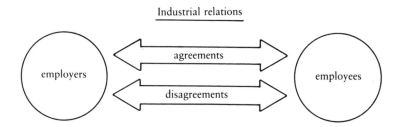

Figure 13.1  Communication

*Task*

Can you give examples of things that employers and employees will generally agree about. Give examples of things that they sometimes disagree about. Why does this difference of interest arise?

From the employer's point of view, industrial relations are about making sure that relations are smooth, while having the right to manage. The management will want to be able to plan for the future, to organize new projects, to make profits and to keep shareholders happy.

From the trade unions' point of view, the aim will be to secure the best possible conditions of work for members. Unions know that the decisions a

**Figure 13.2** Bill Morris, General
Secretary of Transport and General
Workers Union

firm makes will affect the livelihoods of workers and their families. Unions will
therefore try to increase the say they have in how a company runs.

Figure 13.3 sets out a diagram showing some of the main aims of a trade
union. Collect newspaper articles and show examples of how trade unions
today are pursuing these aims.

## The early days of trade unions

In the nineteenth century people worked for very long hours and working
conditions were sometimes degrading and unacceptable by modern standards.
Groups of employees joined together in the early unions to try and protect
their members. Over the years unions grew in strength and numbers. By using
the strike weapon and other methods, they were able to push up the wages of
members and improve working conditions.

In recent years, however, the number of people belonging to trade unions
has declined. In the later 1970s there were 12 million trade union members. In
the early 1990s there are fewer than 9 million.

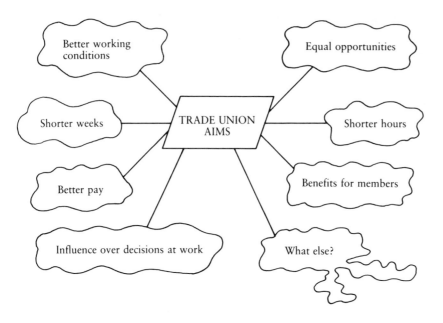

**Figure 13.3** The aims of trade unions

There are a number of reasons for the decline of trade union membership:

1. Trade unions are particularly popular in large factories and plant. Today there are far fewer manufacturing units employing thousands of people. Make a list of the units that have disappeared, e.g. coal mines, munitions factories, textile mills, etc.
2. More people today are employed in smaller units, often in the service industries.
3. Today there are far more part-time jobs. Part-timers are less likely to join a union.
4. People are better off today. Some of the early hardships that encouraged people to join trade unions have disappeared.
5. Women are more important in the working population. Statistics show that women are less likely to join trade unions. (Why do you think this is so?)
6. New jobs and skills require more flexibility. Employers may be reluctant to encourage trade unions in their place of work if this reduces flexibility. For example, an employer may want an employee to do lots of different jobs.

The dominance of the blue-collar (manual) workers has been reduced by the decline of manufacturing and the growth of white collar (service) work. Of the working population, 54 per cent is now made up of women, many of whom have part-time jobs. With the growth of skilled jobs more people are now in the higher social group. With higher incomes, their own homes and greater ownership of shares, affluent workers are less likely to identify with the traditional aims of trade unions.

## The main actors in industrial relations

### The union side

#### *The president of the union*

The president is elected nationally to represent the whole membership in dealing with employers, government and other unions.

#### *The full-time official*

An official is appointed and paid by the union and will cover a number of firms in a particular area. The officer has close contact with union headquarters.

#### *The convenor*

Originally the convenor was the shop steward who called for union meetings in a large workplace. Today the term simply means the senior shop steward. It is an important post and most convenors hold the job for long periods of time.

#### *The shop stewards*

Factories in many trades are split up into areas called shops, e.g. the cutting shop, the sewing shop, etc.

Each shop would elect at least one steward to represent them in the workplace. The work would be part-time and hardly ever paid.

### Case Study—A day in the life of a shop steward

Sylvia Holt is a machine operator on production lines making metal packaging at Huntley, Boorne and Stevens. She has been with the company for 20 years. She is also a shop steward for the GMB.

| | |
|---|---|
| 7.15 a.m. | Clock in for work. |
| 7.30 a.m. | Start work on line. |
| 8.55 a.m. | A worker complains that her bonus has been underpaid. She explains to me what job she was doing and how many trays she has done. I explain the situation to the supervisor who then takes it further. |
| 9.05 a.m. | I return to my job. |
| 9.20 a.m. | Supervisor returns informing me that the worker is owed £1.05 |

| | |
|---|---|
| 9.45 a.m. | Tea break—I also inform the worker of the amount she is owed. |
| 10.00 a.m. | Tea break over—start back on line. |
| 11.05 a.m. | Another worker comes to me. He has caught his trousers on a broken wooden box. I take him down to the personnel department to report the accident. He is given the option of buying a new pair, with the firm paying a percentage, or getting them repaired at the firm's expense. I then go back up on to the shop floor and investigate whether the broken box can be repaired or needs to be thrown away. |
| 12.20 p.m. | Lunch break. |
| 12.50 p.m. | Lunch break over—start back on line. |
| 14.00 p.m. | A worker tells me he has been working alongside two other men for over a week and that they have been offered one hour's overtime a night, but he has not been offered any. I tell the worker to go back to his job and assure him that I will go and see the supervisor. I explain the situation to the supervisor and I am told that the worker is only helping out in the department. I then state that if he is good enough to work on the line in the daytime with them, helping out, it is only fair that he should be offered the overtime as well. The supervisor agrees and the one hour overtime is given. I then inform the worker of his overtime. |
| 14.20 p.m. | I return to my work. |
| 16.30 p.m. | Clock out—day is over. |

*Questions*

1. What do the letters GMB stand for? What type of employees does the union represent?
2. Does Sylvia work full-time for the union?
3. What is the leading shop steward in a large workplace called?
4. How many hours did Sylvia work? How much of this time was spent in her work as a shop steward?
5. Does the company pay Sylvia for her union work? How does the company benefit from Sylvia's union work? How important is it to the company to have shop stewards?
6. Who does Sylvia represent? How does this group benefit?
7. Who does Sylvia negotiate with in the case study?
8. Do you think that Sylvia is powerful in the workplace? Explain your answer.

### The management side

*The board of directors*

This is a committee chosen by the shareholders to represent their interests.

*The managing director*

This is the senior director with the responsibility for the day-to-day running of the business.

*The personnel manager*

This is the manager responsible for recruitment, training, welfare and safety. The personnel manager will be at the hub of day-to-day dealings with the unions.

*The charge hand*

This is a working supervisor responsible for a particular group of employees in an organization.

## Day-to-day industrial relations

On a daily basis the main industrial relations bargaining takes place between the personnel department and a shop stewards' committee. Normally they would meet regularly once a week and thrash out issues such as the following:

1. Pay
2. Bonuses
3. The working environment
3. Disputes
4. Work schedules
5. Grievances
7. Health and safety at work
8. Hours
9. Production targets

## Major industrial relations issues

As well as local bargaining which is concerned with small-scale industrial relations, larger issues may be thrashed out on an industry-wide scale. Wages for government employees, for example, are normally agreed upon at an annual pay award. The parties involved will normally be the central executive of a union and employers' leaders.

- An **executive** is a body given the power to put decisions into effect, i.e. to make things happen.

## Union organization

This varies considerably, but a typical form is shown in Fig. 13.4.

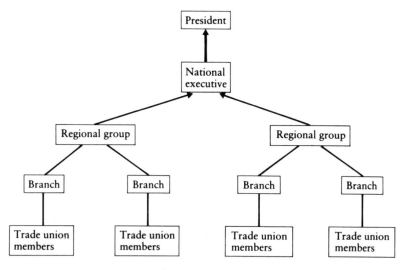

**Figure 13.4**  A typical union structure

Groups of workers are members of a branch. They choose branch officials to represent them. The branches also choose representatives to represent them at a regional committee. Regional groups then choose representatives to go to an annual conference. The annual conference makes decisions relating to the industry and chooses a full-time body of officials known as the national executive. The top official in the union is the president.

The National Union of Mineworkers is a good example of how a union is organized. The local branch is based on the colliery and the branch personnel deal with the day-to-day problems, disputes and many minor matters. Shop stewards as such are not found in mining and the branch is based on the pit and includes in its membership all manual and craft grades; the branch officers do the job of the shop steward in other industries. There is one line of communication from the branch up through the area coalfield office to the national centre.

### Official union action

This is action which has been approved by the union's executive.

### Unofficial union action

Unofficial action takes place when members carry out actions not approved by the union. An example of this might be when local stewards call out workers in a lightning strike.

In the UK, most industrial action is unofficial but only short-lived. Union funds cannot be used for unofficial action, because it is not approved by union officials. Unofficial action will generally take place if local unionists feel that the national union is out of touch with their feelings or if they want to act quickly.

### Case Study—Number of strikes falls

In May 1991, the Advisory, Conciliation and Arbitration Service (see page 266) reported that the number of strikes had fallen to a 55 year low. This reflected a shift in power to the employers. Rising unemployment was a cause of the reduction in strike action. Unions were aware of the need to preserve jobs in a period of recession. Employers had become far more self-confident and were prepared to dismiss strikers. Another factor was the government law that made

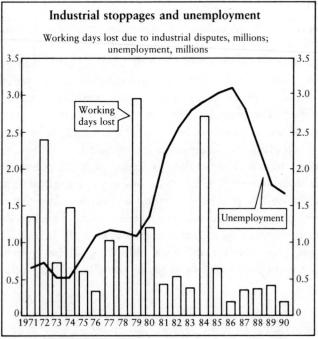

**Figure 13.5** Industrial stoppages and unemployment

The high level of strikes in 1979 was a product of the 'winter of discontent' and that of 1984 was due to the miners' dispute

unions ballot members before calling a strike. Unions had lost one in four members in recent years, especially in traditional industries and were unable to recruit effectively in growing areas of employment.

*Questions*

1.  List five factors which have led to the reduction in the number of strikes. Which of these do you regard to be the most important?
2.  In what year were the most working days lost? How many? In what year were the least working days lost? How many?
3.  How does the level of unemployment affect the likelihood of strike action?
4.  Do you think that it is a good thing that unions should have strike ballots? Explain.
5.  What are the 'traditional industries' that have declined?
6.  What are the 'growing areas of employment?'

# Types of trade union

There are four main types of trade union (see Table 13.1).

1.  Craft unions
2.  Industrial unions
3.  General unions
4.  White collar unions.

It is important to point out that many unions do not fit easily into a particular class. Often they have characteristics common to more than one class.

| Craft unions | Industrial unions | General unions | White collar unions |
|---|---|---|---|
| Musicians' Union | National Union of Mineworkers | Transport and General Workers' Union | National Union of Teachers |
| Pattern Weavers Society | National Union of Railwaymen | General, Municipal, Boiler- makers and Allied Trades Union | Banking, Insurance and Finance Union |
| Associated Metal- workers' Union | | | |

Table 13.1  Examples of the four types of trade union

### Craft unions

The earliest type of union in this country was the craft union. These unions were made up of highly skilled craftsmen in a particular trade. Often these groups were mutual benefit societies before the welfare state came into being. Subscriptions could be quite high and in return the union would provide sick pay, unemployment pay, a pension and other benefits. These unions are less important in the UK today and their membership is relatively small (one or two of these have under ten members).

### Industrial unions

Industrial unionism is common in many European countries, notably West Germany (as was). The economy is divided up into industrial sectors and workers in each sector belong to the industrial union for that sector. Until 1985, the National Union of Mineworkers was often quoted as an example of an industrial union. (However, in 1985, a rival union, the Union of Democratic Mineworkers, was formed and also there are smaller unions such as the pit deputies' union NACODS.) The advantage of an industrial union is that it caters for all workers in an industry whatever their job. Negotiation with employers is greatly simplified and all workers are united in their efforts.

### General unions

These are some of the largest unions in the UK today. They recruit workers from several industries. They include semi-skilled and unskilled workers. A particular advantage of this form of union is that it gives strength to workers who would have little power on their own. It gives them the opportunity to belong to a well-funded and organized body.

### White collar unions

White collar workers are non-manual workers such as civil servants, bank workers and teachers, as opposed to blue collar workers, who do manual work.

White collar unions have been the most rapidly expanding groups in the 1980s and 1990s. This has happened with the growth of the tertiary sector of the economy and the expansion of large bodies of office staff in insurance companies, banks, company administration units, the Civil Service, etc.

## Unions and Europe

The Social Charter of the European Community sets out the right of all employees to freedom of association and collective bargaining. All employers and employees within the European Community have the right to join professional organizations freely. In addition, employers and employees are free to bargain and make collective agreements over such matters as wages. In the event of disagreement employees have the right to take collective action such as a strike.

If the levels on which trade unions and employers speak to each other and negotiate wages in the EC are compared, there is no standard picture. In Belgium and the Netherlands talks are highly-organized at national level and cover several branches of industry together. The parties sit at a table, recognizing their joint responsibility for the employment situation. Possible changes in working hours are discussed and, in Belgium, the minimum wage determined. In Germany there would be a storm of protest if the government tried to intervene in wage negotiation, in Italy and the Netherlands the government is sometimes involved.

In principle, employees in all countries have a right to be consulted, to express their views and, in differing degrees, to share in management.

- **Co-determination** involves employees' views being listened to and being incorporated into joint decision making with managers.

The extent to which co-determination operates in Europe varies a lot. Clearly there are many advantages to allowing employees to have a say in order to increase the partnership at work.

In Germany, the right to a say in management decisions, which has existed in the iron and steel industry since 1951, was extended in 1976 to include joint stock companies (private and public companies) employing more than 2000 workers. Since that time, the so-called 'works director' has represented the interests of the employees on the management committee. Workers and salaried employees are represented in equal numbers with the shareholders. In the event of a tie, the vote of the chairperson, representing the interests of the management, decides.

## Union finance

Unions get the bulk of their finance from members' subscriptions. They will also have a number of investments which can be quite substantial if they pay pensions to members. Unions will also try to build up a reserve in order to pay out strike pay and organize publicity in the event of industrial action. Day-to-day union expenditure goes on the maintenance of union buildings, staff salaries, publicity, administration and running expenses such as telephone and electricity bills. Frequently, unions will also run an education section and will make donations to other groups such as workers in similar trades overseas. Some unions will also make a contribution to the Trades Union Congress (TUC).

# Forms of union action

Unionists have a number of types of action available to them to put pressure on employers.

### Picketing

Primary picketing is lawful. This involves members of a union who are on strike standing outside a firm's entrance and trying to persuade other workers not to cross the picket line.

Secondary picketing is not lawful and occurs when workers from one firm try to persuade workers at a firm not involved with the strike not to go to work. Secondary picketing takes place when unionists try to spread the impact of their action.

### Withdrawal of goodwill

This is when workers become obstructive about things which need cooperation.

### Go-slow

Workers take their time over the work they are doing.

### Work-to-rule

Workers stick to the book of rules relating to their particular job in order to reduce efficiency. For instance, railway workers may check that every carriage door is firmly closed at each station.

### Ban on overtime

Workers refuse to work more than the hours laid out in their contract of employment.

### Official strike

Workers cease work with the authority of the union.

### Unofficial strike

A group of workers cease work without the approval of the union.

## Sit-in

The workers occupy their workplace. If a factory has been threatened with closure, the workers may remain at work operating a work-in, i.e. they refuse to stop work.

## Blacking

This occurs when members of a firm refuse to handle particular materials or work with particular machinery.

## The closed shop

Unions can put pressure on management to operate a closed-shop policy whereby all workers must belong to the same union. Sometimes the employers encourage this set-up because it is easier to bargain with just one union.

## Demarcation disputes

Sometimes unions have disputes with each other about 'who does what' at work. Unions are sometimes very protective about the work their members should rightfully be doing.

# Forms of employer action

The employers can put pressure on trade unions to accept their authority in several ways. The most obvious way is to threaten to stop privileges such as bonuses. Employers can also threaten to close down a plant which they think is making a loss. They may say that a pay rise would make the firm uncompetitive. If there were no other jobs in the area, the union would be in a weak position.

### Other weapons that employers can use

*The sack*. The employers cease to employ certain workers.
*Suspension*. Workers can be laid off without pay. This could be to encourage fresh thinking about the dispute, or as a form of punishment.
*Lockouts*. Employers refuse to let workers on to the premises.

### Case Study

Look at the article overleaf in Fig. 13.6.

# Crunch talks at strike firm

### By RICHARD SPENCER

CRUNCH talks were due to be held yesterday in a bid to try and resolve a strike which has stopped production at a Harrogate engineering company.

More than 170 steelmen from Octavius Atkinson, in Prospect Road, Starbeck, went out on strike on Monday over a pay dispute with management.

Pickets at the factory gates yesterday morning said their shop stewards had agreed to meet with management for the first negotiations since the strike began.

The results of the negotiations would then be put to the striking workforce by union leaders at a mass meeting at lunchtime today.

The dispute started just before Christmas, when a four per cent. pay offer was rejected by the workforce in a secret ballot.

The unions want an £18 a week rise and say the four per cent. offer — amounting to £3.50 a week—is an "insult."

Pickets on duty at the factory gates have turned away delivery lorries all week and production inside has ground to a halt.

"The lads thought the pay offer was not enough," explained shop steward, Mr. Bob Roddam.

"There have been flat weeks for the past eight months and the men haven't been earning bonus or overtime payments.

"Average earnings are less now than they were three years ago and we are prepared to stay out until we get a reasonable offer.

"The flat wage rate is so low a married man is entitled to a Family Income Supplement.

"This is not a militant place but we have been pushed into taking action."

Octavius Atkinson's managing director, Mr. Michael Reffitt, said there were about 40 men in the factory carrying out maintenance and a limited amount of work.

Mr. Reffitt warned that if no agreement could be reached the dispute could hit the order book.

"We are dealing with a very serious situation. In today's market there is the risk that clients may decide to cancel orders.

"We won't turn away orders but we can lose them very easily."

Mr. Reffitt said annual pay and conditions negotiations had not been concluded but were broken off by the strike decision before the company had made its final offer.

Mr. Reffitt said he was "anxious" to reach a settlement with the striking workforce and put an end to the damaging dispute.

**Figure 13.6** Newspaper article about a dispute at Octovius Atkinson in Harrogate (Source: Harrogate Advertiser)

*Questions*

1. What is the dispute about?
2. What is meant by the following terms:
   pickets          overtime payments
   pay offer        flat wage rate
   bonus            dispute
3. What factors give (a) the union and (b) the management, strength in this particular dispute?
4. Use a computer newspaper package to produce your own report on the settlement of the dispute. You are allowed to use a maximum of 300 words.

## The Trades Union Congress

This is the annual meeting of the trade union movement. All the major trade unions are members of the TUC and send a number of delegates to the conference depending on the size of their membership. The annual congress takes place in September every year, at seaside resorts like Scarborough and Blackpool, where there is a lot of hotel space after the holiday season is finished and where large conference halls are available. The conference lasts for a week and during this time a number of motions and issues are debated.

The TUC chooses full-time officials including a president and vice-president and has its own headquarters offices. The TUC is an important organization because it reflects the general feelings of the trade union movement. It is particularly active in negotiation of industrial disputes. It offers advice and help to unions with problems and tries to iron out disagreements between unions. It acts as a pressure group trying to influence government and employers.

The annual congress discusses many things. The TUC is not just concerned with wages. The congress will discuss subjects as varied as education, the Third World, privatization, AIDS and alcohol.

The TUC does not have a great deal of power. Individual unions are not bound by its decisions and the only threat it can use is to expel a union from the TUC.

## Professional associations

Many workers belong to a professional association. These are organizations that do many of the same things as trade unions but are not registered as a trade union. They tend to cover better-paid, white collar workers. An example is the British Medical Association (BMA) which negotiates for doctors. Professional associations also try to set standards for members and to insist on a high qualification for membership.

## Employers' organizations

Like trade unions, employers' organizations do many things, the most important of which is collective bargaining. Faced by large and powerful trade unions small employers would be at a disadvantage if they had to stand alone. An employers' association bargains on behalf of many firms. Other things that it does include:

1. Pooling ideas and funds for research.
2. Setting up industry training schools.
3. Discussing common interests and problems, e.g. the threat of competition from other countries.
4. Providing a collective voice to raise industry-wide problems with government and other bodies.

## The Confederation of British Industry (CBI)

The CBI is the employers' equivalent of the TUC. It too has permanent officials and an annual conference. The leader of the CBI is its elected director-general. The CBI is represented on government working parties looking at industrial matters. Leaders of the CBI, the TUC and the government meet to discuss industrial policy.

The CBI produces a number of booklets about health and safety, international trade, small firms and other matters. It is the mouthpiece of employers and its views on such things as taxation, inflation, unemployment, etc. are closely followed by the press and the government. For example, in 1991 the director-general of the CBI hit the headlines with his criticism of high interest rates.

## The government and industrial relations

This topic is dealt with in more detail in Chapter 15. Government has passed laws on industrial relations concerning:

- Health and safety at work
- Discrimination
- Training
- Employment of the disabled
- Employment of young people
- Dismissal and redundancy
- Pay
- Industrial action
- Restrictions at work such as the closed shop

A closed shop is an agreement between employer and employees that an employee must belong to a particular trade union.

## The Advisory, Conciliation and Arbitration Service (ACAS)

This body can be used by both employers and employees. It was used in the ambulance drivers strike in 1990, as well as in over 50 000 disputes involving individuals and groups that year.

ACAS is managed by a council of nine members—three chosen by the TUC, three chosen by the CBI and three who are independent.

In an industrial dispute in which there is deadlock, the parties can ask ACAS to help. Sometimes the parties might allow ACAS to look at the problem and come up with a solution that is 'binding'. At other times, ACAS might simply be asked to make recommendations.

Arbitration is the process through which parties in a dispute allow a third party to make a decision for them.

### Case Study—Gloom in Germany over seven per cent wage deal

In May 1991, the employers and the engineering workers union in Germany agreed to a seven per cent wage increase. The employers felt that giving in to the demand was better than facing a full-blown industrial conflict.

The government felt that the settlement was a disaster because the wage increase was higher than the level of productivity and would set the standard for other industries. It would undoubtedly push prices up.

One of the employers said that the effect of the rise would be to reduce employment and to make it difficult for firms to invest in the

east. Seven per cent would now be the target for all smaller unions and sectors.

*Questions*

1.  What evidence is given in the article that the wage rise could cause problems?
2.  How might the wage increase affect the following?
    (a)  Engineering workers
    (b)  Engineering employers
    (c)  Other workers
    (d)  Other employers
    (e)  Consumers
    (f)  Other countries that compete with Germany
    (g)  The German economy
    (h)  People living in eastern Germany

# Questions

1.  Complete the following sentences using the terms below:

Shop steward                 Craft union
Unofficial strike            Industrial union
President                    Branch
General union                Official strike
White collar union

(a)  A strike that is recognized by the executive of the union is called an . . . . . . . .
(b)  A . . . . . . . . is made up of highly-skilled workers.
(c)  Local workers in a particular union are members of a . . . . . . . . of the trade union.
(d)  The executive officer who acts as the figurehead for the trade union is known as the union . . . . . . . .
(e)  An . . . . . . . . tends to be short and can flare up with little notice.
(f)  Factory-floor workers will be represented by a . . . . . . . . in day-to-day negotiations with management.
(g)  A . . . . . . . . is made up of workers from several different industries.
(h)  Clerks, teachers and bank employees would all be examples of workers who could be members of a . . . . . . . .
(i)  An . . . . . . . . is made up of all the workers in the same industry.

2.  The following are all examples of industrial action that could be used by a trade union.

(a)  Strike                  (c)  Blacking
(b)  Work-to-rule            (d)  Overtime ban

Explain which you would use in each of the following situations and why you would use the particular method. (Perhaps you would do something different.)

(a) You are the shop stewards' leader in a company producing confectionery. Your firm has an important order to meet for an overseas buyer. Currently your firm is refusing to allow a six per cent wage increase which is equivalent to the rise that workers in a competing firm have just been given.

(b) You are the shop stewards' leader in a firm that has just introduced some new highly advanced machinery. The machinery will increase output but the management is expecting workers to use it at the old wage rates. Introducing the new machinery will make it necessary to make 10 workers redundant.

(c) You are the union representative in a large office. It is a particularly hot summer and you have asked for an extra quarter of an hour break in the middle of the afternoon. The management side argues that this is not necessary.

(d) You work in a leisure centre in which there are only a few members of your union. The management is insisting that you work at the weekend as well as during the week.

3. Suggest how each of the following might 'work to rule'.

(a) Check-out operator at a supermarket
(b) School caretaker
(c) Schoolteacher
(d) Refuse collector
(e) Footballer
(f) Taxi driver
(g) Prime Minister
(h) Actor

4. The following is a list of employees at the company that you work for. Enter this information into a computer database.

| Name | Age | Years with company | Department | Weekly wage | Overtime pay | Days away |
|---|---|---|---|---|---|---|
| Jones | 53 | 25 | Production | 150 | 50 | 6 |
| Patel | 34 | 10 | Production | 120 | 40 | 2 |
| Creek | 61 | 40 | Production | 160 | 20 | 74 |
| Byers | 61 | 40 | Production | 160 | 40 | 1 |
| Deer | 42 | 12 | Sales | 200 | 20 | 3 |
| Cant | 38 | 18 | Sales | 200 | 20 | 14 |
| Peters | 49 | 2 | Office | 150 | 0 | 30 |
| Davis | 60 | 1 | Production | 120 | 0 | 12 |
| Cribb | 24 | 4 | Accounts | 300 | 0 | 6 |
| Marks | 45 | 20 | Accounts | 450 | 0 | 0 |
| Hood | 23 | 3 | Marketing | 400 | 0 | 0 |
| Ali | 27 | 7 | Accounts | 400 | 0 | 1 |
| Plodd | 30 | 6 | Production | 300 | 20 | 5 |
| Dunn | 35 | 1 | Production | 200 | 50 | 14 |

(a)   Sort the database into alphabetical order.
(b)   Sort the database into descending order of absence from work.
(c)   Sort the database into descending order of pay per week.
(d)   Imagine that you have been asked to cut down the labour force by two employees. Who will you cut out? Produce a report to justify your actions to the managing director.
(e)   Remove the two employees that you have decided to make redundant from your database. Another group of students can now search the database to find out who you have removed. They could represent the trade union. They may disagree with your decision. This could form the basis for a role play activity.

5.   For this activity the class must work in two groups. One group represents the management negotiation team of the West Wales Assurance Company and the other group represents the union negotiators.

The union and management are worried about absenteeism and illness. The workforce has been suffering from headaches, dry skin and a general feeling of drowsiness at work. Outside experts have been called in and they have reported on a number of 'building-related illnesses'. (See Fig. 13.7.)

The building is air-conditioned, windows cannot be opened and the air that is recirculated makes workers feel sick and drowsy.

The glue in the carpet contains formaldehyde, which causes headaches and the photocopier produces toxic fumes. Water in the pipes has become contaminated and produces bacteria which seep out into the air system. Eye complaints stem from the various chemicals present in the air which react with the rays that come from fluorescent lighting.

You are told that this sort of situation is not uncommon in modern offices. In 1984, there was an outbreak of illness at the Public Records Office in West London. The problem was traced to the air-conditioning system. More than £100,000 was spent on the clean-up and the building was closed for 10 weeks.

Each side must decided what the key issues are. Why is the situation a problem to the people you represent? What solution would you like to see? Try to negotiate.

# Coursework

1.   Find out what contribution a shop steward makes to his or her workplace. Pose the coursework as a question: 'What contribution does the shop steward make to industrial relations?' Make sure that you interview the shop steward and other relevant people. A similar assignment could be done on a personnel manager.
2.   What is the industrial relations machinery at a local plant, office, or factory? Carry out research to find out how negotiations are organized between employers and employees.

**Figure 13.7**  Some causes of 'building-related illnesses': 1. contaminated air from the air-conditioning. 2. Chemicals in the air reacting with the rays from the fluorescent lighting. 3. Windows that cannot be opened. 4. Toxic fumes from the photocopier. 5. Formaldehyde from the glue in the carpets. 6. Bacteria from contaminated water in the pipes

3.  What happened in a local industrial dispute? Study a local dispute over pay or conditions. Use newspaper cuttings and eye witness accounts to build up your data bank.

# 14

# Business in an international setting

Business activity takes place against a wider background of world trade.

1. Many businesses based in the UK are owned by overseas shareholders or are offshoots of foreign companies.
2. Many UK firms buy raw materials and supplies from overseas.
3. Many UK firms face overseas competition.
4. Many UK firms sell their products or services overseas.
5. Many UK businesses have offshoots overseas and foreign companies have UK shareholders.

In recent years we have become particularly aware of the impact of the world market on business life in the UK. When the world market prospers, international economies benefit, companies in those markets benefit and individuals benefit.

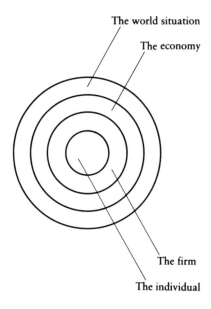

**Figure 14.1** The world market impacts on business life

## Imports and exports

For centuries the United Kingdom has gained enormously from international trade. We purchase goods and services from other countries and in return we sell them goods and services produced here.

- An **import** is a purchase by UK citizens from overseas.
- An **export** is a sale by UK citizens to a member of another country.

### Visible and invisible trade

For the purposes of classification we call the tangible goods (things that you can touch and see) that we trade, visible items. We call the services that we trade, invisible items.

*Task*

Which of the following are visibles (goods) and which are invisibles (services)?

| | | | | |
|---|---|---|---|---|
| Whisky | Cars | Banking | Textiles | Insurance |
| Furniture | Stationery | Transport | Metals | Post |

### Why do countries trade?

Countries trade in order to benefit from each other's resources and skills. In the UK we are very good at producing whisky (mainly because of climate), Land Rovers (because of skill and efficiency) and insurance policies (because of long years of experience). We are not so good at producing rice (because of climate), motorbikes (because of lack of efficiency compared to other countries) and snow tyres (because of lack of experience).

International trade is an example of how we can gain from specialization. Let us look at specialization to see how it works.

A tennis player is not only good at her sport, she is also a top class accountant. However, she concentrates on her tennis and hires an accountant to do her bookwork because tennis is her best line. It would take her a week to do all her paperwork. In this time she would lose £5,000 in earnings, whereas it only costs her £800 a year to hire an accountant.

In the same way, in the UK we concentrate our resources into our most efficient lines of production such as banking, insurance and microtechnology. By trading these goods on world markets we are able to buy things which we could only make in an inefficient way when compared to other countries such as cricket bats, pineapples and washing machines.

Other reasons why we trade include the following:

1.  Some items, such as scarce minerals, are impossible to obtain naturally in the UK.
2.  To foster good relations with other countries.
3.  To earn foreign currency.
4.  Because we cannot fully supply our own market in many items.

## The balance of payments

Exports bring money into the UK, whereas imports lead to an outflow of money.

The UK has always done well on her invisible trading account. This is because we developed a worldwide reputation for commercial services. Some of our major invisible earnings come from the following:

1.  Selling insurance policies overseas.
2.  Banking services to foreigners.
3.  Carrying goods for foreign companies by sea and air.
4.  Tourists spending money in the UK.
5.  Money earned on investments overseas in the form of interest and dividends.

On the news every month we hear that the UK has made a surplus on invisible trade, showing that we have sold more invisible services than we have bought. The figures for a particular month might be, for example:

| | |
|---|---|
| Invisible exports | £100 billion |
| Invisible imports | £80 billion |
| Invisible surplus | £20 billion |

At the same time, the UK frequently makes a loss on her visible trade. In the early 1990s the UK ran a very high loss on its visible account. For the first time since the industrial revolution, the UK has started to import more manufactured goods than it sells. There are a number of reasons for this. For example, we need to import goods that are difficult to produce in this country, e.g. agricultural products such as grapes, oranges and sunflower seeds. It has also been argued that UK manufacturers have failed to produce goods and services at competitive prices and have neglected some important non-price factors such as after-sales service and meeting delivery dates. It is also argued that insufficient attention has been given to the development of new products and services. In addition, it is also said that high interest rates have discouraged investment and that consumers have sucked in too many foreign imports.

- The **visible trade balance** is the sale of visible goods minus the purchase of visible goods.

The current trading account of the balance of payments is made up of the visible and invisible balances, as shown in the table below.

**Figure 14.2** Visible and invisible balances in the current trading account

| Visible exports | 500 | Invisible exports | 400 | Total exports | 900 |
|---|---|---|---|---|---|
| Visible imports | 650 | Invisible imports | 200 | Total imports | 850 |
| Visible balance | −150 | Invisible balance | +200 | Current balance | +50 |

## Ways of solving balance-of-payments problems

While it is typical today for the UK's visible balance to run at a loss, this is greatly helped by our surplus on invisibles. There are no easy ways of solving balance-of-payments problems. Because we are a member of an international community, actions we take at home will have effects on other countries and their actions will likewise affect us. The following are ways of improving the balance of payments.

### Becoming more competitive

If we produce more up-to-date products than other countries, produce goods more cheaply, offer better after-sales service and meet required deadlines, then we will find our products selling well.

### Import tariffs

If we tax foreign imports then they will be more expensive to home buyers, who will switch to buying more goods produced in the UK. However, the danger of such a policy is that other countries will retaliate and tariff barriers around the world reduce world trade so that everyone loses.

### Import quotas

We sometimes limit the quantities of foreign goods entering this country such as Japanese cars and East European suits. This can be done by a voluntary agreement between trading countries or by law. Once again such a policy leads to retaliation and foreign companies get round it by setting up factories in this country.

## Subsidies

The government could give financial help to UK companies to make it easier for them to sell their products at lower prices. This normally leads to retaliation and the breakdown of trading.

## Exchange control

In most countries the central bank, which is controlled by the government, keeps the central pool of foreign currency. If the government wants to cut back on imports it will instruct the central bank to reduce the amount of foreign currency it will supply. Usually this will mean that the central bank will only readily supply currency to important users. For example, importers of important raw materials will find it easy to get hold of foreign currency, whereas citizens wanting to holiday abroad may find that they can only take out of the country a limited amount of foreign money.

## Buying home-produced products

The government might run a campaign encouraging citizens to buy just their own home-produced products. This has been done in the UK from time to time and is used throughout the world as is illustrated by the photograph from Pakistan in Fig. 14.3 below.

**Figure 14.3** Pakistan encourages its citizens to buy home-produced goods (Source: Denis Doran)

## Trade restrictions

International trade exposes businesses to foreign competition. This can be a major problem if businesses are competing with subsidized imports or with dumped products.

- **Dumping** occurs when a firm sells goods at lower prices overseas than in its home market. It is an illegal practice.

Another major problem for firms is in exporting to markets that are protected by customs duties and taxes.

### Case Study—Sugar-based sweet imports to New Zealand
(*Source*: Southern Examining Group)

In 1985 the New Zealand government lifted all import controls on sugar-based sweets. This opened the 'floodgates' to cheap imports, mainly from South American countries. The chart below shows the increase in the quantity of sugar-based sweet imports to New Zealand between 1983 and 1988.

*Questions*

1. By how much did New Zealand's imports of sugar-based sweets rise between 1985 and 1988?
2. Why do countries import goods?
3. What is an import control?
4. Give **one** example of an import control, explaining briefly how it works?

**Figure 14.4** Graph showing the increase in imports of sugar-based sweets

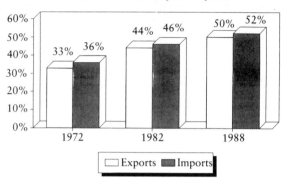

UK TRADE WITH THE EC
(as a % of total Imports/Exports)

Exports   Imports

**Figure 14.5**  The rise in UK trade with the EC

5. What action/s could New Zealand's sweet manufacturers take to keep their share of New Zealand sweet sales?
6. How might the lifting of import controls on sweets have affected New Zealand's current account balance?

Wherever firms export goods, they must get the following right:

- Price
- Quality
- Delivery

The exporters must know their market. Information about overseas markets can be obtained from two main sources:
1. The government
2. Banks

The government and banks play a major role in overseas trade because of their experience. They will help to organize finance, give advice, help with insurance and assist with foreign currency.

It is not surprising that some businesses are reluctant to engage in international trade. Problems include:

1. Uncertainty
2. Language differences
3. Differences in tastes
4. Paperwork
5. Customs duties
6. Extra transport and insurance costs.

The reader should try to think these through in terms of, for example, sending to Italy a vanload of fashion dresses made in the UK.

## Documents and payment in international trade

The exporter needs to do a lot of paperwork because many documents may be needed.

One of the most important of these documents is the bill of lading. This document has two purposes.

1. It forms a contract between the exporter and the shipping company. The ship's captain will sign it to show the state of the goods when he or she takes them aboard. If they are undamaged he or she will sign to say it is a 'clean bill'. If they are not in perfect condition the captain will note their condition on the bill (a 'dirty bill').

2. A copy of the bill is sent ahead of the goods by air to the importer. This paper gives the importer proof that he or she is the owner of the goods. When the goods arrive in port the importer can present the document and claim the goods (see Fig. 14.6). If the goods are sent by air the document is called an airway bill and the importer must prove his or her identity to claim the goods.

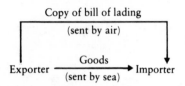

**Figure 14.6**   A bill of lading is sent by air so that the importer can claim the goods being sent by sea

### Open-account payment

International trade payments can be made in a way which is similar to trading within a country. The Irish Whiskey Company regularly sells goods to an importer in Canada. At the end of each month the importer is sent a statement of account. The importer arranges for the sum of money to be withdrawn from her account with the Royal Bank of Canada and transferred to the Bank of Ireland branch in Dublin used by the Irish Whiskey Company.

### Bills of exchange

With many trading deals, more risk is involved than in the home trade. The bill of exchange is a common way of making payment for credit deals. The exporter sends goods to the importer and only expects payment after a certain period—generally three months, but sometimes one month or six months.

The exporter draws up the bill of exchange and sends it to the importer, where it is signed for and accepted.

Figure 14.7 shows a bill of exchange made out for £5,117.65, which must be paid within three months of being presented. The bill has been drawn up by Edward Angus of Scottish Cosmetics Ltd (the exporter) and has been signed and accepted by Sonia Ramos of the US Import Agency, Boston (the importer).

The exporters, having sold goods on credit, might find themselves with a cash-flow shortage. They need money to carry on business and yet they have to

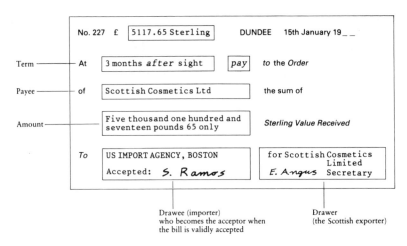

Term ——— At    3 months *after* sight    pay    to the *Order*

Payee ——— of    Scottish Cosmetics Ltd    the sum of

Amount ——— Five thousand one hundred and seventeen pounds 65 only    *Sterling Value Received*

No. 227  £  5117.65 Sterling    DUNDEE    15th January 19 _ _

To    US IMPORT AGENCY, BOSTON    for Scottish Cosmetics Limited

Accepted:  *S. Ramos*    *E. Angus*  Secretary

Drawee (importer) who becomes the acceptor when the bill is validly accepted

Drawer (the Scottish exporter)

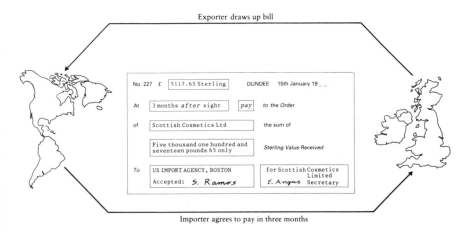

Exporter draws up bill

Importer agrees to pay in three months

**Figure 14.7**  An example of a bill of exchange, and how it works

wait for payment for goods sold on credit. To ease this problem they could do one of the following:

1. Sell the bill of exchange for less than its face value to a bank or other body dealing in money. There is a well organized market in bills of exchange.
2. Borrow money from a bank using the bill of exchange as security for the loan. (See Fig. 14.8.)

## Other documents used in international trade

Exporters can get tied up with endless paperwork. Small companies might employ a specialist firm to handle their paperwork. Large firms have a specialist exporting department but, today's uncertainty regarding the exchange rate has encouraged many multinationals to set up plants and offices overseas. Documents used in international trade include the following:

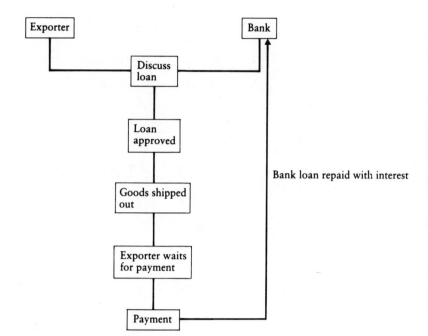

**Figure 14.8**  An exporter may have to borrow money from a bank while waiting for the payment promised in the bill of exchange

1. *Invoices*. International trade invoices are similar to those used in the home trade.
2. *Certificates of insurance*. These cover various risks, mainly risks involved in transport.
3. *Certificates of origin*. Because the amount of import taxes paid varies according to where goods have come from, most shipments of goods must carry a certificate of origin for inspection by customs officers.
4. *Import licence*. This is issued by the importer's government, giving permission for goods to be imported.
5. *Export licence*. This is needed for certain goods such as firearms and works of art.

## The government and exports

The government of nearly every country tries to encourage exports for the following reasons:

1. They create business contacts and opportunities to make further sales.
2. They help to create jobs.
3. They earn foreign currency.

The British government organizes trade fairs and 'British Weeks' overseas. It provides information and advice about foreign markets and currencies and vital statistics about trade. It helps with the translation of documents and materials.

The Department of Trade and Industry also runs the Export Credits Guarantee service. The Export Credit Guarantee Department performs two important functions:

1.  It provides grants and low-interest loans to help exporters get contacts off the ground.
2.  It provides an insurance service against non-payment of debts by the importer (see Fig. 14.9).

## If an overseas buyer failed to pay you, would you see red?

In the event that a buyer is unable to pay you, getting angry will be the least of your problems.

One bad debt can cause havoc with your cashflow and turn the tide on profits.

The non-payment of, say, a £20,000 contract could erode the profits on a much larger piece of business. All that work wasted when the £20,000 could have been covered for as little as £80.

In such an unpredictable trading environment, the cost of ECGD insurance seems a small price to pay compared to the damage caused by a bad debt.

ECGD is used by 4 out of every 5 companies who insure their export sales, and can tailor a competitively priced package to suit your individual needs.

See your local ECGD Regional Director, **ECGD** before you see red.    Export with confidence.

**Figure 14.9**  Advertisement for the Export Credit Guarantee Department

Non-payment may be caused by war or bad relations between countries or by civil unrest in the importing country.

**Case Study—The export initiative** (*Source*: Southern Examining Group)

Study the extract from an advertisement for the Department of Trade and Industry 'Export Initiative', below in Fig. 14.10.

## If you need a local rep overseas, just say the word.

Gaining new customers overseas can be a job easier said than done. Especially if your hands are full trying to run the business here at home. Take the Export Initiative from DTI and we'll put you in touch with a reputable businessman abroad.

And we'll check that he's gained all the relevant experience necessary to act as your local sales agent, distributor or importer.

*Extract from DTI advertisement.*

**Figure 14.10**  Advertisement for the Department of Trade and Industry 'Export Initiative'

*Questions*

1. Give *three* difficulties faced by companies wishing to sell goods and services overseas.
2. What actions might a British company take to deal with these problems?
3. (a) What is a local sales agent?
   (b) What is an importer?
4. Why do you think that the Department of Trade and Industry (DTI) wants to encourage an export drive by British companies?
5. Explain how British companies can benefit from increasing their exports.

## Case Study—The Single Market

The goal of a single 'common' market goes back to the Treaty of Rome, which established the European Economic Community. In 1985 the heads of government in the European Community committed themselves to progressively completing the Single Market by 31 December 1992.

For too many years in the EC, despite the elimination of tariffs and quotas, the 'common' market has not been a reality. The movement of goods without restriction has been prevented by a range of national restrictions such as:

- Technical barriers such as different national product standards.
- Public purchasing policies which distort competition.
- Red tape.
- Differences in food law such as on additives and labelling.
- Barriers to the sale of financial products.
- Controls over capital movements.
- Restricted transport movements.
- Limitations on the establishment of professions.
- Differences in company law.
- Competition policies and state subsidies.
- Differences in external trade policy and consumer protection.
- Language barriers.

Removing such trading barriers will open new opportunities for UK business. The creation of a single market for goods and services should cut down business costs, encourage more efficient organizations and thus stimulate wealth and job creation.

*Task*

You work for a small confectionery business and realize that the changes that are taking place could affect your business. Working with a partner, consider what strategy you would take to improve your position in the business environment given such changes. Outline your strategy under the following headings.

- Marketing
- Sales
- Distribution
- Production
- Product development
- Purchasing
- Finance
- Training, languages and recruitment
- Information Technology

## Case Study—Holidaytours

Holidaytours is a United Kingdom travel firm with branches throughout the UK. Details of its sales for 1992 are given below.

| Sales to | £m. |
|---|---|
| UK citizens for holidays abroad | 50 |
| UK citizens for holidays in the UK | 120 |
| Foreigners for holidays in the UK | 30 |

Holidaytours has been particularly successful in promoting holidays within the U.K. where it has worked closely with some local authorities.

Look carefully at the sales figures given above.

1. How would each of these figures affect the United Kingdom balance of payments?
2. What is the overall contribution that Holidaytours makes to the UK balance of payments? Show your working.
3. How could Holidaytours make more people aware of what their company offers?
4. Why would it be sensible for local authorities and Holidaytours to carry out market research?

**Case Study—Europerfume Ltd** (*Source*: Southern Examining Group)

Study the letter below:

S.A.F.R.I.C.O.
B. P. 1258
ABIDJAN
COTE D'IVOIRE

Europerfume Ltd.
Burnt Mill Industrial Estate
HARLOW
Essex CM19 5DS
ANGLETERRE

N/Réf: JB/588                                     Abidjan, le 29 août 1992
Objet: Recherche de Partenaires

Messieurs,

Dans le cadre de la recherche de partenaires britanniques votre
ambassade basée en Côte d'Ivoir nous a conseillé de prendre contact avec
votre firme.

Nous sommes une société de vente et de distribution de parfums et
notre clientèle est surtout composée de grossistes qui veulent élargir leur
gamme de produits. Nous estimons que notre collaboration ne sera pas sans
retombées positives pour nos deux sociétés.

Nous vous serions très reconnaissants si vous pouviez nous envoyer
vos conditions de vente (ex-usine ou livrés-dédouanés) et le meilleur délai
de livraison.

En plus, pourriez-vous nous envoyer quelques échantillons pour que
nous puissions lancer une étude du marché? Il va sans dire que les frais qui
y seront générés seront entièrement à votre charge.

Dans le cas où cette proposition retiendrait votre attention, nous
souhaiterions que les différentes correspondances soient en français.

En attendant une réponse favorable, veuillez agréer, Messieurs,
l'assurance d'une franche collaboration.

Jules Bregha
Directeur Commercial

**Figure 14.11**   Letter to
Europerfume

*Questions*

1.  Who is the letter from?
2.  Where are they based?
3.  What is B.P. 1258?
4.  What is the purpose of the letter?
5.  What is the position of the person sending the letter?
6.  How has Jules Bregha found out about Europerfume Ltd?
7.  What does S.A.F.R.I.C.O. do?
8.  What details is Jules Bregha seeking?

9.  What request does Jules make about the correspondence?
10. What is meant by the following terms?
    (a) Ex-usine (b) grossistes (c) franches collaboration (d) recherche de partenaires (e) étude du marché.

## Questions

1.  Complete the following sentences using the terms below:

    Bill of exchange            Visible trade
    Bill of lading              Invisible trade
    Certificate of origin       Exchange rate
    Export                      Discount
    Import                      Export licence

    (a) A UK product sold to a foreigner is called an . . . . . . . .
    (b) The sale of whisky to Japan is an example of . . . . . . . .
    (c) An importer would present a . . . . . . . . at the docks to claim the goods.
    (d) A . . . . . . . makes it clear where goods first came from.
    (e) A foreign product brought into the UK is known as an . . . . . . . .
    (f) The . . . . . . . is the rate at which one currency will exchange for another.
    (g) When a bill of exchange is bought for less than its face value it is bought at a . . . . . . . .
    (h) To take a valuable painting out of the country you would need an . . . . . . .
    (i) A . . . . . . . is used to sell goods on credit.
    (j) Selling banking services to a foreigner is an example of . . . . . . . .

2.  Work out the visible balance, the invisible balance and the current balance from the following figures:

    | Visible imports   | 1200 |
    | Invisible exports | 1000 |
    | Visible exports   | 1000 |
    | Invisible imports | 600  |

3.  Give six examples of visible and six examples of invisible items of trade.

4.  Which of the following statements are true?
    (a) The UK always runs a surplus on visible trade.
    (b) The current balance will always be a negative figure.
    (c) The UK earns a lot of money from invisible trade.
    (d) Interest, profits and dividends from overseas are a visible trading item.
    (e) The UK buys imports from Third World countries.
    (f) The UK was one of the founder members of the EC.
    (g) The EC is a free trade area.
    (h) Machinery would be counted as an invisible trading item.

(i)    The current account is made up only of visible items.

(j)    The UK sells most of its exports to EC countries.

(k)    A tariff is a limiation on the number of goods that can be imported.

(l)    Exchange control is a method of encouraging exports.

5.    Explain the following trade restrictions:

  (a)    subsidies

  (b)    quotas

  (c)    tariffs

6.    Explain what is meant by 'dumping'. Find a reference in a newspaper to a case of dumping. How might dumping affect (a) UK consumers (b) UK producers (c) employees of the UK companies?

7.    Study the following figure which shows an employee in South Korea assembling a computer.

**Figure 14.12**  Assembling a computer in South Korea (Source: David Hayes)

(a)    What does the picture tell us about the way in which computers are assembled in South Korea?

(b)  Why do we import computers from South Korea rather than making them ourselves?

(c)  Who benefits from such trading?

(d)  Under what circumstances is it beneficial for the UK to manufacture its own computers?

(e)  Under what circumstances would South Korea import computers from the UK?

(f)  List eight problems that are faced by exporters. Given these problems, why do firms export?

9.  How can a rise in exchange rates affect businesses in this country?

10.  Use the map below to identify the twelve member states of the EC. (Are there any new countries which are seeking to join?)

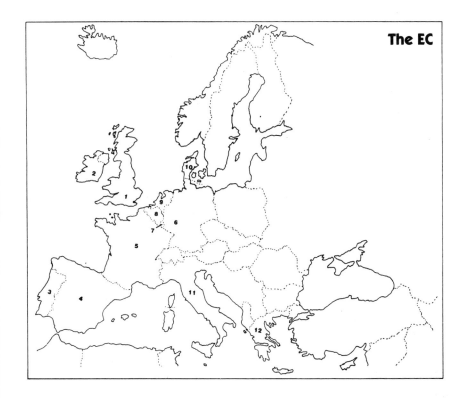

**Figure 14.13**  Map showing EC countries

11. Load a database package and set up a file containing the following information about EC countries. The information will be entered under the following headings: country, capital, date of entry, population (1990, 000's).

| Country | Capital | Date | Population |
|---|---|---|---|
| Spain | Madrid | 1976 | 39 000 |
| Greece | Athens | 1981 | 10 000 |
| France | Paris | 1957 | 56 000 |
| Portugal | Lisbon | 1986 | 11 000 |
| Germany | Berlin | 1957 | 80 000 |
| Luxembourg | Luxembourg | 1957 | 400 |
| UK | London | 1973 | 60 000 |
| Belgium | Brussels | 1957 | 10 000 |
| Eire | Dublin | 1973 | 3500 |
| Denmark | Copenhagen | 1073 | 5200 |
| Netherlands | Amsterdam | 1957 | 15 000 |
| Italy | Rome | 1957 | 60 000 |

(a) Save and print all of the file, record by record.
(b) Sort the file into alphabetical order. Print this list.
(c) Who were the founder members of the Community?
(d) Which countries joined most recently?
(e) Which two countries have (i) the largest populations? (ii) the smallest populations? Sort the file in descending order of population size.
(f) Other European countries would now like to join the Euopean Community. These include: Poland, with a population of 40 million and Czechoslovakia, with a population of 16 million. Assuming that these countries join the Single Market in 1996, add them to your file. Assuming that Norway, Sweden, Austria and Switzerland also join, add them to your file. Print the completed file in a list format.

## Coursework

Why does international trade take place? The following assignment, designed by Peter K Radband of Sandhurst school, can be used to prepare for a piece of individual research in which individual students can explore why countries trade particular well known items.

Split the class into groups. In your groups discuss where things come from and why. Make out lists like those in Fig. 14.14. Try to make some notes which will help you answer the questions that follow.

| FOOD AND DRINK | SMALL CONSUMER GOODS | TOYS AND HOBBY EQUIPMENT |
|---|---|---|
| 1 Tea from Sri Lanka | 1 Camera from Russia | 1 Lego from Denmark |
| 2 Milk from _____ | 2 Telephone from _____ | 2 Bicycle from _____ |
| 3 _____ | 3 _____ | 3 _____ |
| 4 _____ | 4 _____ | 4 _____ |
| 5 _____ | 5 _____ | 5 _____ |

| ELECTRICAL GOODS | GARDEN AND MOTORING | RAW MATERIALS |
|---|---|---|
| 1 Video from Korea | 1 Lawn Mower from Germany | Can you find where these come from? |
| 2 _____ | 2 _____ | 1 Wool from Australia |
| 3 _____ | 3 _____ | 2 Oil from _____ |
| 4 _____ | 4 _____ | 3 _____ |
| 5 _____ | 5 _____ | 4 _____ |
| | | 5 _____ |

Figure 14.14   Produce a list like this of where different products come from

1. Choose one item which is not produced in the UK and explain why not.
2. Choose one item which we consume in the UK which is not imported and explain why.
3. Choose one item which you have found that is produced in the UK and abroad. Explain why this situation arises.
4. With the help of your answers to questions 1–3, explain the main reasons for international trade.
5. With the help of an atlas, complete a world map using a key to show where the goods on your list come from.

## The Single Market and a local business

The Single Market is made up of 341 million people in 12 countries. This represents the world's largest trading bloc, accounting for about one-third of all world trade. The EC is all about the creation of greater economic integration. Member states are working towards producing a unified economic area which is not divided by customs or trade barriers.

In this area, four main economic freedoms are being created:

- movement of goods
- movement of persons
- movement of capital
- and the freedom to provide services.

How are these changes affecting local businesses? Interview a small selection (perhaps two or three) of local businesses to find out the impact upon them. Evaluate the information that you uncover to prepare a more detailed class questionnaire that you can send out to about thirty local businesses.

# 15

# The government and business

This chapter looks at how government affects business in a general way. We have not tried to list every single Act of Parliament or to go into great detail about how government works.

The details of government policy change frequently and it is more important for the student to be aware of:

1. Why the government becomes involved.
2. Ways in which government might become involved.
3. The effect of government on business activity.

- **Central government** governs the whole country. Citizens choose Members of Parliament. The MPs belong to political parties which have leaders. Central government passes new laws in Parliament. Civil servants run the day-to-day activities of the State such as collecting taxes.
- **Local government** looks after only a small part of the country, e.g. a county like Somerset or a heavily built-up area such as Manchester. Citizens vote for councillors to represent them at local-government level.

## Why does the government get involved in the economy?

To understand the part played by the government, take a walk in a group along a road outside your school or college. List ways in which the government influences everyday life. For example, who has paid for the roads, street lighting and maintenance of the pavements and parks? Why are drivers wearing seat belts and why are lorries only allowed up to a certain size? The list you end up with will be a long one (far longer than if you had simply sat and thought in the classroom).

1. Some goods and services are provided by the government because it is felt that all citizens should share in the public provision of such items. For

example, most people in the UK believe that all children should have some form of health care and education.

2. Some goods and services from which everyone benefits can only be produced by the government if they are going to be properly provided. An example of this is the police force.

3. Some people believe that the government should try to reduce inequality. This might involve taxing some people at a higher rate than others and giving more benefits to those who are worse off. Of course, there are others who believe that inequality is not such a bad thing because it gives people a motive to try to better themselves.

4. The government might also try to make the economic system run more smoothly. For example, it passes laws against monopolies to protect consumers and it takes measures against pollution and other antisocial practices.

A very important role played by the government is to set the 'rules of the game' within which business activity takes place.

These rules are constantly changing and each time they do some people will lose out and others benefit. It is important to think about the following questions:

1. Who makes the rules? (For whom?)
2. Why do the rules change?
3. How do they change?
4. Who loses and benefits when they change?

*Questions*

Who would lose out and who would benefit as a result of the following changes in the rules? (Why have these rule changes been made?)

1. A new law is passed so that lorries must contain a tachograph showing how many hours a lorry driver is at the wheel at one time.
2. Sunday trading is made legal.
3. The government publishes a list of drugs and medicines limiting the types that doctors can prescribe on the National Health Service.
4. Schools are given control over their own spending.
5. The government passes a law making it compulsory for all businesses to publish their accounts for public inspection.
6. The government passes a law allowing doctors to advertise their services in newspapers.
7. Importers and exporters within the Single Market have paperwork reduced to a single form.
8. The government passes a law laying down tighter controls on safety standards at sporting grounds.

# Ways in which the government becomes involved in the economy

There are a wide number of areas in which government involvement in the economy is particularly felt and you should have a general understanding of these broad areas. Many of them are dealt with in greater detail in other sections of the book.

Major areas include the following:

1. Employment policy
2. Industrial policy
3. Regional policy
4. Inflation policy
5. Trade-union policy
6. Education policy
7. Taxation policy
8. International policy
9. Establishing the rules of the game

Government policy is an area of the course where it is particularly useful to take up-to-date notes on developments from newspapers.


## Employment policy

In the 1920s and 1930s unemployment in the UK created terrible human, social and economic problems. Living through this period made a very big impact on people who were later to be in a position to make policy decisions. After the Second World War politicians of all parties saw full employment as being a major goal of government policy. A major policy used between 1945 and 1979 was for the government to spend money to try to boost jobs in the economy. The government built up its spending projects so that eventually about half of all the money spent in the country was by the government. The government also became a major employer of labour, for example, in the National Health Service, the Civil Service, and in nationalized industries such as electricity and gas.

The government pumped money into the economy by spending more than it took in taxes. This is called a deficit budget. The government borrowed money to make up its budget deficit.

After 1979, the Conservative Government tried to cut back the part the State played in running the economy. It believed that the best way of creating and keeping jobs was to allow businesses to compete because this makes them more efficient. In the 1980s and early 1990s central government pulled back from major spending policies to create jobs. At the same time there were many small-scale projects, often run by local government to create jobs.

On a national level, interesting schemes of the 1980s and 1990s have included:

1.  *The Youth Training Scheme.* This guarantees a period of work experience and training for all school-leavers. The scheme subsidizes employers who take on workers under the scheme.
2.  *The Enterprise Allowance Scheme.* The government pays wages to unemployed people setting up their own business for the first year of its operation.
3.  *The Employment Action Scheme.* This is a temporary work scheme which is designed to provide opportunities for those who have been out of work for long periods of time. Participants will receive an allowance on top of their normal benefits. Job Clubs have been set up where the unemployed can club together to help each other look for work and to boost their confidence.

*Questions*

Between 1945 and 1979 governments believed that government spending could play a major role in creating employment. After 1979 the government tried to reduce its share of spending. Why do you think that this change came about? How do you think this might have affected the following people?

1.  A taxpayer
2.  A miner in a loss-making pit
3.  An unemployed person
4.  A firm making machinery

What other factors would have influenced how these people fared?

**Industrial policy**

British industry depends in many ways on government support. Michael Heseltine (an industry minister in the mid-1980s), writing in March 1987, said, 'This government, like all its predecessors for at least the last fifty years, is up to its neck in the business life of this country, stimulating one enterprise here, stifling another there and interfering everywhere.' It would be worth while for a class of students to check out this statement by following the television mid-evening news for a week and recording references to the government's relations with business.

The government plays a major part in setting up large projects to develop the UK's economic infrastructure.

*   The **infrastructure** is the skeleton at the base of the economy, e.g. motorways, power stations, etc.

Examples of decisions that the government has made in recent years include the decision to let the channel tunnel go ahead and to improve the motorway facilities of the A1(M).

The government has a partnership with industry in some research and development projects, for example, in energy conservation projects.

The government also subsidizes particular projects and industrial sectors. An example of this is the grants given to farmers to preserve hedgerows and to employ organic farming methods.

The public sector of the economy is also important as a creator of employment, output and incomes. British nationalized industries such as British Rail and British Coal still employ over half a million employees (1992). Over the years government objectives for the nationalized industries have changed. Since the Second World War these industries have increasingly been expected to show profits on investments, although they still get a subsidy for social benefits (e.g. running some cross-Pennine railway services where other forms of communication are difficult).

The most recent policy for nationalized industry has been that of privatization. This involves selling off shares in state industries so that they become part of the private sector. One of the main arguments for this is to make them more competitive so that they cut out inefficient parts and expand efficient ones. There is the belief that if a business is open to the threat of 'bankruptability' then it will be spurred on to greater efforts.

## Regional policy

Central-government policy in relation to the regions is covered in the chapter on external influences on businesses. In the UK today there is also a very strong thrust of policy at a local level. Local councils compete with each other to create employment within their region. This leads to extensive advertising of regional advantages. Councils will research the employment needs of the local situation and will organize the building of office and factory units to encourage industrialists in.

Areas which are situated in government designated development and enterprise zones will be at a considerable advantage, but it must be remembered why these areas are felt to be in need of help in the first place.

## Inflation policy

Inflation is all about rising prices, but we must bear in mind that different prices affect different people in different ways.

*Questions*

If the price of petrol went up how would this affect the following people?

1. A pensioner living in an old people's home.
2. A mobile-discotheque owner.
3. Someone living on an agricultural commune.
4. An insurance agent.
5. The government.
6. A petrol retailer.
7. An oil company.

The government, however, is concerned with the general level of inflation. It becomes concerned if prices generally start to rise, because of the following consequences:

1. UK goods become more expensive and difficult to sell.
2. People become unsure about prices and this can cause uncertainty and unrest. For example, employees might want more wages to keep up with price rises.
3. Some people lose out while others benefit and this might not be thought to be fair. For example, somebody who lends £10 at a time when this would have bought two compact discs would not be happy to find that when the money was repaid to him or her it would only buy one compact disc.

## Policy to control inflation

The government can use many different policies to try to control inflation. Policies that might affect business would include the following:

### Raising interest rates

This policy would make it more expensive for business to obtain money. This increased cost could and does help to cause bankruptcies. It will also lead to cutbacks including the creation of unemployment. Unemployment helps to reduce inflation because consumers (who are wage earners) will have less money to spend.

### Discouraging spending

If the government carries out policies that cut back on the spending of money, such as making it more difficult to buy goods on hire purchase, this will hit the sales of a lot of businesses.

### Controls on wages and prices

If the government sets limits on the amounts by which firms can raise their prices, or on wage increases, this will reduce profits so that firms will cut back their workforces.

*Trade union policy*

Different governments have different policies on trade unions. Some people think that trade unions have too little power while others think they have too much power. In the 1980s and early 1990s there have been several rounds of trade union laws and most people would recognize that these have reduced union power. For example, today secondary picketing is illegal, as are secondary strikes (where people strike in sympathy with someone else's dispute when their own firm is not involved). Today all unions must ballot their members before calling strike action. Courts can freeze union assets if they break the law.

## Education and training policy

Education and training is seen in the UK as having an important contribution to make to business life. The government plays a part in researching the contribution education can make and in encouraging schools and colleges to move in various directions. In recent years the government has subsidized the use of computers in schools and encouraged the teaching of business studies and information technology.

In the 1990s the government is emphasizing the importance of work-related qualifications being given equal status to academic ones. Today there is greater emphasis on the curriculum being related to the world of work. Work experience is expected to be part of the learning process of all pupils in the upper years of schools and those studying in colleges. Technology has become a compulsory subject for all pupils up to the age of 16 and pupils are also expected to study Economic and Industrial Understanding and Information Technology from 5–16. The new TECs (Training and Enterprise Councils), which are organized by local industries, will place great emphasis on providing training opportunities for all people in a particular area. The TECs are organized in partnership with government.

## Taxation policy

Businesses can make valuable contributions to the community by the taxes they pay. Businesses in return benefit from government spending on projects like airports, roads, research and development, aid to developing countries and many other items.

The four main taxes that affect businesses are:

1. Profit taxes
2. Value Added Tax
3. Customs and excise duties
4. National Insurance

*Profit taxes*

Someone who is a sole trader or in a partnership will pay income tax, while companies pay corporation tax on profits over a certain amount.

A director in a limited company would pay income tax on his or her salary and on any sum of money withdrawn from company funds.

*Value Added Tax*

The standard rate of value added tax is seventeen and a half per cent in the UK. If a small firm bought in £1,000 of inputs in a year and sold its output for £11,000, it would have added £10,000 to the value of the product. It will then add seventeen and a half per cent as value added tax on the value it has added to the goods or services. In total, therefore, it will hand over £1,750 of tax to the government which it charges to its customers' bills.

Firms send the VAT payments to the government every month or quarter. A firm that buys goods or services with VAT on them can claim the VAT contribution back. For example, Sally Jones Ltd hires a solicitor to help with some paperwork. The solicitor charges £1,000 + £175 VAT. Sally Jones Ltd will hand over the VAT but the amount can be reclaimed from the government at a later date.

*Customs and excise duties*

Customs duties are duties charged by the government to protect home industries. They would normally be placed on goods from non-EC countries that compete with UK goods.

Excise duties are taxes placed on goods for the purpose of raising revenue for the government. Taxes are a great bone of contention with many businesses. For example, the UK whisky and cigarette industries have formed strong pressure groups arguing that they are over-taxed.

*Questions*

Study Fig. 15.1.

1. What percentage of a bottle of whisky goes in tax?
2. If a bottle of whisky cost £14, how much of this would be paid to the government in tax?
3. Do you think that the tax is (a) high (b) low (c) about right? Justify your arguments.
4. What do you think would be the effect of raising the tax?
5. What do you think would be the effect of lowering the tax?
6. Why do you think that taxes are placed on whisky?
7. What should the tax revenue be used for?

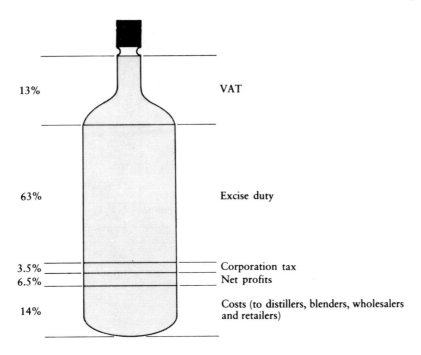

| | |
|---|---|
| 13% | VAT |
| 63% | Excise duty |
| 3.5% | Corporation tax |
| 6.5% | Net profits |
| 14% | Costs (to distillers, blenders, wholesalers and retailers) |

Figure 15.1 Diagram showing what percentage of the price of a bottle of whisky goes to different recipients

### National Insurance

As well as deducting National Insurance from wages, employers also have to pay a contribution to the National Insurance Fund.

## International policy

This topic has been dealt with in the chapter looking at business in an international setting (Chapter 14). The government may try to promote trade, encourage exports or reduce imports.

The exchange rate is an important influence on UK trading. The government therefore tries to control the exchange rate wherever possible.

The value of the pound sterling has an important effect on the price of Britain's imports and exports. Known as the foreign exchange rate, the more the pound is required to pay for exports, the higher its price.

The price is lowered when it is needed to pay for more imports. The value of the pound is expressed in terms of its value against another currency, e.g. so many D Marks/Francs/Pesetas to the pound. In 1990, the pound joined the European Monetary System. This means that the government has less power to alter the price of the pound because it is tied to other EC currencies.

Governments of all political parties believe that a healthy world market is good for the UK and that we have an important contribution to make in helping the development of other countries.

An important principle laid down in EC policy for its aid programme is that aid should not be limited to sending small amounts of surplus grain and dairy products to poor countries (which tends to damage the markets there for the products of local farmers). Instead we should use the same money to buy from, and thus support, poor-world farmers with surpluses available for sale.

### Establishing the rules of the game

The government sets out the rules of the game in many areas of business life. A few examples of these would be rules on the following matters:

1. Setting up a business and making information available.
2. The protection of records and data.
3. Health and safety.
4. Monopoly and competition.
5. Nuisance, noise and other social costs.
6. The rights of buyers and sellers.

The student only needs to have a general awareness of these rules because the actual fine detail is very extensive. Health and safety regulations, for example, stretch into thousands of pages.

It is worthwhile, however, for the student to look at a particular subset of rules and follow through the effects of changes in the rules. Interesting examples are changes in competition rules and consumer-protection laws.

Students should investigate these areas by seeking information from the appropriate government departments. For example, the Office of Fair Trading provides an excellent publication entitled *An outline of United Kingdom Competition Policy*. It can be obtained from Office of Fair Trading, Competition Policy Division, Field House, 15–25 Bream's Buildings, London EC4A 1PR.

## The effect of government activity

This will vary from business to business but, inevitably, all businesses will come across the government in a wide number of ways. The government is thus a key institution influencing the way in which businesses behave.

## The main areas of government spending

Government spending has become an important fact of life in the twentieth century and, with the growth of welfare services, the amount spent has continued to increase. The biggest single item of government spending is social security, of which the largest part is pensions. In the UK today we have an increasing number of elderly people and this group of people will continue to need an increasing share of resources for the remainder of the century.

| Spending programme | Is central or local government mainly responsible? | Examples of spending |
|---|---|---|
| Social security | Central | Pensions, unemployment pay |
| Defence | Central | Army, Navy, Air Force |
| Health and personal social services | Central and local | National Health Service, Social services |
| Education and science | Central and local | Schools, colleges, research |
| Industry, energy, trade and employment | Central | Development grants, training schemes |
| Law, order and protective services | Local | Police, fire and prisons |
| Housing | Local | Repairs to council houses |
| Agriculture, forestry fisheries and food | Central | Subsidies to farmers |
| Overseas aid and overseas services | Central | Aid to poor countries and contributions to EEC |
| Transport | Local | Roads |
| Other environmental services | Local | Refuse collection, parks |
| Arts and libraries | Central and local | Libraries |
| Government lending to nationalized industries | Central | Lending to British Coal |
| Other | Central and local | Help to Wales, Northern Ireland and Scotland |

**Table 15.1**  Government spending

Table 15.1 lists the main areas of government spending and states for each area whether central or local government is mainly responsible.

### Case Study—The Channel Fixed Link

The notes below are derived from various newspaper reports:

THE CHANNEL FIXED LINK

'The Prime Minister and President Mitterand announced . . . on 20 January (1986) their decision to facilitate the development . . . of a fixed link across the Channel by the Channel Tunnel Group (CTG) in partnership with France Manche (FM), if the project is able to mobilise the necessary finance from the private sector. No support is proposed from public funds or by government financial guarantees . . . '

' . . . The shuttle trains will provide a no-booking, drive-on, drive-off service . . . the peak frequency will be one train every 5 minutes or less . . . '

' . . . The journey will take about 30 minutes, frontier controls and security checks will be co-located so that the formalities of both countries are completed before travellers board the trains . . . '

' . . . A major difference from the proposals for a Channel crossing made . . . in 1973 is that the current proposals are for a private sector project. Private markets . . . will take all the risks and have a very strong incentive for cost-effectiveness and completion on or before schedule . . . '

' . . . The purpose of a fixed link is to provide a way of crossing the Channel which is quicker, cheaper and/or more convenient for some users than ferry or air services. These savings in cost and time can be expected to increase traffic between Britain and . . . Europe and to contribute to economic growth and employment throughout the UK . . . Consumer choice would be widened.'

## Tasks

1. Write a memo to the Chairman of your local Chamber of Commerce outlining *either*
   (a) the advantages
   *or*
   (b) the disadvantages
   *or*
   (c) the advantages and disadvantages
   of the Channel Tunnel Fixed Link project for business users or other businesses in the UK affected by the project.
2. State and explain **four** different problems which might be encountered by the Channel Tunnel Fixed Link project organizers.

## Questions

1. Read the article in Fig. 15.2 and indicate by a tick or a cross whether the following statements are true ($\sqrt{}$) or false (X):
   (a) The total number of people employed rose between March 1988 and March 1989.    . . . . .
   (b) Not everyone is affected equally by the new situation.    . . . . .
   (c) Women and the long-term unemployed are doing better.    . . . . .
   (d) The percentage of unemployed is greater than the percentage in 1984.    . . . . .
   (e) Those who are already unemployed are the first to benefit from the improvement in the economy.    . . . . .
   (f) The number of males unemployed has gone down.    . . . . .
   (g) Fewer women between 25 and 49 are now employed.    . . . . .

MARCHÉ DU TRAVAIL

# Emploi: une reprise certaine, des inégalités croissantes

*L'Insee confirme la reprise de l'emploi, mais souligne le fait que les deux cent cinquante mille créations ne profitent pas de la même façon aux hommes et aux femmes.*

Avec une sensible diminution du chômage et une augmentation de 250 000 de l'emploi total entre mars 1988 et mars 1989, le marché du travail se porte mieux. Pourtant, l'enquête « emploi » de l'Insee, effectuée auprès de 65 000 ménages, montre que cette amélioration ne profite pas à tout le monde. Les principaux oubliés sont les femmes et les chômeurs de longue durée.

Le nombre des chômeurs est passé en deux ans de 2 567 000 en 1987 à 2 308 000 en 1989, et le taux de chômage global est en 1989 de 9.6% de la population active, c'est-à-dire le niveau de mars 1984. La croissance du nombre des ouvriers indique la bonne santé de l'industrie. Mais la reprise économique ne profite pas à ceux qui sont déjà chômeurs.

Au contraire elle profite avant tout aux hommes: le nombre de chômeurs masculins baisse d'environ 120 000, tandis qu'il reste stable pour les femmes. La progression du taux d'activité des femmes de 25 à 49 ans ralentit, tandis que le travail à temps partiel stagne. L'Insee explique ce phénomène par le fait que « *les nouveaux emplois émanant de l'industrie et du bâtiment ne favorisent pas les femmes, contrairement aux années précédentes, où les créations d'emploi provenaient essentiellement des secteurs tertiaires* ».

**Figure 15.2**   French newspaper article (Source: Oxford and Cambridge Board)

(h)   The amount of part-time work for women is increasing. . . .

(i)   Work now available in the building industry favours men.

. . . . .

(j)   In the past most new jobs were in the service industries. . . .

### Case Study—Warnings on cigarette packets

Stark warnings on the dangers of smoking, including the words 'Smoking kills' started to appear on the front and back of cigarette packets at the end of 1991. The warnings are in much larger type than previous messages on the sides of packets. The new messages are much blunter.

The British Medical Association welcomed the change saying that it was wrong to allow the product to continue to be advertised. The previous warnings included such bland statements as :'Smoking can cause fatal diseases'.

The new ones now include:

**'Smoking kills'**
**'Smoking causes cancer'**
**'Smoking when pregnant harms your baby'**

Now cigarette packets also warn about passive smoking, e.g.

**'Protect children—don't make them breathe your smoke'**

There is now also more information provided about tar and nicotine levels. The move followed an EC trade harmonization directive.

*Questions*

1. What different interest groups will have different views about warnings on cigarette packets? Give examples of what some of these views might be.
2. Why has the government intervened to strengthen the messages provided to consumers?
3. Do you think that the government should act in this way? Justify your arguments.
4. What are the likely costs of this change?
5. What are the benefits?
6. How would you go about assessing whether the benefits outweigh the costs?

## Questions

1. Complete the following sentences using the terms below:

   Central government                  Nationalization
   Local government                    Privatization
   Infrastructure                      Value Added Tax
   Youth Training Scheme               Customs duty
   Enterprise Allowance                Excise duty

   (a) The . . . . . . . . guarantees all 16-year olds a period of work experience and training.
   (b) The . . . . . . . . of a country is the skeleton of its economy.
   (c) . . . . . . . . is a tax levied on the difference in value between a firm's inputs and its outputs.
   (d) . . . . . . . . is responsible for major national policies.
   (e) . . . . . . . . involves the transfer of ownership from the public to the private sector.
   (f) A government levies . . . . . . . . to protect its home industries.
   (g) The . . . . . . . . enables someone to claim a subsidy while starting up his or her own business.
   (h) . . . . . . . . is responsible for making some of the rules in a local area.
   (i) An . . . . . . . . is levied to raise revenue for the government.
   (j) . . . . . . . . involves the government taking over private firms and industries.

2. Study the statements about the government in the UK in Table 15.2. Copy out the table and tick the boxes which you think apply. (A—a statement

| | A | B | C | D |
|---|---|---|---|---|
| (a) The government carries out a high proportion of all spending in the UK. | | | | |
| (b) The government spends too much. | | | | |
| (c) The government should spend more on unemployment. | | | | |
| (d) Inflation is a major problem. | | | | |
| (e) Over a million workers are employed by nationalized industries. | | | | |
| (f) It is necessary to subsidize traditonal farming methods. | | | | |
| (g) Trade-uion officials should be elected by secret postal ballot. | | | | |
| (h) The whisky industry is taxed too highly. | | | | |

**Table 15.2** Table of statements about the government in the UK

based on fact; B—a statement based on opinion; C—something that can be proved; D—a political statement.)

3. Suppose that the government increases its spending by building a new airport. What effect will this have on the following?
   (a) Businesses in the area that are not directly involved with building the airport.
   (b) Long-term unemployed workers in the region.
   (c) School-leavers in the area looking for their first jobs.
   (d) Citizens living in the area of the new airport.
   (e) The firm that plays the major part in constructing the airport.
   (f) Companies that make building and construction equipment.

4. Study the article below:

   **Firm fined over lead level in toys**
   Thousands of Thomas the Tank Engine toys had to be recalled from the shops after it was found that they contained 90 times more than the allowed level of lead.
   The importer, ERTL (UK) Ltd, was fined the maximum £2,000 by Devon magistrates. 130 000 of the toys were brought in from China. The company pleaded guilty and was made to pay court costs of £1,400.
   The prosecutor said that responsibility rested fairly and squarely on the shoulders of the selling company.

   (a) Why is the government involved in the above case?
   (b) How is the government involved in the above case?
   (c) What action is being taken against the firm?
   (d) Do you regard this as sufficient action against the firm?
   (e) What do you think the consequences would be of the government not being involved in such cases?

5.  The following example illustrates the adding of value in the process of producing a product. We are assuming that VAT has not yet been charged.

    Jean produces £100 worth of wheat from seed that she got for nothing. Michael buys the wheat for £100 and grinds it into flour which he sells for £300 to Stan, who converts it into bread which he sells for £350.

    How much value added tax would each one hand over to the government?

6.  List and explain four business taxes that a firm may have to pay to the government.

7.  List six rules that the government use which affect business activity.

8.  The article below is used to illustrate changing rules. Before starting on the piece of work you should do some research into the arguments for and against privatizing bus routes.

### Children 'casualties of Dales bus war'

**EARLY-MORNING passengers bound for Harrogate from Nidderdale—including schoolchildren—are 'casualties of a bus war',** Summerbridge parish council heard on Tuesday.

The West Yorkshire Road Car Company and Wrays Coaches, of Summerbridge and Harrogate, are in competition for passengers on the Pateley Bridge-Harrogate route.

Coun. Nevin Ward told the parish council that the rival companies' buses were competing for the downdale passenger trade before 8 a.m. from Monday to Friday.

"Recently we have had buses coming through the village so early that our schoolchildren going to Harrogate have missed the bus," he said.

"It's become the same for everybody—no-one knows just when the buses will pass through the village on the way to Harrogate.

"In fact, we now see coaches hopping round each other—if one company's bus is at a bus stop, the other company's bus races to the next one where there are people waiting."

The council chairman, Coun. David Smith, said: "It

By HARRY HARDCASTLE

appears to be a free-for-all. We can complain to the bus companies but we know the problem will not go away while they are seeking to make their journeys profitable."

He said the bus services in rural areas had been discussed at last week's Yorkshire Local Councils' Association, and the Rural Community Council was wanting information about gaps in the daily public transport service and wanted suggestion for improving the services with the aid of county council grant aid.

Coun. Kathleen Hulme said the worst gap in the services was that between 12.30 p.m. and 3.20 p.m.

"There are no buses in between those times, either up or down the dale, and it creates problems for people wanting to visit Harrogate hospitals. It also ruins social life because people without cars cannot get to afternoon functions away from their own locality.

"Also anyone going by bus to Harrogate in a morning can't get a bus back until late afternoon."

Borough councillor Richard Whitefield said the county did have some finances for grant aid to bus services which would not be viable otherwise. "It's a matter of making the needs known," he said.

The council agreed to inform the Rural Community Council that an early-afternoon service, and a late-night service was needed. The last buses up and down dale start from Harrogate and Pateley Bridge at 6.20 p.m. and on Saturdays at 5.20 p.m.

Coun. Hulme said: "I wish we could get the companies to stagger their services—it looks ridiculous to have buses arriving in twos and threes as at present."

A spokesman for the West Yorkshire Road Car Company on Wednesday said the company's morning service had started at Pateley Bridge at 7.40 for a long time, and was changed to 7.35 a.m. in last October's reorganisation.

"We issued circulars on our buses informing passengers well in advance of our change in the morning timetable," he said, adding that he had no knowledge of drivers racing each other.

The managing director of Wrays Coaches, Mr. Malcolm Wray, said on Wednesday: "We started off with our Daleslink service morning and evening.

"Our morning service was starting from Pateley Bridge at 7.45, but then the West Yorkshire Road Car Company put on a service starting at 7.40, from Pateley. To be fair we moved ours to start at 7.40 a.m., but now West Yorkshire has moved its starting time to 7.35 a.m.

"I must admit that our drivers began to leave earlier than 7.40 for a day or two when the competition began, but I have now laid down the law—start at 7.40 prompt."

**Figure 15.3** Newspaper article illustrating some possible effects of bus privatization (Source: Harrogate Advertiser)

(a)  How would bus services have been operated before privatization?

(b)  Make a list of all the groups and individuals who will have been affected by the rule change.

(c)  Which of these groups do you think will have benefited from the rule change and which will have lost out?

(d)  Write a short paragraph to represent the views of each group.

(e)  Split the class into at least five sub-groups to represent interest groups involved and have a discussion to try to argue out the issue.

(f)  Do you think that the community was better off or worse off as a result of the rule change? How would you be able to tell?

(g)  Write up individual reports about the bus privatization issue. A suitable heading might be 'Was bus privatization a good thing for the people of Pateley Bridge?'. Alternatively, why not write about your own town or village?

# Coursework

1.  What are the effects of changes in the rules? Study a local example of the effect of a change in the law. This could be a law made nationally or a local by-law. Why has the law been changed? How will people be affected? How can the change be evaluated? There is plenty of scope for both primary and secondary research in this assignment.

2.  How does the government interfere with the economy in any one week? This could be the subject of a groupwork exercise based on newspapers. Sub-groups within the class could look through one day's newspapers and report back their findings.

3.  What are the effects of consumer-protection laws?
    Consumer-protection laws will only be really effective if consumers are aware of their rights and producers comply with the laws. You could also find out how Trading Standards Officers operate, to see how effective they are in checking on standards. In order to carry out this assignment you must first of all research consumer-protection laws. The Trading Standards Office have produced a very good pack of current information.

# 16

# The consequences of business

When a new supermarket opens up in your local town will this make you better off? Of course it depends on how you are affected. Perhaps you will be able to get a part-time job working there. You may find that it provides you with a wider range of goods to choose from than was previously available in the town. But, what if the supermarket is built next door to your house and it is open from first thing in the morning to last thing at night with all the noise of cars parking and trolleys being noisily stacked.

All communities are made up of individuals and groups who may have different views about whether a particular decision is a 'good one' or a 'bad one'. It might be a good idea to build a motorway to a growing industrial area. It is not such a good idea if the route of the motorway goes through your front door.

We therefore need to look at the social benefits and the social costs of business activity to get a clearer picture of net benefits.

- *Private benefits* are all the benefits to an individual or group resulting from a particular activity, e.g. the dividends that shareholders get from the profitable growth of their firm.
- *Private costs* are all the costs to an individual or group resulting from a particular activity, e.g. the cost to an individual of buying a new toothbrush, or the cost to the firm of the raw materials, labour and other costs needed to make that toothbrush.
- *Social benefits* are the private benefits, plus all the good effects for other members of the community, resulting from a particular activity. For example, if I set up as a florist I will (hopefully) receive monies from my sales which are a private benefit to me. But because I am a member of society they are also a social benefit. In addition, other social benefits will include the pleasure that customers receive from purchasing my flowers, the enjoyment of passers by whose day is brightened up, the wage that my assistant receives, the tax that the local council receives, the rent that my landlord earns and so on.

- *Social costs* are the private costs, plus all the bad effects for other members of the community, e.g. the extra traffic congestion caused by vehicles pulling up outside my shop, the clearing up of confetti that I sell as a sideline and so on.

*Task*

Read the following information. Make a list of five groups of people involved in the situation. Show which are the costs and which are the benefits to each group resulting from the activities described.

Every year there is a rock festival just outside Centreville. Typically, 6000 young rock fans converge on the park to spend three days in the sun listening to loud music and meeting up with friends. The event is organized by millionaire 'rock entrepreneur' Justine Villeneuve. Justine runs several rock enterprises and has his own record company. The Centreville festival is always a sell out and the rewards to Justine are lucrative.

Not everyone is happy with the festival however. Local farmers say that crops are trampled, broken bottles are a danger to livestock and have even reported that their cows give a reduced milk yield. Other local residents have mixed feelings. Many young people and even their parents support the festival as a valuable source of entertainment. Others are violently against it describing it as 'three days of filth, noise and declining values'. All police leave is cancelled during the festival and the bill for policing the festival is shared equally between the town of Centreveille and Justine Villeneuve.

# The benefits of business activity

Many people involved in business and industry see its main importance as the creation of wealth. Industry provides all the goods and services that we need. Almost everything that we see around us has been produced by industry—even much of our food.

Industry reacts to people's changing wants. It can only sell those goods that people are prepared to buy. Sometimes industry anticipates consumers demands for new products. (Some people might argue that consumers can be manipulated.) Society did not know that it wanted the video recorder. The product had first to be invented, then tested and researched. Finally, it had to be sold in the market place. When the product became popular it was obvious that it would be a commercial success, but in the meantime industry had to develop the product.

- The **wealth of a society** is the stock of possessions–money, houses, stocks and shares, etc. owned by members of that society. To this we should add **human wealth**, that is, the economic skills of the people which depend on such things as education and training.

In modern society, products are often highly complex and may be assembled thousands of miles apart. The modern motor vehicle is an example of a product whose components are built in many different plants before being finally assembled. Workers often have only a very limited knowledge of what they are making. In a similar way, consumers may have only a sketchy idea of how modern complex products are made and brought to market.

### Case Study—Choosing medical products

The government minister for health said in 1991 that the public should be free to choose new medical products that are on the market. He said that people should buy what they think is best for them.

An industrialist who had worked for many years in the industry said that information that was available to consumers about medical products was too complex for the 'person in the street' to understand. The consumer given free choice could make decisions that were harmful to them.

*Question*

Who do you think is right? What experience do you have of buying medicines? Do you think that you have enough information?

Industry brings together resources to produce wealth. In so doing it produces the following major benefits:

1.  *Industry provides employment.* Millions of people are employed in industry and commerce. Some of them are employed in enjoyable, creative work, while others work in boring, unimaginative environments where work is a burden rather than a pleasure.
2.  *Industry creates income.* The factors of production that produce goods earn factor incomes. Shareholders receive profits, landlords receive rent, lenders receive interest, workers receive wages, etc.
3.  *Industry creates products.* Value is added at each stage of production. A simple example of wealth creation is the carpenter converting relatively inexpensive material into furniture. The difference between the cost of the wood and the price of the finished article is the wealth which he or she has created. (See Fig. 16.1.)
4.  *Industry improves living standards.* Table 16.1 shows that most people became materially better off between 1974 and 1991 and indeed most of us are materially better off than ever before. However, in this chapter we shall go on to consider some costs of growth such as pollution of the environment. We might question whether the modern citizen in Tokyo,

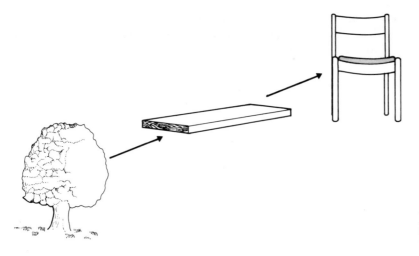

**Figure 16.1** Industry creates products (Source: Understanding Industry)

New York or London is really better off with more material possessions, living with more noise, smoke and high crime figures.

5. *Industry makes it possible for people to enjoy more leisure.* Because of industrial growth, people have more free time on their hands. Hospitals, schools, museums and the many welfare functions we have come to expect, are all supported from the wealth created by businesses in the public and private sectors of the economy.

| | 1974 | 1984 | 1991 |
|---|---|---|---|
| Dwellings per 1000 population | 349 | 381 | 422 |
| TV sets (licences) per 1000 | 308 | 330 | 350 |
| Private cars (licences) per 1000 | 244 | 283 | 320 |
| Telephones per 1000 | 337 | 520 | 610 |
| Refrigerators % of households | 82 | 94 | 97 |
| Pupils per teacher | 20.8 | 17.8 | 16.2 |
| Real income per head at 1984 prices | £3422 | £3898 | £4260 |

**Table 16.1** How standards of living improved between 1974 and 1991

## The costs of business activity

When a firm produces something it has to bear in mind a number of internal costs:

1. Production costs
2. Marketing costs
3. Financial costs
4. Administration costs
5. Other costs

In addition to these, there are external costs, which are costs which go beyond the balance sheet of the firm. These costs are sometimes known as externalities or spillover costs.

- **External costs = social costs − private costs.**

### Pollution

The most obvious social cost of business activity is pollution.

#### Water pollution

It has been standard practice for a long time for industry to locate by canals, rivers and seas. Industries such as paper production, chemicals and breweries not only use water in their manufacturing process, but they also pour out their waste into rivers and the sea. Perhaps the most notorious example of this type of activity is the dispersal of waste products from the nuclear-fuels industry. We have purification and filtration plants where water is treated, but it is difficult to break down the effects of industrial chemicals which destroy water life.

In Hungary, France, Germany and other European countries, firms are charged heavily for causing water pollution. This puts heavy pressure on firms to clean up their water.

Of course one problem of checking on water pollution levels in order to tax firms that pollute, is the cost of administering the system. In the UK, we tend to prosecute firms that break water safety laws. Fines can be imposed and imprisonment ordered in serious cases.

#### Air pollution

This was dramatically illustrated by several events in the 1980s. First, there was a leak of poisonous gas from a Union Carbide plant at Bhopal in India. More than 2000 people died and at least 10 times this number suffered from breathing and eye complaints. The Carbide plant was part of an American multinational producing pesticides to spray on crops. Investigations led to concern over the safety standards at the plant.

Perhaps even more dramatic was the nuclear disaster at Chernobyl in 1986. Here, we have an example of what was a growing, centrally planned economy trying to push through the growth of new power sources rapidly. Again, the safety standards of the nuclear reactor were highly questionable. Wide tracts of land have been declared unfit for farming for several years, threatening the ruin of a whole economy. Livestock of Welsh hill farmers were banned from sale in the market place because of heavy contamination. Emissions from UK factory chimneys and power stations are recognized as major sources of the 'acid rain' which results in the destruction of forests and pollution of lakes in Scandinavia and Germany.

*Eyewitness account*

GN Petrov witnessed some of the effects of the Chernobyl explosion.

'I approached Chernobyl at about 2.30 a.m. I could already see the fire above No 4 unit. The ventilation stack was clearly lit up by the flames. I remember how the flames were higher than the shaft, so that they must have been nearly 200 metres in the air.

I stopped about 100 metres from the end wall of the damaged reactor unit. By the light of the fire I could see that the building was half destroyed: there was nothing left of the central hall, it was a terrible sight. There were fire trucks and ambulances. The air smelled just the way it does after a massive bolt of lightning, a lingering smoke which made my eyes smart and my throat dry.

One of the firefighters climbed on the roof of V block to direct his comarades. Now I realize he was the first person in history to be exposed to that kind of danger. Even in Hiroshima no one got that close to the nuclear explosion as the bomb went off at 900 metres from the ground.

The next day the sun was shining and the sky was blue. Kids were playing in the sand, building houses, making pies. About eleven o'clock our next door neighbour went up to the roof to work on his tan. At one point he came down for a drink and said how easy it was to get a tan that day. He said his skin gave off a smell of burning right away. That evening he began vomiting uncontrollably and was taken to a medical centre.

It was only later, when we were told everything, that I thought back to that night when I drove up to the plant. I remember the potholes lit up by my headlights and the cement factory all covered in dust. For some reason it stuck in my mind. And now it occurs to me that pothole was radioactive, a perfectly ordinary pothole and the entire cement factory and everything else—the sky, my blood, my brain and what I was thinking—all was radioactive. Everything.'

*Dereliction*

If we consider the decision to build a new mine, or to drill for oil or natural gas, we can see that this might destroy areas of natural beauty in a irreversible way. Furthermore, when business pulls out of an area, the effects can be worse, for not only do jobs disappear but the community is also left with derelict land which is unpleasant to look at and sometimes dangerous. These dangerous remains include disused railway tunnels, mine shafts, quarries and old buildings. Generally it has been left to imaginative local councils to redevelop the sites as parks, boating lakes and sites for new industries.

## Case Study—Dereliction

The eyesores shown below might exist in a town near you.

Disused railway line

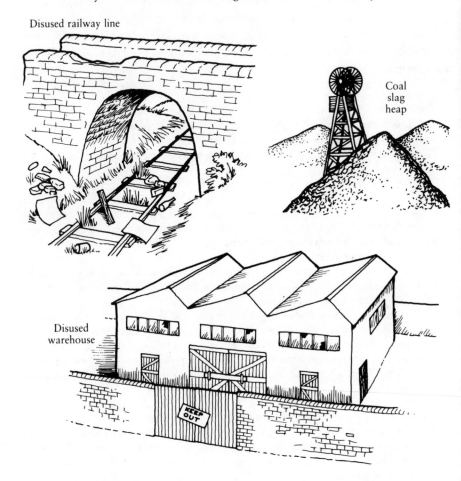

Coal slag heap

Disused warehouse

KEEP OUT

**Figure 16.2**   Familiar eyesores

*Question*

How could each of the sites be redeveloped? Make a list of four suggestions for each. Show in detail how one of these could be developed.

*Traffic congestion*

The speed of business development has put great pressure on our road networks. In 1986, the M25 orbital road around London was opened. By the time it was made fully operational it was inadequate to meet the need for a circular road. It has been described as the longest traffic jam in Europe.

Motor vehicles cause accidents, pour out noxious fumes and are noisy. One way of calculating the cost to householders of modern roads is to compare house prices near a large road with those of similar housing which is placed further away from the road in the same locality.

### Long-term waste

British Nuclear Fuels plc reprocesses nuclear waste at its plant in Sellafield. This waste is collected from many nuclear power stations. A recent report showed that if these power stations were shut down immediately, it would take ten years to reprocess the existing spent fuel.

Highly radioactive spent nuclear fuel is transported by road or rail in nuclear-waste 'flasks'. The resulting waste is then either dumped in the sea or buried in stores underground. It is argued that in this way we are storing up problems for the future.

### Noise

Concorde is a great flag-flyer for British Airways. It is also a considerable nuisance for those citizens who live close to its take-off points. Noise from road and rail traffic can also be a considerable nuisance to householders.

In the UK, noise nuisance is controlled through by-laws made by local authorities covering a wide range of matters from noisy animals and fireworks to radios and televisions. People can be prosecuted for continually making noise. For example, if your neighbours are forever holding parties and banging about in the middle of the night you can complain to the local council. They will send an officer round with a noise recorder. If the noise is above a certain level an order can be made out instructing your neighbours to keep the noise level down or face prosecution.

The activities of businesses and construction firms are controlled and certain areas may be designated by the local authority as Noise Abatement Zones.

### Food additives

Today consumers often want interesting presentation of products and value for money. Artificial colouring and flavourings and synthetic ingredients are used to make food and drinks more attractive and cheaper to produce. The medical profession have pointed out the dangerous spillover effects, particularly in areas such as hyperactivity in children.

**Figure 16.3**   Food additives

*Insufficient testing of products*

To try and become market leaders firms may be tempted to put their new products on the market before they have been thoroughly tested. A well known example of this was the production by the Distillers Company of a drug used by women to reduce the effects of morning sickness in pregnancy. The spillover effect was the terrible side-effect of thalidomide which caused babies to be born missing limbs.

*Weighing up costs and benefits*

Society benefits if resources are used well. When a business makes a decision it weighs up the costs and benefits in private terms. It does so because its prime purpose is to provide profits for shareholders.

The government is more likely to use cost-benefit analysis, for instance, in deciding whether to build a new road.

Cost-benefit analysis has been used to weigh up building a new London Underground line, the siting of the third London airport, the route of the rail link for the Channel Tunnel and even the building of fences to stop sheep from straying into the streets of Merthyr Tydfil.

A simple way of carrying out a cost-benefit analysis is given in the following example. Imagine that you are considering building a new training centre for unemployed workers. You would have to find out who would benefit and who would lose out. You would then have to make measurements in money terms of the loss or gain. For example, you could ask someone who would benefit how much he or she would be prepared to pay to see the project carried out. You would then have to ask someone who would lose out the minimum sum that he or she would be prepared to accept as compensation for the project taking place. We then add up all the gains and all the losses. If the gains outweigh the losses the project passes the test.

## The Environmental Protection Act

New environmental laws passed in 1991 have gone some way towards integrating pollution controls. Before the act, companies dealt with a variety of agencies controlling different aspects of pollution. The National Rivers Authority kept an eye on discharges to water, while Her Majesty's Pollution Inspectorate looked at other aspects such as air pollution. There was often a disorganized approach, with each agency looking after its own concerns, not always in the best interest of either the company or the planet. For example, if the NRA got tough the firm could shift its waste somewhere else.

The new system of Integrated Pollution Control turns the old system on its head. It affects only 'proscribed' sites—depending on the process and substances used—but most of manufacturing industry will fall into the IPC category. Under IPC one main agency will take the prime role in checking on overall environmental concern on an industrial site. In most cases this will be the Pollution Inspectorate.

## Pressure groups

Businesses have to operate against a background in which they are faced by many different competing interests.

Internally, the business needs to make a profit for shareholders and the shareholders need to be kept content with the way in which the business is being run. Externally, the business has more to contend with:

1. Perhaps the biggest pressure is to sell its products. Consumers do not have to and will not buy something they don't want.
2. The business is faced by the pressure put on it by competitors. Competition is often a spur to do well.
3. The government also exerts pressure on business to produce within certain standards.
4. Businesses also have to respond to the influence put on them by organized 'pressure groups'.

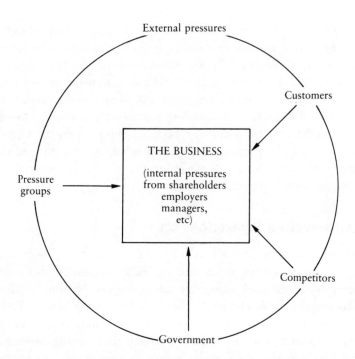

**Figure 16.4** Pressures on the business

### Types of of pressure group

The two main types of pressure groups are:

- *Protection groups* which are set up to fight a specific issue, such as danger on a local road caused by construction traffic building a local airport. In other words, local residents are protecting their interests against an outside threat.
- *Promotional pressure groups* are more formal groups which are sometimes highly-organized and fight campaigns on a wide range of issues. Examples of the latter would include Greenpeace and Friends of the Earth. Business might also find that a political party exerts strong opposition to some of their policies, e.g. selling products to South Africa.

*Consumer pressure groups*

A well known and powerful consumer group is the Consumers' Association, which produces the magazine *Which?*. The group is funded by subscriptions from members who buy the magazine. The Consumers' Association uses its funds to test a wide variety of products on which it then produces reports in its monthly magazine. It also produces books on consumer related matters.

The influence of the Consumers' Association goes beyond its publication of *Which?* because its reports are frequently reported in the national press.

Consumer programmes also get fair coverage on national television, the most famous being Esther Rantzen's 'That's Life'. Typical media coverage involves the investigation of complaints and the comparison of goods and services.

Nationalized industries also have Consumers' Councils, examples of which are:

- Post Office—Post Office Users' National Council
- British Rail—Transport Users' Consultative Committee

The government makes provision for the continuation of these groups when industries are privatized.

### Consumer boycotts

Consumers are sometimes organized into groups to stop buying certain products. In 1986, Barclays Bank sold off their South African branches. Throughout the 1970s and 1980s there was pressure put on Barclays customers by opponents of apartheid, to use other banks. It is arguable that this sort of pressure helped to finally influence Barclays' decision. In a similar way, animal rights pressure groups have used advertising campaigns and more direct persuasion to stop consumers using animal furs and products of modern factory farming.

As an extension of these activities sabotage has been used as an extreme form of protest against some forms of industrial production. Within the area of animal experimentation in the food, chemical and drugs industry, there are several animal rights protest groups including:

- The Royal Society for the Prevention of Cruelty to Animals (RSPCA)
- The Animal Liberation Front
- The National Anti-vivisection Society

Quite clearly this can cause adverse publicity for businesses operating in this area and raise operating costs. Animals have been freed, premises attacked and businesses have to spend money on the employment of security, such as the specialist security firm 'Control Risks' which specializes in risk assessment and kidnap negotiations.

### Local lobbying

There are several reasons why local residents may want to put pressure on a business to change its operations including:

1. Traffic danger
2. Emission of fumes
3. Emission of fluids

4. Litter and noise
5. Safety hazards such as tips, pits, etc.

Normally, a pressure group will develop out of letters to the press and protest meetings. The pressure group will then try to encourage the firm to change its policy, after which point it will put pressure on local and central government to influence the activities of the firm. Enlightened firms will try not to antagonize local feelings which bring adverse publicity for the business.

### Other organized pressure groups

Sometimes groups run themselves in a highly-organized way to influence public opinion. They will try to get a wide number of people to accept their views to exert pressure on the business community. Trade unions use this method of persuasion quite often. Groups like the teachers, the miners and the printworkers, have used national advertising to try and win support from the public and political parties for their cause. Picketing and industrial action is another way of trying to put pressure on business.

The employers' organization, the CBI, and the unions' organization, the TUC, also exert influence.

Other promotional pressure groups, such as the campaign for lead-free petrol and the anti-smoking lobby, use similar techniques. Sometimes groups use less peaceful methods to impress their views on the public. Demonstrations, protest marches and sit-ins often lead to publicity on television or in the press.

### Business response to pressure groups

There are a number of ways businesses can respond to pressure groups:

(a) Ignore them using the argument that consumers can choose whether to buy the product or not, and in the meantime make sure that production takes place within the bounds of legal requirements.
(b) Run a counter campaign to win public support. This is the policy which has been used by British Nuclear Fuels plc. 'Come to Sellafield. Look around the place. See for yourself how safe it is.' This, loosely paraphrased, is the message of a multi-million pound advertising campaign which has been commissioned by British Nuclear Fuels. The campaign is being shown on television as well as in newspapers.
(c) Take advice from consumers in order to compromise and win public support in this way.

**BRITISH NUCLEAR FUELS PLC**

*request the pleasure of
your company to view their Sellafield
Exhibition Centre.
Open from 10am-4pm every day of the
week,
Easter—end of October
or 10am-4pm Monday–Friday,
November–March.*

*Exhibition Centre, British Nuclear Fuels plc, Sellafield, Cumbria.
(Off the A595 at Calderbridge between Millom and Whitehaven)*

**Figure 16.5**   Advertisement –
British Nuclear Fuels PLC

## Employment and unemployment

Another consequence of business is the creation and destruction of employment. There are more people working in the UK today than ever before, as a consequence of the rise in the population. Over 70 per cent of the population today work in the service sector of the economy. Service occupations have displaced many of the old manufacturing jobs, as well as jobs in agriculture and mining.

In the 1950s exports of manufacturers were over three times bigger than imports. Today, we import more manufactured goods than we export (see Fig. 16.6).

Factors causing this decline have been low quality and an overconcentration of producing low-value products which many other countries now also produce.

Unemployment can be seen as a consequence of the failure of business to keep up-to-date. The government's chief scientific adviser has continued to warn that 'industry is not spending enough on research and development. History shows that we are a very innovative nation; what we lack is development—the knack of exploiting the ideas that we produce.'

Another cause of unemployment is new technology. In industries as different as banking, car production and brewing automation, information technology and robots are able to do the work previously done by humans. However, information technology and other new developments also create new jobs. With the extra income that we earn from producing more we are able to enjoy more leisure—creating a further demand for services and service

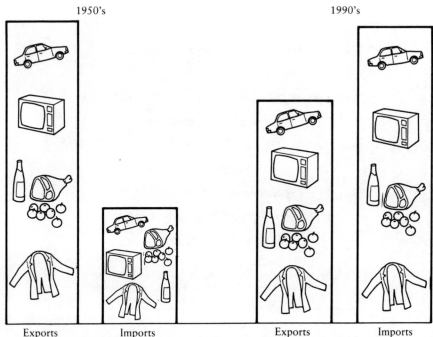

1950's                                         1990's

Exports        Imports              Exports            Imports

**Figure 16.6**  Ratio of UK exports to imports

occupations. Today, jobs usually require more skill and training. A survey in the East Midlands in 1990 showed that for every 100 unemployed general labourers there were only 5 vacancies. For every 100 unemployed electronics engineers there were 140 vacancies.

## Business and the community

Centres of population develop around work. As these centres become established a community comes into being. Very strong communities develop where people share similar jobs, working together and experiencing similar life styles. Mining communities, farming communities, and fishing communities are well known for the strong bonds that tie people together.

In modern society, people tend to move further to get work and modern housing estates are characterized by people doing a wide range of different jobs. Inevitably this tends to reduce the bonds that hold people together.

## Conservation

Modern business depends on the use of non-renewable resources, particularly in the use of energy. Modern technology is particularly dependent on three main fossil fuels—oil, coal and natural gas. Together they account for over 90 per cent of the world's energy supplies.

- **Non-renewable resource**: one for which only a limited stock exists on the planet (not necessarily totally discovered by humans) and for which the creation of new stock over time is zero.

Some commentators are very worried about the way in which non-renewable resources are being used up. D. H. Meadows and his associates, in their book *The Limits to Growth*, argued that if resources continue to be used up in the way they are today, then within the next 100 years a crisis will occur because certain resources are limited namely: arable land, coal, oil, aluminium, copper, iron and other minerals.

When this crisis point is reached, they predict 'the breakdown of society and the irreversible disruption of life support systems of this planet'.

The problem of conservation is both a national and an international one. Businesses are more concerned with relatively short-term profits than with the future of society. Multi-lateral agreements have been signed between countries limiting whaling and fishing. On a national scale, governments have used subsidies as a means of encouraging farmers to preserve hedgerows and use more traditional methods of farming. Commercial farming has tended to encourage farmers to use chemicals as pesticides and fertilizers to increase yield per acre. Pollution of water by nitrates has increased since the Second World War as farmers have ploughed more and more fertilizers into the land. This is particularly true in areas of heavy cereal production. Rain has then washed the chemicals into the water supply. The Wildlife and Countryside Act has provided scope to compensate farmers to encourage them to consider the environment rather than simply to aim for a profit.

Over the last few years, report after report has stressed the gravity of world utilization of resources. *Global 2000* concluded that we face a world 'more polluted, less stable ecologically, more vulnerable to disruption than ever before'.

- **Ecology**: the relationship between living things and their environment.

The Brandt Report stated: 'Few threats to the peace and survival of the human community are greater than those posed by the degradation of the biosphere on which human life depends.'

- **Biosphere**: the regions of earth's crust and atmosphere in which living matter is found.

Day by day we witness the accelerating loss of land, fertile soil, fresh air, clean water, forests, non-renewable fossil fuel and precious raw materials.

Case Study—Cities for people

**Figure 16.7** Anti-pollution
advertisement

*Questions*

1.  What are the benefits of the motor car?
2.  What costs of the motor car are mentioned in the article?
3.  Draw up a report weighing up the costs and benefits of motor cars.
4.  What is a pressure group?
5.  What is the pressure group in the above advertisement in Fig. 16.7?
6.  Find out more about this group.

Case Study—Trolley folly

# Trolley folly clampdown

IT'S WAR on the trolley wallies!

Reading Borough Council is set to take action against stores which own the wire eyesores discarded around the town.

They have taken on the powers outlined in The Berkshire Act of 1986 to help deal with the problem.

And if you think the council's off its trolley, think again. Already the problem of abandoned trolleys has been 'drastically reduced' thanks to the Cleaner Reading Campaign.

But now the wheels are in motion to step up action against the little metal monsters, which can turn up in the most unlikely places.

Reading Borough Council wants a shopping showdown with stores in the Reading area, and have invited them to a special meeting at the Civic Offices in January, and want all stores using trolleys to attend.

The council hopes that using the powers outlined in Section 13 of the Berkshire Act will help curb the problem of discarded trolleys.

They explain: 'This Section allows the borough council to carry out its own collection of trolleys left abandoned on the streets and to make a charge to return these to the stores.'

'The main responsibility for the retrieval and control of the use of shopping trolleys rests with the shops providing them for customer use.'

'The borough council expects frequent collections in areas of high use and from the surrounding area with attention to a wider area as well.'

The act empowers the council to move in if regular collections from stores in the area are not up to scratch and if trolleys have become so damaged they cannot be used any more.

Shops and stores wanting more information before the meeting should contact Assistant Chief Environmental Health Officer Derek Tomlin on Reading 55911 extension 2305.

*Questions*

1.  How has Reading Borough Council the powers to deal with the problem outlined above?
2.  Who is responsible for trolley pollution?
3.  Who is going to be made to pay?
4.  Do you think this is a good solution?
5.  In what other areas do you think this solution to social costs could be applied?

### Case Study—Chernobyl

Six months after the nuclear disaster at Chernobyl, the plant was once again producing nuclear power. The Russians estimated that it cost $3 billion to clean up the site and rehouse the refugees in a new area. They were quite open in admitting that the design had been wrong and that human error had been involved.

The accident occurred on 26 April 1986, but within months the plant was back in production.

The Russians expected to build a further six pressurized water reactors by 1990. The damaged reactor, unit 4, at Chernobyl employed 3500 workers who worked in two-week shifts and lived 20 miles away from the plant to reduce the danger from radiation.

The costs will be felt for a long time. Electricity prices were set to rise by over 10 per cent in the Soviet Union and in early 1987 there was a severe energy shortage. Street lighting was run at a dim level. The Russians were forced to make changes to 14 plants similar to Chernobyl.

*Questions*

1. What are the benefits of the nuclear-energy programme to the Russian economy?
2. What have been the costs of the Chernobyl disaster?
3. Is it possible to accurately measure these costs?
4. Who should be responsible for these costs?
5. What pressures would you expect to have been put on the Russian government as a result of this disaster? By whom?

### Case Study—The Nationalized Industries' Consumer Councils

In 1987, British Rail was considering bringing back its first class day-return tickets as a result of pressure put on it by commuters.

The first class day-return had been stopped in 1983, but ever since there had been a storm of pressure to bring it back. An experiment was being planned in the South East to bring back the ticket and, if it went well, the ticket would go on sale nationwide. There had been a lot of pressure put on British Rail by the Central Transport Consultative Committee which is the watchdog of how British Rail runs its affairs.

An executive said, 'All my friends were furious when they stopped the ticket. Often we do not travel at peak times and why should we pay the full price to sit on an empty train? Many people have switched to cars.' A train driver said, 'We need all the passengers we can get.'

Mr Len Dumelow of the Transport Committee said, 'I don't see how British Rail can ignore the market. Now they are beginning to see the light, but only after a long period of pressure. A study by the committee showed that first class carriages are often underused and that there would be a big demand for the ticket.

*Questions*

1. What is the consumer council mentioned in this article?
2. What do you think that it does?

3. Will this group have any influence?
4. What sorts of complaints might you make to this group?
5. What are the advantages of having such a group?
6. Do you think that such a group would represent all rail users' views equally?
7. Do some research to find out if other students or members of the public are aware of the existence of such groups. Has anyone ever made a complaint to such a group? Was it taken up?
8. Do you agree with the views of:
   (a) The executive?
   (b) The train driver?
   Why do you think they have these particular views?

# Questions

1. Complete the following sentences using the terms below:

   | | |
   |---|---|
   | Conservation | Non-renewable resource |
   | Pollution | Pressure groups |
   | Externalities | Cost-benefit analysis |
   | Private cost | Regional imbalance |

   (a) The wages a firm has to pay out are an example of a . . . . . . . .
   (b) Businesses often have to face opposition from . . . . . . . . which try to influence the way the firm runs from outside.
   (c) The government might carry out a . . . . . . . . exercise before building a new road.
   (d) . . . . . . . . are the difference between private and social costs.
   (e) Oil is an example of a . . . . . . . .
   (f) . . . . . . . . is a result of the way industry moves to the most profitable locations.
   (g) Dumping of waste products is an example of . . . . . . . .
   (h) . . . . . . . . involves carefully saving up resources for the future.

2. Which of the following would you classify as private costs, private benefits, social costs and social benefits, from the point of view of a firm manufacturing chemicals?
   (a) Local jobs
   (b) Wages
   (c) Purchase of raw materials
   (d) Heating costs
   (e) Destruction of local beauty spot
   (f) Revenue from selling products
   (g) Waste fumes
   (h) Noise from construction traffic
   (i) Wider range of products on the market

3. In East Bay there is a meat processing plant producing dog food. It employs 200 workers and is the largest local employer in a town of just 1200 inhabitants, with a 15 per cent unemployment rate.

The smell coming off the plant is very strong and is a major source of complaint for residents. House prices around the plant sell for on average £4,000 less than the market value elsewhere. Wages in the factory are well below the national average.

When a residents' committee took their complaints to the firm they were told that the firm was considering closing down this factory and converting it into an automated warehouse employing six workers.

(a) List **five** social costs and **five** social benefits to the community from the food processing plant.

(b) Would East Bay be better off if the buildings were converted into an automated warehouse?

4. Study the article from *The Economist*—'Oh deer'. (See Fig. 16.8.)

You are a Laplander writing a letter of complaint to the Russian Embassy.

Structure the letter to highlight the problems of your people.

### Case Study—Nos amis les animaux

Un kilogramme d'ivoire est racheté 50 F au braconnier (POACHER). Ce même poids sera revendu 1,000 F à Hong Kong ou à Tokyo. Dans le parc de Ruaha, en Tanzanie, on tue le plus grand mammifère terrestre pour 150 F et on abandonne sa viande—au soleil. Pour les rhinocéros, dont la corne recèle soi-disant des vertus aphrodisiaques, c'est pire. En 1972, il y avait 500 rhinocéros dans le Ruaha. Aujourd'-hui, il en reste 10. Pour risquer leur vie en luttant contre les braconniers—mais quels risques prennent-ils?—les gardiens gagnent 120 F par mois et sont logés, pas nourris. Ils ont droit à une petite prime lorsqu'ils arrêtent un pauvre hère qui chasse pour se nourrir, de 150 F pour un chasseur d'ivoire et 300 F si ce dernier est ramené avec son arme.

*Questions*

1. By how much is ivory marked up, from the price that the poacher sells it for, to the market price in Hong Kong and Tokyo?
2. What happens to the elephant's meat?
3. Why is the rhinoceros' horn so valuable?
4. How much do the gamewardens get paid as a standard wage?
5. Do they receive any non-money perks?
6. How much do the game wardens receive for catching poachers?
7. What evidence is given in the article that the animals at Ruaha are in danger?

## Oh deer

FROM OUR NORDIC CORRESPONDENT

Rudolph the Red-Nosed Reindeer may have an unusual glow to his nose this Christmas, if his summer home is in those areas of Norway and Sweden contaminated by radioactive fall-out from the Chernobyl disaster. Local experts think that up to a third of the animals killed in this year's autumn season will be unfit for human consumption. That is tough, but not absolutely disastrous, for the Lapp people of sub-arctic northern Scandinavia.

About 30,000 Lapps and 200,000 herded reindeer live in Norway and 17,000 Lapps and 250,000 reindeer in Sweden, where some 40,000 wild reindeer are also preserved for hunting. In both Norway and Sweden something over 2,000 Lapps make their living from reindeer-herding. They are no longer nomads; although some do follow the herds to the summer pastures (where they also entertain the tourists), all have permanent, hard-roofed homes where they spend the cold months, comparatively in the Lapp of luxury. Each year they slaughter 60,000-80,000 animals, whose lean dark meat has a specialised market.

In the late 1950s, the Lapps and their animals were exposed to high doses of strontium-90 from Russian nuclear tests. The Chernobyl fall-out, mostly of caesium-137, is about 50 times as high. The 1950s fall-out seems to have had no measurable effect on the Lapps' health. This year's exposure lasted a much shorter time, but reindeer moss may prove to have been very efficient at capturing caesium from the atmosphere, so the after-effects of Chernobyl could be long-lasting.

Sweden and Norway are taking no chances. The World Health Organisation says there need be no restrictions on eating food with radioactive levels of under 2,000 becquerels per kilogramme. Sweden has set an upper limit of 300 becquerels per kilogramme, Norway of 600. Some reindeer in Norway have registered 40,000 becquerels; but the average in the Norwegian affected areas is probably nearer 10,000, and in Sweden it is much lower.

As for the Lapps, restrictions on sales of the meat will hurt their traditions worse than their incomes. About one-third of them still speak their ancient language, which is of the Finno-Ugrian family, originating in central Asia. Its vocabulary is not extensive, and a remarkably large proportion of its words refer to reindeer and products derived from them. Now the Lapps' governments have promised to buy up the uneatable dead animals, which will very likely end up as food for mink.

**Sniffing the caesium**

**Figure 16.8**  The effect of Chernobyl (Source: *The Economist*)

8.  Who benefits from the preservation of the animals at Ruaha?
9.  Is it important to conserve the animals?

## Coursework

Select an issue which you are particularly concerned about. It may be something that you are directly involved with or have heard about through the media.

It may involve:

- a new road/motorway
- a local/national/or global environmental issue
- local services
- health service facilities
- another issue.

Make a record of all the information you can collect on that issue.

Try to record all sides of an issue. Interview people face-to-face. Write to people like MPs and councillors who are difficult to meet face-to-face.

Look at the costs and benefits of any changes that are taking place. Who gets the benefits, who suffers the costs?

What are the alternative ways of looking at the issue?

What comments can you make about your findings?

# 17

# Services to business

The individual business is heavily dependent on other groups within its environment; the government provides it with a legal framework, consumers provide it with a market and other producers provide it with competition. Business is also dependent on business services provided by other specialist firms. Without the specialist services illustrated in Fig. 17.1, businesses could not function.

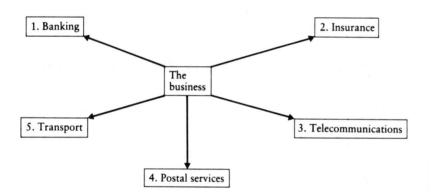

Figure 17.1 Diagram showing the services needed by businesses

*Task—Do businesses need services?*

Working in groups, look at the services indicated in the chart above. Make a list of the reasons why businesses need such services. Briefly describe what might happen to trade if such services were not generally available.

## Banking services

Banking services today are provided by *financial intermediaries*. In the past, the market for banking services was straightforward. If you wanted banking services you automatically went to a high street bank such as National Westminster, Lloyds, Barclays and the Midland; if you wanted a mortgage you went to a building society and, if you wanted insurance, you went to an insurance company. Increasing competition in the 1970s, plus legislation in the 1980s, has meant that, in the modern market for banking services, such services are available from a variety of institutions and that banks themselves have radically expanded their role to provide a wider range of services for their customers and become a one-stop supermarket for financial wares.

Financial intermediaries are organizations which channel funds, from those who have a surplus and wish to deposit their money, to those who wish to borrow. One of their most important functions is to accept money from the public and then lend it on. They, therefore, provide a link between borrowers and lenders and by charging a rate of interest to borrowers slightly higher than they pay to lenders, intermediaries make their profits. (See Fig. 17.2.)

**Figure 17.2** How banks use depositors' money to make loans to borrowers

There are many different providers of banking services in the UK including:

1. *The Bank of England.* This supervises the other banks and controls the banking system. It issues new notes and destroys old notes and holds accounts for the clearing banks and for the government.
2. *The clearing banks.* The membership of the Clearing House used to be restricted and only included the large commercial banks, but today membership has expanded to include a larger number of banks involved with 'cheque account' banking, for example, National Girobank and TSB. A significant event took place in 1988 when Abbey National became the first building society to become a member.

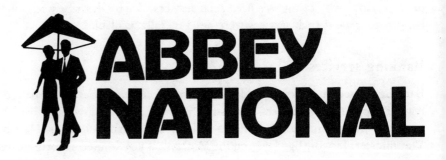

**Figure 17.3** Abbey National logo

- **Clearing** is a highly automated system of sorting cheques and settling debts.

3. *Merchant banks.* These are old-established trading banks, such as Morgan Grenfell and Kleinwort Benson, whose main functions today include finance, advice and dealing. For example, a major part of the their work involves lending to companies and governments, issuing new stocks and shares, factoring, leasing and buying and selling on the commodity and exchange markets.

4. *Building societies.* These are the banks' largest competitor for deposits. Whereas the banks' share of consumer deposits has decreased over the last 10 years, the building societies' has increased. In the past the role of building societies was to take in funds from customers and lend to others for house purchase. Today, building societies can lend for other purposes and provide cheque accounts, as well as many other services more normally associated with high street banks.

5. *Moneyshops.* Over recent years these have been set up by American banks to provide a more informal approach to banking for customers, e.g. Citibank, Boston Trust, etc. Though the main area of moneyshop activities is lending, they also provide a wide range of financial services designed to make it easy for customers to transact.

*Task—What do you require from a bank?*

Assume that you have just started a small sports shop in the centre of your nearest town or city. Make a list of the services which you feel a business of this type will require. Briefly explain why this business might require each of these services. Compare your answers with those of others in your class.

There are many types of banking services.

## A safe place for money

Banks provide a place where customers can put their money in safety. A business can put its daily takings into the bank by sending out an employee with a paying-in book or, alternatively, depositing after banking hours by placing a money pouch in the night safe.

## A source of loans

Lending money to customers is the banks' most profitable activity. Banks will lend for a wide variety of purposes, to both personal and business customers. There are five principles which all banks will follow when lending money:

- *Purpose*  —What will the loan be used for?
- *Amount*  —Is the amount requested enough?
- *Repayment*—Can the borrower make the repayments?
- *Term*  —How long is the loan for?
- *Security*  —Is there security against default?

Assessing each of these five areas will help the bank to calculate the risk involved.

### Case Study—Working as an advances clerk

Imagine that you work as an advances clerk at your local high street bank. Your main responsibility is to recommend decisions to your manager concerning loans to customers at your bank. In order to help you make such decisions you use a decision sheet. Look at the two decisions sheets below and explain how you would feel about lending money to each of these customers. Use Purpose, Amount, Repayment, Term and Security, to help you recommend your decision.

```
                        Decision Sheet
Customer's Name ......William Anderson............ Age 34
Address ...5 Rose Street, Walmley, Sutton Coldfield
Customer's account held for .........3 years.............
Has the account been satisfactory?   YES/NO
If NO, why? ....Overdraw once without permission.....
INCOME (monthly)               £ 1000
EXPENDITURE (monthly)          £ 900
Purpose of loan .......Holiday................
Nature and cost of project ........£1500...........
Amount from customer ...........-...............
Amount of loan .......£1500.................
Length of loan .......24 months................
Repayment ......£77.84 per month..............
Security ...........NONE...................
Decision ...............................................
.................................................
```

**Figure 17.4** Decision sheet (1)

**Decision Sheet**

Customer's Name ... *Marshall Dillon* ... Age *42*

Address ... *5 Kentucky Drive Water Orton*

Customer's account held for ... *23 years*

Has the account been satisfactory? YES/~~NO~~

If NO, why? ...

INCOME (monthly) £ *2300*

EXPENDITURE (monthly) £ *1100*

Purpose of loan ... *To purchase a car*

Nature and cost of project ... *£10000*

Amount from customer ... *£2000*

Amount of loan ... *£8000*

Length of loan ... *60 months*

Repayment ... *£221.10 per month*

Security ... *Customer has a mortgage with this bank*

Decision ...

**Figure 17.5** Decision sheet (2)

A *loan* enables a business person to buy a fixed asset, such as a piece of office equipment or a motor car. This is an agreed sum of money, borrowed and paid back over a number of years. The bank will only be prepared to make the loan if it is reasonably satisfied that the flow of cash coming into the business will cover the repayments.

An *overdraft* helps customers to overcome any temporary cash shortfall by allowing them to draw more from their account than they have in it. The bank will fix an overdraft limit up to which the customer can draw cheques. Charges are made by the bank on the amount overdrawn.

## A way of transferring money

Whereas in the past whenever a transaction took place funds were transferred using coins or notes, today the majority of transactions involve automated systems which transfer an amount directly from one account to another, without any direct movement of cash.

*Cheques*

A cheque is a written instruction by the account-holder (the 'drawer') to the bank to make a payment to somebody else (the 'payee'). The most common form of cheque used is a crossed cheque which must be paid into a bank account. A crossing on its own is called a general cross. (See Fig. 17.6.)

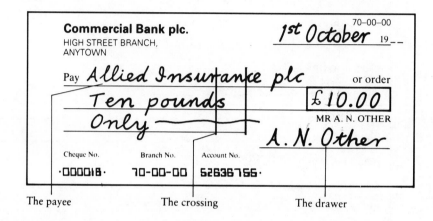

**Figure 17.6**   Crossed cheque

Sometimes businesses use other crossings (see Fig. 17.7).

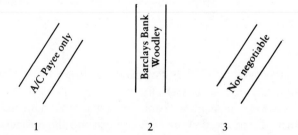

**Figure 17.7**   Three special cheque crossings used by business

1. A business might ask its customers to write 'A/C Payee only' in the crossing. This is to ensure that the money is paid only into the account named on the cheque (i.e., the business' account). The cheque cannot be signed over (endorsed) to some other account.
2. The second crossing means that the cheque can only be paid in at a specific branch of Barclays, i.e. the business' branch at Woodley.
3. The third crossing shown in Fig. 17.7 is a warning to the person the cheque is paid to. The words 'not negotiable' mean that if the cheque was stolen and then passed on, the person receiving the cheque has no legal right to it.

**Figure 17.8**   Cheque guarantee card

*Cheque guarantee cards* (see Fig. 17.8) increase the acceptability and use of cheques as a means of payment. Where the customer follows the conditions of use and the card number is put on the back of the cheque, the cheque cannot be stopped from payment. Most cards guarantee a payment up to £50, but some are for larger amounts, i.e. £100.

## Standing orders

A standing order is a written order by a bank customer to the bank to make a payment of a certain amount on a certain date. The order stands until the customer stops it. For example, a business could pay its rates bill of £300 per quarter in this way.

- A **standing order** involves a set amount which needs to be paid at regular intervals.

The standing order in Fig. 17.9 overleaf, is made out by J. Scott ordering her bank to make a payment for rates every quarter to Darlington Council.

## Direct debits

This is similar to the standing order, apart from the following features:

1. The payment can vary in amount and date.
2. The firm to which the payment is made informs the bank what the size of payment will be.

An example of the use of a direct debit could be for the sale of a vehicle on credit. The finance company might ask the customer to sign a direct-debit form giving their permission to make payments when requested to do so by the finance company.

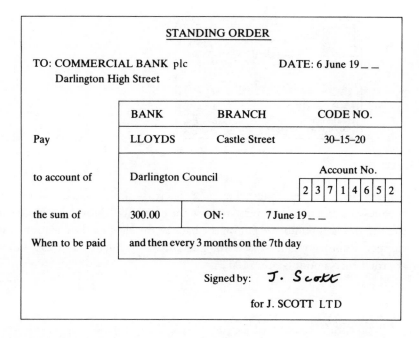

**Figure 17.9**  Standing order

*Bank giro credits*

Often customers wish to pay money into someone's else's bank account. This can be done through the system of bank giro credits which allows transfers to anybody's account in any bank in the country.

A form for a single bank giro (see Fig. 17.10) is made out to make a payment into a single account; a multiple giro makes a payment into several accounts.

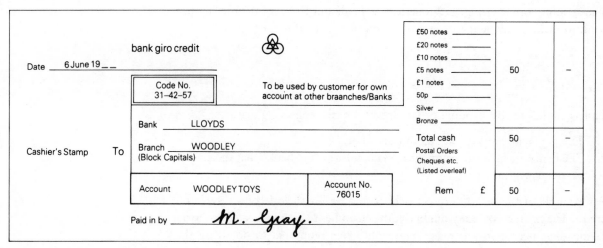

**Figure 17.10**  Form for a single bank giro

For example, anyone can transfer money into a single account simply by walking into a bank or post office and handing over cash or a cheque and filling in a giro form for that amount.

A business might also use the system for the payment of its bills. When sending a customer a bill, a business might enclose a pre-printed giro form as part of the bill. This practice is commonly used for gas, electricity and telephone bills.

A multiple giro allows one payment to be made to many people. This system is used by employers to pay wages and salaries to their staff. A business will pay a cheque into a bank and fill out a multiple-giro form listing the names, account numbers and banks it wants money to be paid into. This paper system is gradually being replaced by Bankers Automated Clearing Services (BACS). The aim of this system has been to reduce the level of paper in the system and replace it with a system of electronic transfer of funds. Information is sent to the bank in the form of magnetic tape, diskette, disc, or through a telephone line. The information is then processed by BACS and the appropriate transactions are recorded.

## Bank drafts

A bank draft is made up by a bank and signed by the bank manager. It is used for making payments of large sums of money. For example, if a business is selling an expensive item it will not allow the customer to take the item away immediately if the customer is paying by an ordinary cheque.

It will, however, accept a bank draft because it knows that payment is guaranteed.

## Credit cards

Over recent years the use of credit cards has dramatically increased. Most schemes are run by companies owned by the banks, e.g. VISA, Access. Credit card customers are given a credit limit and can buy goods and services up to that limit. Goods and services can be bought at any outlet which displays the appropriate credit card sign. For example, if Sandra Bailey buys £20 worth of petrol from a garage, she will show the garage her card and then sign a sales voucher with the details of the sale on it. The credit card company will then settle the bill with the garage, keeping back a percentage of the bill, normally between one per cent and five per cent, as an income from the retailer charged as a commission for the sale. At the end of the month Sandra will receive a statement from the credit card company.

The advantages to businesses of the credit card scheme are that it helps solve their cash-flow problems (when they buy using a credit card) and allows them to make more sales (when they allow customers to pay by credit card).

## Other bank services

Banks provide a wide range of other financial services:

1. They will provide regular *statements* of bank balances.
2. Many bank customers have documents or valuables which they need to keep in a secure place. Boxes can be rented out allowing valuables to be stored in vaults.
3. Banks provide international services. An important area is the provision of services to business customers as either exporters or importers. They might buy or sell foreign currencies in exchange for sterling, to enable a business either to buy or sell goods which are priced in foreign currencies. Banks also help businesses by providing them with advice on documentation, as well as methods of payment and settlement in international trade. Banks will also provide traveller's cheques and Eurocheques for international travel. Traveller's cheques are safer than foreign currency and are available in fixed denominations either in sterling or foreign currencies. Eurocheques operate just like a cheque book and can be used with a Eurocheque Card to make purchases overseas.

### Case Study—NatWest Eurocheques

Read the extract below:

NatWest Eurocheque Service is one of the simplest and most convenient ways of spending money abroad because it works with your UK current account. It provides you with a special cheque book and card which guarantees your cheques and allows you to withdraw currency from cash machines. This means that when you are travelling in Europe, your current account travels with you. So you can:

- obtain cash in banks
- pay for goods and services by cheque
- withdraw cash from cash machines

The NatWest Eurocheques Service is part of the eurocheque scheme which covers more than forty countries throughout Europe, the Mediterranean and North Africa. Some 250 000 banks and over 5 million retail outlets currently take Eurocheques and Eurocheque cards can be used in nearly 30 000 cash machines. To locate the banks and retail outlets that welcome the NatWest Eurocheque Service, whichever country you happen to be in, just look for the distinctive blue and red 'ec' logo on windows, doors and cash machines.

# NatWest

# eurocheque Service

**Figure 17.11**   National Westminster logo (By kind permission of National Westminster Bank)

*Questions*

1. Make a list of the benefits of using eurocheques.
2. Why would it be useful to use cash machines in another country?
3. Briefly describe the alternatives to using eurocheques. If you were going abroad on business how would you organize your financial arrangements?

4. Banks provide a *factoring* service for businesses. This provides finance for a business by mobilizing the amount due to it by its debtors. Banks will take a business's invoices from it in return for cash and will collect the money when it is due. A commission is charged for the service and this can lead to the bank's managing the debtors of the business.
5. Business customers often turn to the banks for *advice* on a wide range of issues. Advice may be sought upon businesses finances, legal matters, insurance, tax problems, seeking to expand the business, status enquiries on new customers, etc.

## Insurance services

- **Insurance** is the business of taking on other people's risks.

Most businesses have valuable property and equipment which is subject to many risks. They can cover themselves against many of these risks by taking out insurance policies.

To take out an insurance policy costs money but, if anything should happen to the business or its possessions, the insurance company will compensate it. The money we pay to an insurance company is called a *premium* and we can illustrate how insurance works by using a simple example.

Imagine that there are 20 students in a class, each with a bicycle worth £40. Each year, one of the bicycles gets stolen and the unfortunate person has to pay out £40 for a new bicycle. One of the students has the idea of starting an insurance pool. The idea is that each student should put £2 into an insurance pool so that there is £40 in the pool. Whichever student loses his or her bike that year claims the £40 to buy a new bike. Every year therefore they will put £2 each in premium into the central pool of funds. Of course, if their bike is not stolen they will not get any money out of the pool but they will be a lot less worried about losing their bikes.

A business is exposed to a wide range of risks ranging from fire to non-payment of debts. With all of the insurance policies available, business people are able to sleep a lot more easily at night, knowing that by paying out fairly small premiums they are covering themselves against the risk of having to pay out large amounts should anything happen to them or their possessions. (See Fig. 17.12.)

**Figure 17.12** Insurance protects businesses against risks such as fire

Insurance companies are not in business to take risks. They calculate very carefully the chances of accidents happening and then set the premiums the public have to pay.

## Stages in taking out insurance

Figure 17.13 summarizes the steps involved in taking out an insurance policy.

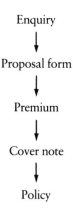

Enquiry

Proposal form

Premium

Cover note

Policy

**Figure 17.13**   Steps in taking out insurance

When a business has chosen the insurance policy it wants, it will fill in an application form for insurance called a *proposal form*. The proposal form will ask a number of important questions so that the insurance company can work out the amount of premium that should be charged. Of course, the proposal form should be filled out with complete honesty. This is termed *utmost good faith*. Obviously the level of risk involved will determine the amount of premium paid.

You will only be able to insure something in which you have an *insurable interest* (i.e., something which will cause you to lose money if anything happens).

Insurance can be obtained from:

- the insurance company directly.
- an insurance agent who work for an insurance company.
- an insurance broker who will work independently of insurance companies and will provide a range of policies so that clients can choose the policy which offers best value for money.

A *cover note* will cover the insured until the policy arrives. The *policy* is evidence of a contract between the insurance company and the insured.

The details of what is covered are laid down in the *schedule*—a section of the policy which indicates the name or description of the business, the complete list of items covered and, possibly, the maximum or minimum claim allowed.

Contents insurance, for example, might cover a firm for carpets, fixtures and burst pipes to a total value of, say £5,000.

When an insurance company has to pay out money this is called *indemnity*. Indemnity should return the insured to the position they were in before the event which caused the loss took place.

## Types of business insurance

Whatever the business, it will require a series of policies.

### Motor insurance

Insurance will be required for the business's vehicles. It might insure them all together under what is called *fleet insurance*. Businesses will usually have *comprehensive insurance*, which covers damage to the business's vehicles and also covers the business against claims made for damage caused by its vehicles.

### Case Study—Maxine Chung's taxi business
(*Source*: Southern Examining Group)

Maxine Chung runs a taxi business using her own car. She drives the car herself. She keeps the car in a private garage in central Manchester.

In August 1985, Maxine took out a comprehensive motor insurance for her taxi. The taxi was brand new at the time and cost Maxine £8,000. In 1985, the annual premium was £350.

Table 17.1 below shows the premiums paid by Maxine for comprehensive insurance in the following years.

**Table 17.1**

| Year | Annual Premium |
|------|----------------|
| 1986 | £320 |
| 1987 | £400 |
| 1988 | £370 |
| 1989 | £350 |
| 1990 | £355 |

In December 1989, Maxine was involved in a serious car accident. Maxine was responsible for causing the accident. Her taxi was a complete 'write off'.

The insurance company only paid Maxine £4,000 to replace the car.

*Questions*

1. What is an insurance premium?
2. How would the size of Maxine's premiums be affected by the fact that
   (a)  she kept her taxi in a garage?
   (b)  she kept the taxi in central Manchester?
3. Suggest reasons why Maxine's annual premiums changed each year between 1985 and 1989.
4. Why did Maxine only receive £4,000 in compensation for the loss of her taxi?
5. What protection would Maxine get from having a comprehensive motor insurance policy?
6. Suggest reasons why Maxine's premium only increased by £5 in 1990.

*Goods-in-transit insurance*

If a firm is transporting goods, it will want to cover against them being damaged on the way.

*Fire and flood insurance*

The firm will want to insure against buildings, goods or machinery being damaged in a fire or by a flood.

*Consequential-loss insurance*

A business might lose its profits as a consequence of a fire or other damage. Compensation can be claimed for money lost.

*Public liability insurance*

A firm can cover itself for the money it has to pay out if it is sued by someone who is hurt on its premises. (See Fig. 17.14.)

*Employers' liability insurance*

A firm can cover itself for the money it has to pay out if it is sued by one of its own employees who is hurt while working on the company's premises. (See Fig. 17.15.)

**Figure 17.14**   A member of the public who is hurt on business premises may sue – public liability insurance protects the business against this

**Figure 17.15**   An employee hurt on the employer's premises may sue – employers' liability insurance protects the business against this

*Fidelity guarantee*

An organization can cover itself against one of its employees stealing from the company.

*Product liability*

A firm can insure itself against being sued by a consumer who suffers injury or loss caused by the firm's products.

*Plate-glass insurance*

A firm like a jewellery shop could insure its plate-glass windows.

*Freezer insurance*

Large supermarkets will insure against losses which might occur if their freezers went out of action.

*Bad-debts insurance*

Firms selling goods on credit might insure against non-payment of debts. Exporters would use the government's Export Credit Guarantee Department (ECGD) for this purpose.

*Theft insurance*

Firms can also insure against items being stolen from their shops.

Firms *cannot* insure against not making a profit or holding goods that do not sell—these are non-insurable risks.

### Case Study—The insurance industry

The British insurance industry is a highly-technical, diverse international industry which holds the key position in the UK economy as the largest contributor to our invisible earnings. Most large insurance companies have extensive branch networks and subsidiaries around the world, as well as vast investment in the UK.

Each area of insurance has experts and specialists. Many work for the large companies which get involved in many aspects of insurance business. Others prefer to work for small firms which concentrate on specialist insurance services.

Insurance companies are quite literally made of money. They collect money in the form of premiums and pay it out when claims are made on policies. This means that at any one time they have billions of pounds in their hands, invested for a range of periods, in markets across the world.

Insurance touches almost every aspect of our lives from cars, houses, factories, buildings sites, to industrial action, political crisis, world cup, terrorism and earthquake, making it one of the most exciting and ever-changing fields of commerce.

*Questions*

1.  Explain what 'the largest contributor to our invisible earnings' means.
2.  Why are insurance companies made of money?
3.  How will you expect insurance to affect your life when you start working?

## Telecommunications services

Modern business relies on telecommunications services for a massive range of links with customers, suppliers and other parties. Many of these links are covered in the chapter on communication (Chapter 9).

Improvements in telecommunications over recent years have provided the business community with the opportunity to improve their efficiency, as well as open new markets and communicate almost instantly with almost all parts of the world. Some of the changes have included the revolution caused by the fax machine, mobile telephones, competition for telecommunication services, telephone credit cards and phone cards, as well as a wide selection of business information services.

### Case Study—Mercurycard

Mercuryphones are now located in over 700 main Post Offices, as well as over 4000 other conveniently located places throughout the country. Just as with the BT services, you can call any other phone system in the UK and the world using a Mercuryphone.

*Questions*

1.  What are the benefits for the customer of having more than one organization competing to provide telecommunication services?
2.  Explain why phonecards are so useful?

## "I'm not one for gossip but she's got one of those new-fangled Mercurycards..."

## "She hasn't?" "She has!"

**Mercurycards are available now at the counter.**

Figure 17.16  'Mercury card'

# Postal services

The Post Office provides a range of services which act as aids to business. The main service of the Post Office is in the field of communication. Up and down the UK there are numerous post offices. Some are main post offices; others, especially in villages and more remote places, are sub-post offices. The sub-post offices usually occupy part of a small general store or small independent shop.

## Letter services

### Letter post

The Post Office offers a two-tier system, with first and second class letters. A higher price is paid for the faster service.

### Post restante

Packets can be sent to a Post Office in a particular town and picked up from there. This is useful if a business person is travelling and does not know the address he or she will be staying at.

### Certificate of posting

The Post Office will issue a certificate to show the date on which a packet was posted. It can be used as proof of posting.

### Business reply service

This service makes it possible for firms to enclose an unstamped reply card or envelope in any magazine, book or direct mail correspondence. The firm must get a licence from the Post Office. The cards or envelopes can carry first or second class postage and the firm will only be charged for the replies that are returned.

### Freepost

As an alternative to the business reply service, this facility removes the need for the business to provide a pre-printed card or envelope and is therefore ideal for advertisers on television and radio and in the press. The organization arranges with the Post Office for the public to be able to add the word 'Freepost' to the firm's address; they are then charged for each letter delivered. This service operates only on a second-class basis.

### Recorded delivery

A business will use the recorded delivery service if it needs proof that a letter has been received. The letter will be signed for on delivery. It would be a useful way of sending a summons to appear in court or a note requesting prompt payment of a debt.

### Registered post

This is a method of sending valuable items through the post. If the package goes missing the Post Office will compensate the sender for the value of the packet. The service provides:

1. A certificate of posting.
2. A record of delivery.
3. Compensation for loss or damaged items.

### Swiftair

For an additional fee, letters can be given express air treatment for quick delivery.

*Special delivery*

This priority service offers assurance of next day delivery. If items arrive late there is a money back guarantee.

## Services for parcels and packets

Royal Mail Parcels has recently started operating under a new name: Royal Mail Parcelforce. This new service claims to look beyond handling parcels and consignments to how distribution helps to improve sales, production and marketing, as well as almost every aspect of a business. Services include:

- Royal Mail Parcelforce.
- Datapost—guaranteed next-day delivery to all major UK business centres and by noon to almost everywhere else.
- Parcelforce 24—guaranteed next-day delivery to 95 per cent of all UK business addresses.
- Parcelforce 48—guaranteed two day delivery to 95 per cent of all UK business addresses.
- Standard service—delivery normally within three days to every address in the UK.
- Royal Mail Parcelforce International..
- Datapost EMS—guaranteed timetabled delivery to 160 countries world-wide.
- Standard service—delivery to around 200 countries worldwide.
- Economy service—low-cost option to most longer distance destinations.

*Task—Post Office parcel services*

Working in groups construct a list of reasons why the Post Office splits its parcel operations into such a wide range of services. What other parcel services do you feel the Post Office could offer?

## Franking machines

A business can hire a franking machine from the Post Office to replace sticking stamps on envelopes. A frank can be made out for any amount. The user will pay a specific sum to the Post Office and will then be able to frank its mail up to this amount. Many organizations have special franks created which also serve to advertise their product.

## Transport

Transport is an essential service for business. The success of modern transport has followed from a clever combination of road, rail, sea and air transport. Containerization of loads has made possible the integration of these different forms of transport.

- To **integrate** means to join together.

Over recent years routes and services have been simplified to cut out wasteful duplication. An example of wasteful duplication would be two half-full airliners running the same route, at the same time.

### Case Study—Geest plc
(*Source*: Southern Examining Group)

Geest plc is a major producer and distributor of fresh fruit (including bananas, apples, pears and grapes) and fresh vegetables (including carrots, mushrooms and cabbages). Geest's own fleet of lorries play an important part in distributing its products in the United Kingdom. The diagram below shows how Geest can quickly distribute its products in the United Kingdom to reach the final consumer within 24 hours.

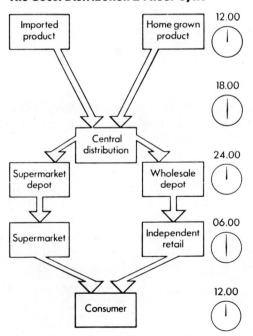

**Figure 17.17**  Product distribution cycle

*Questions*

1. Why is it important for Geest to distribute its products within 24 hours?
2. What is the difference between:
   (a) a home grown product?
   (b) an imported product?
3. Why are supermarkets able to sell Geest products at lower prices than independent retailers?
4. What advantages are there to Geest from using its own fleet of lorries?
5. How can computers help Geest to distribute its products efficiently?

# Other services to business

### Chambers of commerce

Most towns and cities will have a chamber of commerce, which is a pressure group and interest group looking after the well-being of business people in the area. The group will meet to discuss matters of mutual interest concerned with developments in the area. It may, for instance, have an interest in the subjects being offered in schools, or in plans to change the routes of local roads, or in the provision of car parks.

### Chambers of trade

These are similar to chambers of commerce except that whereas the above include all sorts of business people, chambers of trade are mainly made up of shopkeepers.

Both bodies have a national committee which makes suggestions to the government and other groups.

### Industrial research associations

In most major industries leading firms club together to establish a combined research association so that they can benefit together from advances.

### Case Study—Translation

Combine the following French words referring to business services into a short story about a business trip to France.

bagages                          envoyer
banque                           téléphonique

assurance                    retenir
station de taxis             taux de change
région                       expédier

## Case Study—Setting up a garden centre

Alvan Whittaker is just about to open up a new garden centre in Manchester. The garden centre is made up of a complex of eight greenhouses and a large showroom area and is centred on a plot of eight acres of land. Alvan will be employing six workers and the firm will have two delivery vans. Alvan has asked for advice on insuring the business and his insurance broker has told him that the best deal will be gained from taking out a comprehensive business insurance policy which will cover all the main business risks.

### Questions

1. Make a list of the main risks which you would expect to be covered under a comprehensive business insurance policy.
2. How will Alvan benefit even if he does not have to make any claims under the policy?

## Case Study—The Channel Tunnel

The impact of the completion of the Channel Tunnel in 1993 is expected to be wide-ranging on a number of different areas of the UK economy. The project involves three parallel tunnels under the English Channel—two railway tunnels and a central service tunnel. The Tunnel will carry:

- shuttle services for road vehicles on trains between Folkstone and Calais.
- passenger and freight services between Britain and mainland Europe.

### Questions

1. What are (a) the costs and (b) the benefits of the Channel Tunnel?
2. Consider how the Tunnel will affect:
   (a) the economy of the south-east of England
   (b) the economy of Scotland
   (c) the environment
   (d) residents in Kent

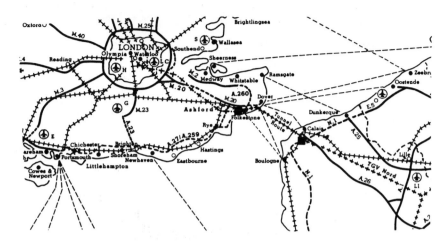

**Figure 17.18**  Channel Tunnel link map

    (e)   our relationships with EC neighbours

    (f)   employment opportunities

    (g)   international trade.

3.   Explain how important good transport links to the Tunnel are, if the project is to be successful.

### Case Study—Using the services of a bank

Tonia Yiannapas set up a taxi firm in Cardiff using the name 555 cabs because the telephone number of the firm was 555111. Her business was able to benefit from many of the services offered by her local bank. She was able to pay her rates bill by standing order and the telephone and electricity bills by direct debit. Some of her larger clients such as local businesses paid their bills at the end of the month using a credit scheme that she offered and she was able to cover herself by using the bank to factor her debts. The firm employed eight drivers who received the bulk of their wages cash in hand but were paid a monthly bonus by bank giro.

*Questions*

1.   Explain the following services which were mentioned in the case study:

    (a)   Standing order

    (b)   Direct debit

    (c)   Factoring of debts

    (d)   Bank giro

2.  Explain how Tonia might also have made use of the following:
    (a)  A business loan
    (b)  An overdraft facility
    (c)  A banker's draft

### Case Study—The statistical basis of car insurance premiums

For the insurance company working out the premium is a statistical exercise. For example:

1.  Cars are classified by *numbers* ranging from Fiestas and Minis in Group 1, to Lotuses and Ferraris in Group 17.
2.  The country is divided into *areas*. Rural areas are charged lower rates than cities.
3.  Premiums depend upon *age*. People between the ages of 17 to 24 are three to four times more likely to have an accident than those over 35.
4.  *Hot hatchbacks* such as XR2s and XR3s face an additional loading.
5.  An element of the premium *compensates* road traffic accident vicitims who have been injured by someone without insurance.
6.  The *use* of the car will affect the premium, for example, taxi drivers pay about three times the normal premium.

*Questions*

1.  Why will statistics be useful when working out premiums?
2.  Comment on the use of each of the factors mentioned for calculating premiums.

## Questions

1.  Complete the following sentences using the terms below:

    Cheque card            Bank draft
    Credit card            Bank loan
    Night safe             Bank giro
    Factoring              Standing order
    Overdraft              Direct debit

    (a)  The bank service used for depositing money after bank closing hours is a . . . . . . . .
    (b)  A business would accept a. . . . . . . .for £1,000 in immediate exchange for a product.
    (c)  . . . . . . . . makes is possible to deposit money into any known account.

(d) ........ of debts involves allowing a bank to collect payment for your invoices.

(e) A business might take out a ........ to buy an expensive piece of equipment.

(f) A ........ is a good way for a business to collect regularly debts of irregular sums.

(g) A ........ would be a good way of paying regular quarterly insurance premiums.

(h) A ........ guarantees a cheque payment up to a set amount.

(i) If a business is prepared to accept payment by ........ this should increase its sales.

(j) A cheap way of borrowing money to ease cash-flow problems in the short term is by ........

2. Make a list of the business services you might require if you set up as a florist in your neighbourhood shopping centre.

3. What methods of posting would you use in each of the following situations?

(a) A jeweller wants to send a small, fairly valuable item of jewellery.

(b) Ross Frozen Foods needs to send documents to its travelling salesperson to await her arrival at a certain town.

(c) Overnight door-to-door delivery is needed of some computer data to a centre for processing.

(d) An insurance broker needs proof that she has despatched important policies to her customers.

4. Freezfree Ltd is based in a small town in East Anglia and makes windows and patio doors. Its products are sold locally, to business owners and householders. At present it buys its glass from a British firm, but the directors are considering whether to obtain future glass supplies from abroad.

The market town is expanding. British Rail is improving the rail service to London and the local council has recently set up a 'business park' to encourage firms to move to the town.

(a) Identify and comment on **two** factors which will help the directors to decide whether or not to import the glass.

(b) Suggest **one** way in which Freezfree's marketing strategy towards business owners will differ from its strategy towards householders.

(c) Explain how the policies of British Rail and the local authority are likely to affect Freezfree Ltd.

(*Source*: London East Anglian Group)

5. Gareth is employed as a driver by a small private company which exports most of its products to France and Italy. What is **one** advantage to Gareth's company from having its own lorries to transport its goods,

rather than hiring lorries from another company?
(*Source*: London East Anglian Group)

6. The Post Office offers a banking service. What is this service called? In what ways is this service (a) similar, and (b) different, from services offered by the high street banks.
7. Describe the services offered by British Telecom. What rival services are there?
8. Describe the Freephone and Freepost services.
9. What changes have taken place in the transport network in the area in which you live over recent years? Comment on the changes.
10. How important is insurance for local businesses? Make a list of the benefits of insurance.

## Coursework

1. Investigate a local business to find out how they benefit from the availability of local business services. Find out what sort of improvements, if any, they would like to see.
2. Make a comparison between the business services offered by various banks.

# Index

Abbey National, 61
Accountants, 206–207
Accounting, 206–218
Accounts department, 24
Acorn, 8
Adding value, 39–40
Aministration department, 23
Advertising:
    agencies, 148–150
    controls over, 151–152
    example of, 38
    persuasive, 147
Advertising Standards Authority (ASA),
    152
Advice note, 193
Advisory, Conciliation and Arbitration
    Service (ACAS), 258, 266
Agenda, 168
Aims of a business, 43–44
Articles of Association, 23, 53–55
Assets, 211
Attendance records, 102–104

Balance of payments, 273–276
Balance sheet, 211–213
Bank:
    drafts, 339
    of England, 62, 332
    giro credits, 338–339
    loan, 204, 333–335
    overdraft, 204, 211, 335
    reference, 197
    services, 331–341
Bar codes, 156
Batch production, 125
Big Bang, 59
Bill of lading, 278
Bills of exchange, 278–279
Blacking, 263
Brainstorming, 2

Break-even analysis, 215–219
British Code of Advertising Practice, 151
British Nuclear Fuels PLC, 315, 320–321
Broker/dealers, 64–65
Building societies, 61–62, 333
Bulk discounts, 86
Bulk-increasing industries, 80–81
Bulk-decreasing industries, 81
Business plan, 61, 204

CADCAM, 127
Campus 2000, 175–176
Capital expenditure, 204
Cash:
    budget, 202–203
    cycle, 211–212
    flow forecast, 202–203
Central government, 77–78
Central planning, 37–38
Certificate of Incorporation, 54–55
Certificate of insurance, 280
Certificate of origin, 280
Chambers of commerce and trade, 353
Channel tunnel, 354–355
Cheques, 336
Closed shop, 263
Commercial services, 40
Companies:
    Acts, 53
    Private, 53–54
    Prospectus, 55
    Public, 54–59
    Registrar of, 53–54
Company Secretary, 23
Competition, 76–77
Computer-aided design (CAD), 127–128,
    155
Computer integrated manufacturing
    (CIM), 127
Computer numerical control (CNC), 127

Confederation of British Industry (CBI), 265
Conglomerate, 89
Conservation, 322–323
Constant tax, 107
Consumer boycotts, 319
Consumers' Association, 318
Contract of Employment, 232, 243
Contribution, 215–216
Convenor, 254
Co-operatives, 60–61
Corporate identity, 122
Corporation tax, 298
Cost-benefit analysis, 316–317
Credit cards, 339
Credit control, 196–197
Credit note, 195
Credit reference agency, 197
Credit sales, 204
Customs and excise duties, 298

Darlington, 83–84
Databases, 13–14, 146–147, 155, 179–180, 190
Data Protection Act, 13, 180
Debit note, 195
Decision making cycle, 3
De-layering, 29
Delivery note, 193
Demand, 74–76
Demarcation disputes, 263
Democratic system, 27
Desk top publishing, 12, 191
Direct debits, 337
Direct services, 40
Diseconomies of scale, 91–92
Dismissal, 238–239
Distribution, 153–154
Dividends, 56, 60
Double-entry system, 208
Dumping, 276

Ecology, 323
Economies of scale, 85–88, 126
EFTPOS, 156–157
Electronic:
  data interchange (EDI), 174
  mail, 175
  office, 172–176
  Point of Sale (EPOS), 156
Employers organizations, 265
Employment:
  agencies, 228
  creation of, 321
  Department of, 228
Enterprise, 1

Enterprise Zones, 83
Environmental Protection Act, 317
Equal opportunities, 239–241
Equal Pay Act 1970, 239
Ergonomics, 129
European Community, 185, 282
Export Credit Guarantee Department, 281, 347
Export licence, 280
Exports, 272
External business environment, 72

Facsimile transmission, 175
Factoring, 197, 341
Fixed costs, 215
Flexitime, 103–104
Flowcharts, 16
Flow production, 126
Footer, 10
Franchising, 61, 63–64
Free market, 38–39
Fringe benefits, 111

Germany, 41
Going public, 54
Government:
  central, 291
  education and training policy, 297
  employment policy, 293–294
  industrial policy, 294–295
  inflation policy, 294–296
  international policy, 299–300
  local, 291
  regional policy, 295
  spending, 300–301
  taxation policy, 297–299
Graphical User Interface, 9
Graphics, 11–12, 155, 182–184
Gross Pay, 105

Hanson PLC, 90–91
Header, 10
Health and safety, 73, 125, 234–235
Health and Safety at Work Act 1974, 235
Hierarchical system, 26–27
Hire purchase, 204
Horizontal integration, 88
Huntley, Boorne land Stevens, 42–43, 130–131, 230, 243

Icons, 8–9
Ideas, 1–2
Import lkcence, 280
Imports, 272

Income tax, 107–108
Independent Television Commission, 152
Industrial tribunal, 238, 244–246
Infrastructure, 82–83, 294
Inland Revenue, Department of, 73,
    107–108, 206
Insurance:
    policy, 343
    premium, 341
    proposal form, 343
    types, 344–347
Integration:
    conglomerate, 89
    horizontal, 88
    lateral, 89
    vertical, 89
Interdependence, 42–43, 72
Interpretation of accounts, 214–215
Interrelationships, 72
Interview, 229–231
Invisible trade, 272–274
Invoices, 193–195, 280

Job:
    centres, 227–228
    production, 125
    satisfaction, 225, 242–243
    sharing, 241–242
    splitting, 241

Kimball tags, 156

Lateral integration, 89
Launch, 121
Leadership, 28
Leasing, 205
Letter of enquiry, 191–192
Letters, 170–172
Liabilities, 211–212
Loan capital, 56–57
Local government, 63, 78
Location of the business, 79–84

Management, 28–30
Managing director, 22–23
Manufacturing, 40, 119
Markets, 76–77, 135
Marketing department, 24
Marketing mix, 142–145
Market-makers, 65
Market research, 138, 145–147
Marks and Spencer PLC, 25–26, 49–50
Marks sense documents, 155
Mass production, 126
Meetings, 31, 168–169
Memorandum, 169–170

Memorandum of Association, 23, 53–55
Menu, 9
Merchant banks, 333
Method study, 129
Midland Bank, 58
Minutes, 168
Mixed economy, 39
Modem, 174
Monetary rewards, 232
Moneyshops, 333
Monopolies and Mergers Commission,
    78
Monopoly, 77
Morris Bill, 252
Mortgage, 61
Multinationals, 59–60
Multiplier, 95
Municipal undertakings, 63

National insurance, 108–109, 299
Nationalization, 51
National Power PLC, 66
National Union of Mineworkers, 257,
    260
National Westminster Bank PLC,
    340–341
Net pay, 105
Nissan Motor Manufacturing (UK) Ltd,
    236–238
Non-monetary rewards, 232
Non-renewable resources, 323
Notices, 170
Nuclear Electric PLC, 66

Offices, Shops and Railways Premises
    Act 1963, 235
Opportunity cost, 35–36
Organic growth, 88
Organization charts/structures, 16–17,
    22–26
Organogram, 22–23

Paperless office, 173, 190
Partnerships, 52–53
Patent, 120–121
Pay:
    attendance records, 102–104
    flexitime, 103–104
    gross and net, 105
    rates, 101–102
    sick pay, 110
    voluntary deductions, 109
Payroll, 111
Personnel department, 24, 224–249
Picketing, 262
Planned obsolescence, 120

Plant, 124–125
Postal services, 349–351
Post Office Users' Council, 63
PowerGen PLC, 66
Pressure groups, 317–319
Prestel, 175
Primary data, 146
Primary industries, 40, 119
Private costs, 308
Private benefits, 308
Private limited company, 53–54
Private sector, 45
Privatization, 51, 62–63, 65–67
Production department, 24
Production function, 39–40, 123
Product research, 139
Professional associations, 265
Profit and loss account, 210
Progressive tax, 107
Prospectus, 55
Prototypes, 120
Public corporations, 62–63
Public limited company, 54–59
Public sector, 45, 62–63, 295
Purchasing department, 24, 128

Quality control, 128–129
Questionnaire, 6–7
Quotas, 274
Quotation, 193

RAC, 3
Race Relations Act 1976, 242
Rates of pay, 101–102
Ratio analysis, 214–215
Recruitment, 226–231
Redundancy, 238
Registrar of Companies, 53–55
Registrar of Friendly Societies, 61
Regressive tax, 107
Reports, 170
Research and development, 119–121,
    138–139
Return on capital, 56, 215
Revenue expenditure, 204
Risk capital, 56–57
Robots, 127
Rolls-Royce, 34
Rover Group, 174

Safety, (see health and safety)
Sales, 152–153
Sales department, 24
Sales maximization, 44
Sampling, 146
Save-As-You-Earn, 109

Scarce resources, 35–36
Secondary data, 146
Secondary industries, 40
Sex Discrimination Act 1975, 240, 244
Shares, 57, 204
Shell UK Ltd, 241
Shop stewards, 254–255
Sick pay, 110
Single European Market (SEM), 185,
    282, 289
Social benefits, 308
Social costs, 308, 312–317
Sole trader, 52
Sources of finance, 204–205
Special Development Areas, 83
Spoken communication, 166–168
Spreadsheets, 14–15, 181–182
Standing orders, 337
Statement, 195
Stock control, 128, 155
Stock Exchange:
    broker/dealers, 64–65
    going public, 54
    market-makers, 65
    SEAQ, 65
    shares, 57
    USM, 54
Stock turnover, 214
Strategy, 27
Strikes, 262
Subsidies, 275
Suppliers, 76
Survey, 6–7

Tables, 16
Tactics, 27–28
Target market, 144
Tariffs, 274
Taxation, 297–299
Telecommunication services, 348–349
Telephone, 174
Tertiary industries, 40, 119
Test market, 121
Times Network Systems Ltd, 175
Trade credit, 204
Trades' Description Act, 151
Trades Union Congress, 261, 264–265
Trade unions, 78, 251–263, 297
Trading account, 209–210
Trading Certificate, 55
Training, 129, 232–234, 297
Training and Enterprise Councils
    (TECs), 233–234, 297
Transport, 352–353
Transport department, 24, 157
Trial balance, 208

Unemployment, 321–322
Unlisted Securities Market (USM), 54

Value added tax, 73, 298
Variable costs, 215
Venture capital, 205
Vertical integration, 89
Vickers, 34
Videoconferencing, 176
Visible trade, 272–274
Voluntary deductions from pay, 109

Wealth creation, 39–40, 119, 123,
    309–311
Welfare, 235
Welsh Development Agency, 96
Women at work, 239–241
Word Processing, 9–10, 177–179
Working capital, 212, 215
Work measurement, 129
Work study, 129